KINGSHIP AND COLONIALISM IN INDIA'S DECCAN

KINGSHIP AND COLONIALISM IN INDIA'S DECCAN
1850–1948

BENJAMIN B. COHEN

MANOHAR
2026

First published by Palgrave Macmillan in 2007

This edition (2023) for South Asia is being published by
Manohar Publishers & Distributors in arrangement with the author

Reprinted 2024, 2025, 2026

ISBN 978-81-19139-31-6

Published by
Ajay Kumar Jain *for*
Manohar Publishers & Distributors
4753/23 Ansari Road, Daryaganj
New Delhi 110 002

Printed at
Replika Press Pvt. Ltd.

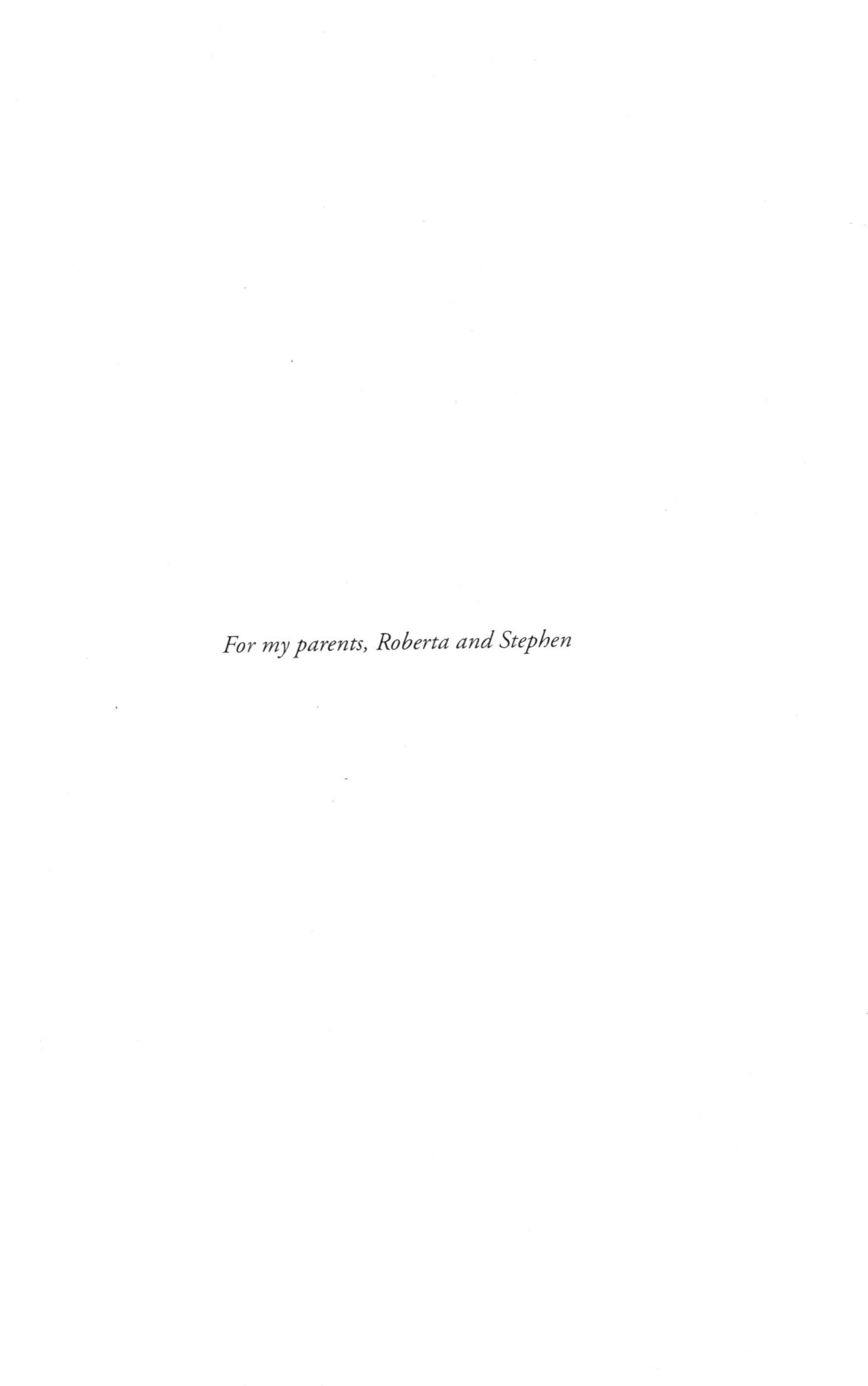

For my parents, Roberta and Stephen

Contents

List of Illustrations, Maps, and Tables

Illustrations

Maps

Tables

Acknowledgments

This book has benefited from the help of many individuals and institutions. Of the latter, the University of Wisconsin, Madison, and the University of Utah's Departments of History have provided supportive academic homes over the past decade. On several occasions, the American Institute of Indian Studies has assisted with visa and other logistical needs I encountered when doing research in India. I am particularly grateful to Pradeep Mehendiratta and Purnima Mehta for their patience and assistance. The Center for South Asia at the University of Wisconsin, and in particular Sharon Dickson, have been a continuous source of support. Libraries and archives in the United States, United Kingdom, and in India deserve special thanks as these are the repositories of material most historians cannot do without. The university libraries at Wisconsin and Utah, and in particular the staff of the interlibrary loan offices, have been invaluable in procuring printed material not available on site. The Oriental and India Office at the British Library has on many occasions been a welcome layover and destination on trips between the United States and India. I am deeply grateful for their assistance. In India, the staff at the Andhra Pradesh State Archive provided exceeding warmth and patience with me; I remain humbly grateful for this. At the Andhra Pradesh Secretariat, I was invaluably helped by Dr. P. Krishna Murthy. I thank the staff at the National Archive, New Delhi, and the Tamil Nadu State Archive, Chennai, and the Nehru Memorial Library, New Delhi for their assistance. Somewhat hidden in Hyderabad are the Court of Wards papers, and I am extremely grateful to K. Mangapathi Rao and the staff of the Court of Wards for their assistance.

While at the University of Utah, several colleagues have provided invaluable support—intellectual and otherwise—while this book was being completed. Mary Ann Villarreal, Tracy McDonald, and Erika Bsumek (visiting from the University of Texas, Austin) all read early versions of early chapters, and I am grateful for their comments. Wes Sasaki-Uemura and Janet Theiss have both been a constant source of friendship, support, and intellectual interaction. Friends in the academy and elsewhere have patiently cajoled me toward completion of this project. Special thanks to: Scott Levi, Chandra Mallampalli, Kevin Downey, James Hoover, Ashok Rajput, Bob Simpkins, Chris Chekuri, Ian Wendt, Venkat Dhulipala, Rajagopal Vakulabharanam, John Roosa, Dana Lightstone, and Brendan LaRocque. To all of them, thank you. Also thanks to: Sanjit Sethi, David Joiner, Kristen Laise, and Rebecca and Dyon Stefanon. A special thanks to Vimala Katikaneni and the entire Katikaneni family. In Hyderabad I benefited from the time and generosity of many of the city's scholars: Dr. Vasant Bawa, Dr. A. Murali, Dr. P. Ramulu, Professor Y. Vaikunthum, Professor M. Radhakrishna Sarma, and Narendra Luther. Also in Hyderabad I wish to deeply thank members of some of the samasthans who shared their time, enthusiasm, and support: Adithya Rao, Shanta Rameshwar Rao, Nandini Rao, Sreelatha Bhupal, and Keshav Bhupal. Back in the United States, I owe a debt of gratitude to David Morgan, Joesph Elder, Richard Eaton, and Phil Wagoner. A very special thanks to: V. Narayana Rao, André Wink, and most of all, Robert Frykenberg.

Nadja Durbach gingerly waded into the world of Hyderabad, and in doing so, has been a constant source of intellectual support as this project reached fruition. She has also forged a permanent and personal partnership with this scholar, and for that, no amount of gratitude would suffice.

My siblings have always carried me, near or far, with them in an enveloping cloud of affection and support. I am deeply proud to be part of our own "great generation," and a participant in the next. To Edward, Jeffrey, Kimberly (Loudon and Posey), Peter, Andrea (Sebastian), Tamara, Matthew (Lucas and Nora) and Susan, again, *thank you*.

Of course, any errors are solely my own.

Salt Lake City,
March 2006.

Notes on Text

In addition to the Common Era (CE) calendar system, documents from the Deccan frequently used two other systems. The first is the Hijri (H) calendar, which begins with the flight of Muhammad from Mecca to Medina. The calendar is lunar and begins from 16 July 622 CE. The second calendar system is the Fasli (F) ("harvest") calendar. This was devised by Mughal Emperor Akbar. The Hijri calendar did not correspond to the agricultural year, nor the fiscal administration, so farmers were pressed to pay taxes out of sync with the administrative calendar. The Fasli calendar was designed to correspond with the agricultural seasons—one crop (*rabi*) in the spring, and the second (*kharif*) in the fall. The Fasli calendar is solar, and thus has slowly diverged from the lunar Hijri calendar. Whenever possible I have converted dates to their CE equivalent, or when necessary, provided the equivalent along with the original Hijri or Fasli date.

Scholars of South Asia will be familiar with Indian vocabulary used, thus I have omitted diacritical marks. Terms are given in italics, and can be found in the glossary for clarification. Indian terms that have become part of the English lexicon are not italicized, such as raja or durbar. The exception to this is the term "samasthan" because of its frequent use. I have used common spellings for places, thus Hyderabad and not Haiderabad, and used the English "s" to signify plurals, rather than the Telugu or Urdu equivalents, thus, "*samasthans*" rather than "*samasthanlu*." All maps and translations are by the author.

Abbreviations

APSA	Andhra Pradesh State Archive, Hyderabad
B.G.	British Government (currency)
CW	Court of Wards, Hyderabad
F	Fasli date
GOI	Government of India
H	Hijri date
OIOC	Oriental and India Office Collections, British Library, London.
NAI	National Archive of India, New Delhi
NML	Nehru Memorial Library, New Delhi
Rs.	Rupee
TNSA	Tamil Nadu State Archive, Chennai
WFP	Wanaparthi Family Papers, Hyderabad

Introduction

In February 1937, the American weekly magazine *Time* featured a cover picture of Osman Ali Khan. He was the Nizam of Hyderabad and the wealthiest man in the world. It is not surprising that he commanded the attention of the magazine during America's Great Depression. Readers would have found his estimated wealth of 1.4 billion dollars a staggering sum.[1] His vast princely state—larger than France—held a key position in south central India, a region known as the Deccan, and was surrounded on all sides by the territories of the British Raj. They would have seen a Muslim whose descendants traced their ancestry back five centuries. In short, the Nizam and his palace-filled capital of Hyderabad presented to the reader a magnificent example of potentates and "oriental splendor." However, the reader might have been surprised to learn that, while the city of Hyderabad was predominantly Muslim, and Urdu speaking, the rest of the state was Hindu and spoke mostly Telugu. In 1909, with a population of 11.1 million, roughly 85 percent of the state was Hindu, about 10 percent was Muslim, and the remaining a mix of Christians, tribals, and others.[2] If the inquisitive reader had wanted to know more about those people and places beyond the city of Hyderabad, their search would have yielded almost nothing.

Thus, Hyderabad State has largely been presented as having a sole center of power, dominated by the Nizam, his minister, and a handful of British officials. However, this impression is misleading. In fact, the state had multiple centers of power and multiple participants who negotiated their power within the state. Amongst those participants dotting the countryside were the capitals of the samasthan (Hindu kingdoms) kings whose origins predated the arrival of Muslim rule in the Deccan. These kingdoms began as military service providers to the Kakatiya and Vijayanagar empires of the fourteenth to sixteenth centuries. As the Deccan came under Indo-Muslim rule, they negotiated their power and authority with their new masters. Over time, their survival and resilience led them to become the oldest members of Hyderabad's polity. At the same time, they shared their position within the Nizam's dominions with other nobles. Some of these were landholders with vast estates not unlike the samasthans, while others were ethnic communities (Arabs, Africans, Afghans, etc.) who wielded economic and military influence across the state, but were generally not large landholders. As the Deccan and Hyderabad State were home to a variety of ethnic, religious, and political communities, each began to incorporate ideas and practices from the other. Due to their longevity, the samasthan kings came to be composites bearing multiple identities. These complex identities drew upon a continuity with their "ancient" pasts, while over time they were quick to adapt and adopt change.[3] While the Nizam held this multiethnic cadre in his political orbit, he and these participants continuously negotiated their positions in a variety of military, ceremonial, and legal ways over several centuries.

For Hyderabad and the Deccan, there has been a long history of seeing a "synthesis," hybridity, or syncretism of politics, religion, and culture.[4] These suggest a melding of two or more entities, and the creation of something new. However, the samasthans, their rulers, and Hyderabad's political milieu in the nineteenth and early twentieth century might alternatively be viewed as composites. A composite has two or more elements, separate, yet forming a larger body. Rather than forming new identities, they forged composite, multiethnic and multicultural identities, each wielding and having access to power deployed at different times and for different purposes.

This work suggests a new perspective on Hyderabad State and the role of local power holders, specifically the samasthans, in a multiethnic and multitiered political system. These polities provided valuable military, fiscal, and ceremonial support to Hyderabad's Nizams, while at the same time maintaining their identity and autonomy within the state's polity. In their territories, they pursued military, administrative, and social practices that both gestured to their origins and came to incorporate newer Indo-Muslim and European practices that surrounded them. Thus, while previously ignored by Deccan and Hyderabad historians, these kings and their states played a vital part in the local-regional dynamics of India's largest princely state. They provide a case study for the ways in which power was negotiated in a multiethnic state, and over time, how identity (individual and political) became increasingly composite in nature.

An example of this composite identity comes in physical form from the statue of a samasthan raja. A few miles north of the Krishna river, which marked the boundary between Hyderabad State and the Madras Presidency, is the town of Kollapur, in modern day Mahbubnagar district. At the center of town is a walled palace compound. Just beyond the imposing gate is the statue of Raja Lakshma Rao. Cast in the early 1930s, the statute pays tribute to one of Hyderabad's multiple power holders. It incorporates in fixed form the composite Hindu, Muslim, and European culture and politics that permeated the state, something neither reflected in the *Time* article nor in much of the scholarship surrounding the state. The king stands as a life-size statue, raised on a plinth and protected by an ornate gazebo. He wears a turban, an Mughali styled long coat with tight pajama pants, English lace-up shoes, and sports a walking stick. On the plinth are his birth, ruling, and death dates carved in the languages that surrounded him: Telugu, Urdu, English, and Persian. The statue not only memorializes one of Hyderabad State's leaders, but also reflects the diversity and composite culture embodied in the state's structure.

Lakshma Rao and his kingdom were one of the samasthans, sometimes also called "little States."[5] These kingdoms were led by rajas and sometimes their wives, *ranis* (queens). Hyderabad State had fourteen samasthans, as seen in map 1, which in order of prestige were: Gadwal, Wanaparthi, Jatprole, Amarchinta, Paloncha, Gopalpet, Anagundi, Gurgunta, Narayanpet, Domakonda, Rajapet, Dubbak, Papanapet, and Sirnapalli.[6] As table 1 indicates, their combined lands formed nearly 10 percent of the state's territory; their populations topped 1.2 million people, or about 10 percent of the state's total population; their annual combined income was over six million rupees; and their *peshkush* (payment, tribute) to the Nizam was nearly one-third million rupees.[7]

As rulers within the Nizam's dominions, and as neighbors to British India, the samasthan families negotiated their power vis-à-vis the Nizam's government, and at times, *through* the Nizam with the British. Both the Nizams and British officials struggled to understand the position of the samasthans within Hyderabad State, and within south India. Two incidents bear out the tripartite negotiation over the samasthans' position and powers.

First, for British officials in the neighboring Madras Presidency, it was a delicate process of recognizing the position of the samasthan families, but in doing so, not subverting the authority of the Nizam whom the samasthans were ultimately subordinate to. One such negotiation occurred in the summer of 1914. At that time, the raja of Wanaparthi purchased a home from Salar Jung, minister of Hyderabad State, in the hill station of Ootacamund. Princes, chiefs, and notables were required to obtain permission to own a house in Ootacamund, and the raja ran afoul of British policy as he purchased it directly from Salar Jung and not through official channels. The question at hand was whether the law,

Map 1 Cities, Samasthans, and Towns of Hyderabad State

Table 1 Area, Villages, Population, Income, and Tribute of Some of the Samasthans

Samasthan	*Area (Miles)*	*Villages*	*Population*	*Annual Income (Rs.)*	Peshkush *(Rs.)*
Gadwal	817	122	968,491	1,704,607	86,540
Wanaparthi	605	150	62,197	1,332,105	83,862
Jatprole	429	86	31,613	1,207,750	71,944
Amarchinta	161	69	34,147	614,155	6,363
Paloncha	3,090	70	38,742	678,382	45,875
Gopalpet		35	16,301	315,213	22,663
Anagundi		78	4,295		
Gurgunta		38	19,937		7,050
Narayanpet			59,967	130,000	

which applied to "chiefs" and "notables," also applied to the raja. Recognizing the importance of the samasthan, and writing to the raja's defense was Major Minchin, first assistant to the Resident at Hyderabad. Citing the entry for Wanaparthi in the *Imperial Gazetteer of India*, (itself a source of authority) Minchin concluded, "there can be no doubt, in Mr. Fraser's opinion [then Resident at Hyderabad], that the raja must be regarded as a 'Notable' or 'Personage' of the Hyderabad State."[8] The raja took possession of the house without further difficulty.

British authorities decided what position the Wanaparthi raja held. However, an incident a few years later brought to light a moment when the Nizam chose an opposite tact, in short, erasing the samasthans from maps of the state, and thus—in a sense—negating or downplaying their very existence.[9] Maps of nineteenth-century and early-twentieth-century India generally illustrate large areas of the subcontinent under British control, while the remaining territories were governed by the princely states.[10] Maps of Hyderabad State displayed the towns and villages of the state along with roads, rivers, railways, etc., but fail to reveal Hyderabad's complex political geography. In fact, it seems to have been the policy of the Nizams, at least that of Osman Ali Khan, to actively discourage the mapping of Hyderabad's different political entities, including the samasthans.[11] In June 1923, the British Residency, then under Charles Russell, wrote to the Nizam's secretary, Nawab Fasih Jung, to request on behalf of a Survey of India team to show the boundaries of the Gadwal, Wanaparthi, and Amarchinta samasthans on the Survey of India maps. If shown, the boundary would have been "undemarcated and approximate" and of no value in a court of law.[12] Fasih Jung replied that the Nizam's government, "very much regret their inability to accede to the request." No further explanation is given. This policy—stated or not—had a twofold effect. In viewing a map of Hyderabad State only a sole center of power—Hyderabad city—is visible. The Nizam cast himself as *the* power in the state, and controlling cartographic representation was a way to exercise this power. Second, this cartographic imbalance has reinforced the historiographical tilt toward Hyderabad city itself. As no other political entities were adequately mapped, historians have largely failed to examine the state's periphery, although it constituted 95 percent of the population.[13]

The samasthans and their towns and villages, demarcated or not, reflect the religious and linguistic composition of the state as a whole. The populations of the samasthans were distributed amongst Hindus, Muslims, tribals, and a few Christians, Sikhs, and Jains.[14] Accordingly, the samasthans had language speakers that included Telugu, Marathi, Kanarese, Urdu, and English. The overall ratio of each religious group mirrors that of Hyderabad State or, about 85 percent Hindu, 5–10 percent Muslim, and the remainder a mix of other faiths. Each samasthan had both temples and mosques scattered throughout its territories. Frequently the grandest temples and largest mosques were located in the samasthan capital towns. Both temples and mosques often received the support of the ruling family, and within Wanaparthi, we can add Christian missionary establishments to the list of religious institutions that received support.[15]

A royal palace generally anchored capital towns in the samasthans. These structures were sometimes originally forts that had been modified over time, while others were built as royal residences. Most were two or three stories in height with grand staircases marking their entrances. The façades had a mix of arches and beams, and the roofline had elaborate finials. The palaces were set in gardens, and those were in turn surrounded by walls and a system of gates. The main gates were often elaborate structures designed more for awe and inspiration than for practical purposes. The palace at Wanaparthi had large lions set at the base of the steps. The palaces had durbar halls (a ruler's court) where the raja would receive guests, conduct business, or be otherwise entertained. Over time, these rooms and the structures themselves were adjusted to accommodate new technology. Electric lights replaced candles and torches, while outside, motorcars replaced horse or elephant-drawn carriages.

Beyond the palace gates, samasthan capital towns fanned out in all directions. In Wanaparthi and Kollapur, rows of shops and noble residences lined the main street leading up to the palace. In his Telugu account of the ruling family of Jatprole, V. Sadasiva Sastrulu provides a list of the offices and amenities available in Kollapur in the first decades of the twentieth century. These included: "line" houses, a magistrate's office, *taluk* (district, division of an estate) office, post office, school, police office, and jail, while further afield other communities resided that were typical of the time including weavers, potters, merchants, etc.[16] The laying of the foundation stone for these structures was often occasion for a guest—usually a Hyderabad official, both Indian or Briton—to be in attendance. The heads of the samasthans recognized the symbolic authority granted to them, and reciprocally offered by them, to these guests. For instance, in Kollapur on 1 June 1930, Maharaja Kishen Pershad (president of the Nizam's Executive Council) was in attendance at the laying of the Lakshmaraya School's foundation stone. Six years later, Richard M. Crofton (director general of Revenue in Hyderabad, 1935–1945) attended the laying of the foundation stone at the Samasthan Hospital.[17] Cyril Jones (an assistant engineer and later managing director of the Nizam's State Railways) was lavishly entertained by the rani of the Sirnapalli samasthan. Jones and his companion, George J. Campbell (a railway survey engineer), were greeted by servants of the rani when they entered samasthan territory.

> It was about midday and they had cleared a space in the jungle and laid out a meal. I think I never enjoyed a meal more. About three or four Indian dishes on leaf plates were followed by the most delicious sweetmeats. We then mounted ponies which the rani had sent for us and rode to the palace where the rani received us in durbar. She was a charming middle aged woman but unfortunately was a victim of elephantiasis. I bitterly regretted that I had to rely on Campbell to express my appreciation but he was fluent in Urdu and I was not. She and Campbell got on very well and were obviously renewing an old friendship.[18]

Holidays, festivals, and markets marked the calendar year of the samasthans. In his introduction to the statistical report on such events in the Nizam's Dominions, Mazhar Husain, director of Statistics, comments that, "In the scheme of life, man has wisely provided some useful diversions from the dreary and monotonous routine of the daily life. Such diversions are in the nature of periodic Festivities, Melas and Jatras."[19] These occurred on a weekly basis, while others were only annual events. They marked important moments in the agricultural calendar, or were related to saints, heroes, or evil spirits. These events attracted varying numbers of attendees. For instance, in the Paloncha samasthan the Venkatesh Swami gathering drew only an average of 150 people, the Lakshmi Narsimha Swami gathering at Sangotam in the Jatprole samasthan drew 4,000 attendees, and the Kurmurti Swami gathering at Amapur in the Amarchinta samasthan drew 20,000 attendees.[20] In addition to events associated with temple deities and agricultural life, smaller markets regularly sprung up to serve the needs of villages and townsfolk alike. These markets were frequently located just beyond the palace gates. The markets provided attendees a chance to purchase goods, exchange information, and enjoy a few moments of entertainment that such events inherently offered. Some of the goods sold in these markets were grown in the samasthans including wheat, *jawar* and *bajra* (millet), ragi (grain), maize, and gram. Thus, the samasthans present a picture of towns and villages organized around the capital where the royal family resided, each penetrated by multiple languages, faiths, and occupations, and punctuated by important calendar dates or the occasional visit by a dignitary. All the while, the samasthan families carefully maintained their authority within their own domains, and negotiated their position within Hyderabad's political milieu.

Negotiations beyond Hyderabad

While this work provides a case study for the way in which power was negotiated within the Nizam's multiethnic dominions, this same process had similar antecedents in the Deccan and elsewhere. Over time the process was further complicated by the addition of European participants. In the Deccan, larger regional powers have long made use of smaller subordinate powers, keeping them in their orbit through a mix of military service demands and ceremonial rewards. Thus, it is not surprising to see the names of the samasthan rulers mentioned in both Kakatiya and Vijayanagar empire accounts, as well as in Mughal records. Military need, fiscal acumen, and ceremonial processes undergirded these relationships. For instance, the Kakatiya rulers employed local rulers or chieftains who maintained bodies of armed forces for them, deferring some of the cost of maintaining large armies. These individuals were occasionally called to the Kakatiya capital at Warangal and performed more ceremonial functions at the royal court. Succeeding the Kakatiyas, the rulers of Vijayanagar also made use of local rulers. The kings of Vijayanagar periodically summoned chiefs to their court—rewarding them with land grants, military commands, and increased ceremonial boons. By the sixteenth century, Indo-Muslim military and court practices comingled with those of earlier times, adding new layers of both real military practice (for instance, the extensive use of cavalry) as well as more ceremonial changes (for instance, changes in dress).[21] Again, regional rulers—centered at Golconda—called upon local leaders to provide armed forces, land management, and participate in ceremonies.

Links between local and regional power holders are also present beyond the Deccan. To the north, under Mughal authority zamindars (landholders) close to Delhi and Agra served as clients of Mughal patronage. These zamindars provided armed forces and ceremonial bolstering to the Mughal rulers, and were in turn rewarded with increased *zat* (personal rank held by a Mughal officer). However, while the samasthan rajas bolstered Deccan rulers, the zamindars of the Mughals have been blamed in part for the very collapse of the administration itself.[22] Among the princely states of the north, a comparison with Awadh and Lucknow brings to light the "family" of scholarship this work joins—one with a focus that begins to shift its attention away from the capital cities and toward the countryside. The once princely state in 1901 had a total area was 23,966 square miles with a population of 12,833,077.[23] Like Hyderabad, Awadh had an urban capital surrounded by a *mufassal* (countryside) where lesser rajas maintained their own courts. Different from the practices followed in Hyderabad was the relationship between the urban center and countryside periphery. In Awadh, for instance, at the coronation of Ghazi al Din Haydari in 1819, the rajas of the *mufassal* either sent *nazr* (gifts, usually gold) or redoubled their fortifications, but none was "welcome" at the event itself.[24] In fact, the Awadh administration actively discouraged the rajas from attending the court.[25] By the mid-nineteenth century, under weakened leadership at Lucknow, many of these small rajas fought amongst each other, paid into an increasingly corrupt exchequer, and sought to further strengthen their own military powers. Thus, in 1857 where some of the samasthan rajas of Hyderabad joined with the East India Company (and one, Shorapur, did not), the rajas of Awadh largely joined in the revolt.[26]

Relationships in Hyderabad were much different. The samasthan rajas and the Nizams were locked in a symbiotic dance: the samasthans at the head of the dominantly Hindu population provided an important buttress to the Nizam's royal pavilion. And the Nizams, while more powerful, could not afford to affront the samasthan holders; and thus adopted a tone of cordiality largely free of religious or communal bigotry.[27] Both found themselves allied with the British before and after 1857. The Nizam bestowed gifts and titles on the samasthan rajas, and after the events of 1857, so too did the governor general of India, thus largely cementing their loyalty. Moreover, post-1857, the territorial chieftains of Awadh encountered changes in their relationship to the court and the British, while the positions and prerogatives of the samasthan rajas remained largely unchanged in their loyalties and practices.[28]

Europeans in India also made use of local and regional powers to help further their own financial and imperial aims. It was the princes of India whom the Company tapped to be their supporters in specific regions. For instance, under Richard Wellesley, governor general, the practice of establishing subsidiary alliances with local princes was dramatically increased. Under this system the prince in question (under economic and/or military threat) agreed to a series of clauses that allowed him to hold largely ceremonial power, while at the same time being brought neatly into a growing imperial structure. The princes, including the Nizams, agreed to surrender the right of negotiation, exclude other European forces (especially the French), and maintain a subsidiary force at their own expense. Frequently, to cover this expense, the princes ceded valuable land to the Company, in Hyderabad this included the rich agricultural lands of Berar. This process also occurred at Pune, Baroda, and Gwalior. In addition, as an official of the Company, the Resident was to be posted at the prince's capital to oversee the terms of such alliances. Thus much of South Asia's precolonial and colonial history was dominated by relationships between superior and vassal powers, relationships that criss-crossed religious and ethnic lines, and by the eighteenth century, came to include European powers. While Hyderabad and its samasthans provide a case study of such relationships, scholarship has largely failed to address these participants below the level of the Nizam.

Intellectual Inquiries

As India's largest princely state, Hyderabad has received an overall surprisingly small amount of scholarly attention.[29] Perhaps the lure of Kashmir's snowy peaks, or the sweetness of Awadh's Urdu have made those states the recipients of much princely state scholarship, to say nothing of works on Rajasthan and a few states of the deep south. As William Dalrymple—having made his own contribution to Hyderabad's late-eighteenth-century history—has reminded us, "The history of Hyderabad and the wider Deccan remains a major lacuna: for every book on the Deccan sultanates, there are a hundred on the Mughals; for every book on Hyderabad there is a shelf on Lucknow."[30]

Scholarship on the samasthans of Hyderabad has generally been cursory, as their role in Hyderabad has been considered, "more nominal than real."[31] This work, to some extent, reorients the view of Hyderabad away from that of the Nizams and British—the standard focus for much of the scholarship, and instead shift attention *outward* to the countryside, and *downward* in the political structure to the level at which the samasthan families operated. Scholarly work on Hyderabad has concentrated on the city itself, and the relationship between its Nizams and the British Raj. The result of this narrow focus is that we know little about the samasthans, the *mufassal* territories that they governed, and their relations with each other as well as powers at Hyderabad and beyond. This work decenters old foci, and shifts attention to the samasthans' role in negotiations over power with each other, with the Nizams, with the British Raj, and with other ethnic communities in the state. An overview of the scholarly topography on the samasthans, Hyderabad State, "little kings," and princely India helps to locate them within a broader intellectual context.

On the samasthans themselves oft cited by scholars is the brief introduction to the largest samasthans by K. Krishnaswamy Mudiraj.[32] Mudiraj compiled his voluminous *Pictorial Hyderabad* in the late 1920s and early 1930s, a time when many of the samasthans enjoyed strong leadership. Thus his account of their administration (as well as accounts of the Nizams ruling at the time), is generous in its portrayal of the samasthan families. In addition, from the early decades of the twentieth century, several Telugu works follow a similar pattern of flattery. For instance, specific to the Jatprole samasthan, V. Sadasiva Sastrulu's *Sri Surabhivari Vamsa Charitramu*, published in 1913, is accordingly generous in its portrayal of then Raja Lakshma Rao.[33] It was written during the raja's tenure, and as we shall see, Lakshma Rao was indeed among that samasthan's most enlightened rulers, yet Sastrulu's work is more flattery than analysis. A year after his death in 1928, Ramasubbaravu Rao published a generous portrait of the raja's life in Telugu, *Sri Surabhi Venkatalaksmaraya Nijam Navajyant Bahaddarvari Jivitamu*.[34] Both works provide valuable details of the samasthan and some of its rulers, but both comprise a style of history writing and biography that leans more toward flattery yet lacks contextualization let alone any critique.

More recent scholarship on the samasthans largely relies on the earlier works (especially that of Mudiraj). These works are largely descriptive and flattering in their thrust, but do not position the samasthans in any larger context. In 1948, while the rest of India celebrated independence, and negotiations to bring Hyderabad into the new union were being sorted out, a brief history of the Wanaparthi samasthan was published in Telugu by Krishna Rachayata.[35] Subsequently, three further works have been published, all in Telugu, on the Wanaparthi samasthan. Celebrating the life of one of that samasthan's best-known rajas, Rameshwar Rao I, is a brief account of his life, *Sri Raja Prathama Rameshwara Rayalu*.[36] This has been followed by two histories of the samasthan that provide a more balanced account of its achievements and pitfalls.[37] Subsequently, a major work in Telugu (which covers all of the samasthans of modern Andhra Pradesh, including those in the Telangana region formerly under the Nizam's dominion as well as those in Andhra's coastal districts) is that of Acharya Tumati Donnapa. Donnapa provides brief histories of each samasthan, but his main focus is an examination of their literary contributions. Further, the work in Urdu of Ramanraj Saksena, which is more general in scope, again provides brief histories of some of the samasthans.[38] This appears to be the only work in Urdu concerning the samasthans as the few students and scholars who have taken up the topic seem to come from a Telugu-speaking background. This is an unfortunate linguistic divide, not reflected in the documents of the samasthans themselves that are in Urdu, Telugu, and English. Finally, in more detail (and specific to Wanaparthi) but frustratingly shy with citations, is the work of Harriet Ronken Lynton and Mohini Rajan.[39] Ironically, the Gadwal samasthan, which was the largest of them all, appears to have been least explored by scholars.[40]

Widening our lens one degree from the samasthan territories to Hyderabad city and state, we find what scholarship exists on the state.[41] Much of it concerns Hyderabad's relationship with the British Raj, but has little or nothing to say on the samasthans. A sample of titles illustrates the orientation of these works: Sarojini Regani's *Nizam-British Relations, 1724–1857*, (1963); Nani Gopal Chaudhuri's *British Relations with Hyderabad* (1964), V.K. Bawa's *The Nizam between Mughals and British: Hyderabad under Salar Jung I*, (1986); and Bharati Ray's *Hyderabad and British Paramountcy, 1858–1883*, (1988).[42] These works have stressed the position of "interference" exerted in Hyderabad by the British, the Resident, or his staff.[43] Since the 1980s, scholarship on Hyderabad has largely shifted to monographs on themes within the state's history. Karen Leonard spearheaded this trend with her work on the *kyasthas* (record keepers) of Hyderabad.[44] Following in her footsteps, Margrit Pernau has carefully recounted Hyderabad's internal political and court culture. Yet, her work like much of the scholarship on Hyderabad State remains fixated on Hyderabad city.[45] Another theme with Hyderabad scholarship has been Hyderabad's dénouement in 1948. Lucien Benichou has examined the critical moments before Hyderabad's "integration" with the Indian union, and second, longtime historian of Hyderabad Omar Khalidi has compiled several compelling articles on "Hyderabad's fall."[46] Much older works from the colonial period have provided first-hand accounts of daily life in the Nizam's territory, but largely fail to go beyond the city gates in scope.[47]

Between scholarship on specific princely states, such as Hyderabad, Awadh, or Kashmir, and scholarship that examines the princely states as a whole or collective body, there exists a step-child of both fields that concerns India's many "little kings." In 1962, Bernard Cohn first used the term "little king."[48] Cohn identified four levels of political hierarchy in eighteenth-century India: imperial, secondary, regional, and local. The little kings, he found, were located at the secondary and local levels. They were identifiable as having "an acknowledged head, the Raja." Further he found that little kings transferred power through patrimony. Cohn's analysis fits the political structure of the eighteenth century, but with the growth of the British presence in India, and with the parallel decline of Mughal authority, many little kings became directly engaged with the Company.[49] Charting a different tack from Cohn's work, the examination here of the samasthan rajas reveals "little kings" who were embedded within larger regimes, and thus remained sheltered from direct engagement with the Company or British Raj.

Smaller kingdoms that were engaged in direct relations with the British Raj such as Pudukkottai and Ramnad in Tamil lands have attracted a wealth of scholarship that has examined court practice within these states' durbars, their relationship to the British colonial power, and a host of other topics and subtopics. In his ethno-history of the Tamil kingdom Pudukkottai, Nicholas Dirks has examined ways in which the crown of that little king became "hollow."[50] Dirks argues that previous work on kingship emphasized religion; and he in turn shifts the debate toward the dynamics of power—especially colonial power. Dirks focuses on the "hollowing" effect of British ascendancy, largely discounting elements in the Pudukkottai crown's own inner strength and structure. Taking a different approach, Pamela Price has broadened the debate on little kings in her work on the Tamil kingdom of Ramnad. She asserts that colonialism did not "hollow" the crown; but instead "transformed" it.[51] Price has illuminated elements of continuity between precolonial, colonial and postcolonial institutions. At their core, both arguments are concerned with the changes wrought by colonialism, and continue to argue for a Crown, which whether "hollow" or "transformed," was nevertheless changed.[52]

Widening our lens still further to that of princely India (as represented in map 2)—a banner under which many of the previously discussed works could fit—scholarship has shifted toward themes of continuity.[53] Continuity and change are interwoven themes amongst India's princes at both the highest levels (those princes directly engaged with British India) and within the princely states at sublevels of power, such as that

Map 2 Hyderabad and Other Princely State Areas C. 1900

of the samasthans. At the heart of their story is how princes maintained practices from earlier times, while at the same time adapting and adopting to ever-changing political winds.

As nationalist politics and communal identities gathered force in British India in the decades leading up India's independence, so too did communal clashes occur within the princely states. Communalism has generated its own subset of scholarly work that includes examinations of the phenomenon in the princely states, and in Hyderabad. Ian Copland has demonstrated that communal relations in the princely states at this time (c. 1900–1940s) were vastly better than relations in the provinces and presidencies. This was due in part to smaller Muslim populations, isolation from British India, a degree of "backwardness," a stronger sense of community, and monarchical policies that resembled "fatherly despotism."[54] But positive communal relations in the twentieth century, in Hyderabad, had nineteenth century antecedents, in part fostered by the role of the samasthans as "Hindu" kings within a "Muslim' state.[55] These men (and women) had a direct interest in maintaining communal harmony as their coffers depended on the cooperative productive labor of their subjects, Hindus and Muslims. The rajas had a further incentive: the Hyderabad administration was largely staffed by Muslims, and communal problems in the samasthans would not be well received in the capital. This ability and desire to address local problems explains why when communalism arose in the 1930s and 1940s in one area of Hyderabad's countryside, it did not in a neighboring area.[56] In contrast, a zamindar or *jagirdar* (landholder)—gifted a plot of land and having no real historical or personal connection to that land—had no vital interest except to collect revenue. Local administration became subleted, thus providing space for administrative ills to draw strength from and grow.

Thus, intellectual inquiries into Hyderabad and the Deccan have been less voluminous than that of other regions of the subcontinent. The samasthans, while being the oldest members of Hyderabad's political milieu, have received only light treatment, and that being mostly marked by hagiographic narratives. By exploring their role as power holders, and their negotiations with each other and with their superiors, a better understanding of Hyderabad's larger multiethnic and diverse political composition can be achieved.

Dramatis Personae

An introduction to the participants of Hyderabad's political milieu demonstrates its diversity and sets the stage for negotiations over power explored in subsequent chapters. The samasthans and other forms of nobility comprised the third tier of Hyderabad's pyramidical political structure. At the top of this structure was the Nizam. The first Nizam, Asaf Jah, was appointed as *subahdar* (viceroy) of the Deccan by Mughal Emperor Aurangzeb. Thus, the position of the Nizam itself originated as one of a subordinate power to that of the Mughals. Early in the eighteenth century as Mughal authority collapsed, the Nizam declared independence, and two centuries of rule steeped in autocracy and ringed with splendor followed. Below the Nizam in the political structure was the *dewan* (revenue minister) who was responsible for overseeing the daily administration of the state. As such, the minister was frequently in touch with the state's nobles, with the British Resident, and with his master. Beneath the minister was a wide spectrum of elites including the samasthan rajas; *paigah* nobles whose ancestors were bequeathed land by the first Nizam on a military tenure; *jagirdars* who over time were also granted land for a variety of reasons, and a bevy of *daftardars* (record keepers). Nobles at these ranks held land in the countryside, and often aspired to higher rank by being patrons of artists, musicians, dancers, poets, and pundits.[57] Finally, there were *vakils* (agent, lawyer) who served both patrons and clients, and would represent either or both in day-to-day court business. Outside of this pyramid, but frequently involved in the state's politics, was the British Resident. The Resident served as a local representative of the Company's governor general, and later the Queen's viceroy.[58] Finally, cutting across these landed elites were a variety of other communities who were intertwined with the Nizams, ministers, nobility, and Residents. These communities included Arab moneylenders, African soldiers, as well as Afghan and Rohilla mercenaries. While the Nizams, their ministers, and the British Residents have received the lion's share of scholarly attention, I wish to focus our attention on the samasthans, demonstrating the ways in which they negotiated power—and thus survival—in Hyderabad's multiethnic dominions.

An eyewitness account from the early nineteenth century provides a snapshot of what these areas looked like, and introduces some of the competing powers at play. The account comes from Enugula Veeraswamy's journal *Kasiyatra Charitra*. Veeraswamy was born around 1780 in Madras. He was a Niyogi Brahman, and from an early age studied English, Tamil, Telugu, and Sanskrit. He joined the Company at the age of twelve to work as a translator, eventually rising to "head interpreter" of the Madras Supreme Court.[59] Veeraswamy embarked on a pilgrimage to Benares in May 1830, and returned in September 1831. Along the way, he kept a journal (in Telugu) that provides us with a snapshot of life in India at this time. More specifically, it provides a view of people and towns along the route from Madras north across the Krishna river (see map 3), near the Raichur *doab* (land between two waters), through the Jatprole and Wanaparthi samasthans, and on to Hyderabad.

On 20 June 1830 Veeraswamy reached the south bank of the Krishna river, stopping for some time at the village of Nivruthisangamam. His path to the river was covered in stone and thus easy, and he was further aided by a lack of jungle (both difficult to traverse, and occasionally inhabited by bandits). Although not specifically mentioned, the countryside at the time would have been a buzz with palace building, jungle clearing, and promoting artisan and commercial development. This region had been a pivotal area in larger battles between Kakatiya, Bahmani, Qutb Shah, and Vijayanagar rulers, and as such, "Every village on the way has a ruined fort."[60]

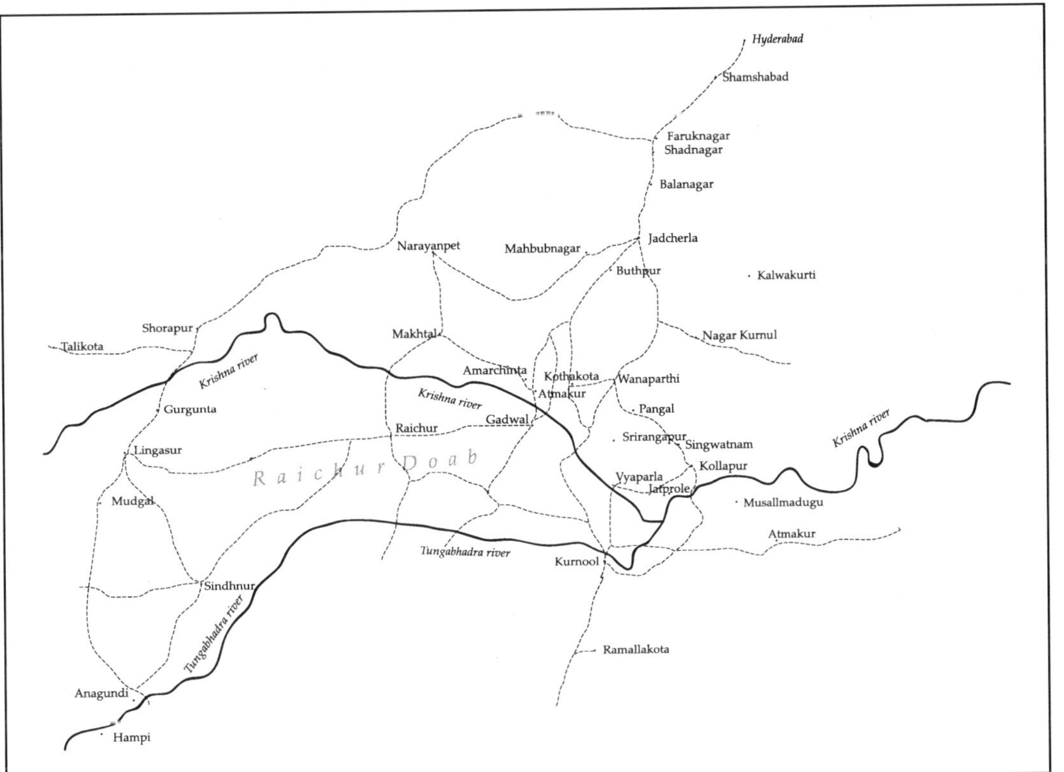

Map 3 The Raichur *Doab* and Major Routes

On the afternoon of the 24th, Veeraswamy reached the village of Pentapalle. This village was under the control of the Jatprole rulers; a point not lost on Veeraswamy who comments that it is under the zamindar of "Kolhapuram." Kolhapuram, also Kollapur, was the capital of the Jatprole samasthan. At Pentapalle, in "an urban village" Veeraswamy found a large temple dedicated to Venkateswara, forty *komati* homes, and provisions for the traveler.[61] Komatis, or Komtis were a trading caste, generally wealthy, and engaged in a variety of small business ventures: grain or cloth selling, banking, moneylending etc.[62]

While passing through Jatprole and Wanaparthi territories, Veeraswamy explained the relationship between the samasthans and the Nizam, and between each other. Initially, in his entry for June 21–24 he referred to these rulers as zamindar*s*, but two days later as he made his way out of Wanaparthi territory and on toward Hyderabad, he used the term "samasthanam." As explained earlier, within the Hyderabad political milieu, the samasthan rulers were different from zamindars. Perhaps for Veeraswamy, coming from the Madras Presidency, any difference was not immediately apparent. His account of Jatprole and Wanaparthi at this time indicates his knowledge of their position as autocratic powers within Hyderabad.

> These zamindars pay limited tributes to the Nizam and enjoy autocratic powers in their estates. The stronger zamindars, it is said, do not pay even this tribute regularly. At such times, the Hyderabad Government pursues them and succeeds in extracting its tribute by force. When these zamindars disagree with each other they not only fight each other to death but also raid each other's villages and cause havoc tormenting the ryots and ravaging the villages. When such tussles arise, instead of enquiring into them and help in the settling of the issues, Diwan Chandu Lal and his followers delight in further aggravating such situations being conscious of the resultant money profit to them. A tussle of this kind is going on between the zamindar of Vanaparti and zamindar of Kolhapuram at the time of my travel.[63]

From Pentapalle Veeraswamy moved on first to Pangal, and then to Wanaparthi town. Veeraswamy says little of Wanaparthi town other than the availability of provisions. He comments that under the "zamindars" of Hyderabad, that is, the samasthan rajas, "People have no security in his State."[64] His observations, both about the "delight" of Hyderabad's minister, Chandu Lal, and the insecurity under the samasthans are not altogether surprising. The early decades of the nineteenth century in Hyderabad State were unsettled, and raiding between the samasthans and possible exacerbation by Hyderabad officials would not have been out of place.[65]

Veeraswamy's account highlights three critical issues relating to Hyderabad. First, the account reveals the confusion over what exactly the samasthans were. Were they zamindars or some other type of landholders? This confusion is not unique to the early nineteenth century, and indeed, haunted the samasthan families well into the mid-twentieth century as they struggled to define themselves against other types of landholders. Second, Veeraswamy walked into a skirmish between the Jatprole and Wanaparthi samasthans. Those noble homes fought amongst each other, but also with other nobles and mercenaries that circulated throughout the state.[66] At this third tier of Hyderabad's political structure, petty warfare dominated relations between the nobility until the mid- to late nineteenth century when growing ceremonialism replaced it. Finally, Veeraswamy was well aware of the power negotiations taking place not only between the samasthans (manifested in armed conflict) but also between the two samasthans and the minister at Hyderabad. On the one hand, Hyderabad officials were actively engaged in keeping the power of the samasthans reduced, either by allowing fighting amongst each other or through reducing their armed forces. On the other hand, they needed the support—both in physical (military) and symbolic terms—from the samasthans to maintain their own position of power. Thus, some definition of the samasthans is required as well as an introduction to the multiple types of power holders within this third tier of the state's hierarchy.

Not surprisingly, no adequate definition of a samasthan has been formulated in recent time. Scholars have relied on older definitions that generally fail to tease out the important differences between a samasthan and other types of landholdings. This is not surprising given the complexity and "veritable jungle" of Indian landholdings and the processes associated with them.[67] A continuing task of this book is to chart the confusion and even reluctance to narrowly define a samasthan. Among the Deccan's nineteenth-century historians, J.D.B. Gribble provides a typically vague account and definition of the samasthans.

> [S]cattered over the country was a large number of indigenous Rajahs and Chiefs who held, most of them, sunnads or grants from former kings, many of which had been confirmed subsequently by the Delhi Emperors. The Rajahs were all recognized and confirmed in their possessions on payment of tribute, being allowed to exercise a kind of semi-independent jurisdiction within the limits of their estates.[68]

These "rajahs" and "chiefs" refer to the samasthan rajas. A working definition of a samasthan in Hyderabad includes five components.[69] First, these territories were geographically contiguous. Territory was controlled from a capital town that contained the residence of the ruling family. Contiguity meant that the samasthans operated as states within a state. Their administrations addressed revenue, judicial, and social facets of a state. In contrast were zamindars and *jagirdars* whose lands were frequently noncontiguous making efficient administration nearly impossible. Second, over time these families acquired royal status receiving increased honors and recognition. With titles such as raja and maharaja, samasthan leaders were able to access ancient notions of kingship and royal behavior, *rajadharma* (duties of a king), that would have been familiar to their subjects. Power was hereditary, passing from father to son, or sometimes to an adopted heir. Occasionally it passed from husband to wife, and then mother to son, as women frequently served as Regents within the samasthans. Third, these rulers were of "ancient" origin, emerging from the pre-Muslim empires of the Deccan. The samasthans traced their origins back to Kakatiya or Vijayanagar times.[70] When those larger empires had fallen, these smaller, more agile and adaptable political units survived. Later, the Bahmanis, Qutb Shahs, and Asaf Jahs had recognized the samasthans' rights and powers and incorporated them into their empires.[71] Their medieval origins and pre-Muslim existence distinguished them from Hyderabad's other nobles. Where *paigahs, jagirdars*, and zamindars were all by-products of the Nizams' rule, only the samasthan rajas could claim pre-Nizamate status. Fourth, the administration of the samasthans was dominantly autonomous. The rajas paid *nazr* or *peshkush*, and participated in court ceremonialism at Hyderabad, but were rarely disturbed in their own territories.[72] As the Resident at Hyderabad, William Barton, wrote of the samasthans in 1925, "[I]t is usual to leave such people [samasthan families] free to administer their own territories without interference so long as the stipulated tribute is paid regularly."[73] This loose connection between local and regional powers allowed the samasthan leaders to more fully administer their states. Finally, the samasthan rulers held simultaneous and multiple positions of power. Embodying composite identities, they found themselves embedded within regional empires of the Deccan and buttresses to those overlords, and at the same time, masters of their own lands. These relationships led to occasional abuses: overlords periodically demanding exorbitant gifts from the rajas who in turn demanded more of their subjects.

While the fourteen estates named were all considered "samasthans," within the group were differences in their relationship to Hyderabad.

The first distinction between the samasthans was whether they were "exempted" or not. An exempted samasthan, while nowhere specifically defined, was generally free from *dewani* jurisdiction (office, jurisdiction, and emoluments of the *dewan*). This gave these estates wide-ranging power in areas such as the police and the judiciary. The exempted samasthans were Gadwal, Wanaparthi, Jatprole, Amarchinta, and Paloncha. Second, while none of the samasthans was held rent-free (like the *paigahs*—examined later), the specific category of rent payment varied between them. The amount of *peshkush* seems to have remained fixed throughout much of the nineteenth and twentieth centuries. With a degree of inflation over time, these amounts would have "shrunk." The Nizams—unable or unwilling to raise the *peshkush*—extracted greater resources from the samasthan families by accepting and demanding ever-increasing *nazr* that substantially added to the amount of funds flowing from the samasthan families to their coffers. Three of the samasthans (Gadwal, Anagundi and Gurgunta) specifically paid *peshkush*.

A second group was held by *pan-maqta*. Here, the land was given to the holder in return for an annual fixed cash rent. This payment was *also* called *peshkush*, and to add to the confusion, for certain influential residents it was also called *bil-maqta*. Wanaparthi, Jatprole, Gopalpet, and Paloncha were held by *pan-maqta, bil-maqta*, or *peshkush*. As the samasthan families "held" their lands prior to the Asaf Jah period, some were defined by additional terminology (*pan-maqta, bil-maqta*, etc.) to distinguish them in rank from the others. Finally, the much smaller samasthans of Domakonda, Rajapet, Dubbak, Narayanpet, Papanapet, and Sirnapalli were subject to *dewani* jurisdiction in addition to some form of payment.

Of the fourteen samasthans, three in particular warrant special attention: Gadwal, Wanaparthi, and Jatprole. In that order, these three were the largest and highest ranking kingdoms within Hyderabad State. They commanded the most respect and prestige within the Nizam's court, and were looked upon by the greater Hyderabad community as leaders in their own right. They were located on the state's southern border, in modern day Mahbubnagar and Raichur districts. In their early years, this location provided them with critical access to geographical resources including diamonds and rivers. Their location was at the "fracture zone" between the Vijayanagar empire and that of the Bahmani and Qutb Shahi empires. By the nineteenth century, their domains bordered that of the Madras Presidency and territories of the British Raj. Their annual incomes all topped the one million rupee mark, and together their domains covered 1800 square miles with a combined population of over two million people that formed a contiguous block along the Krishna and Tungabhadra rivers' juncture.[74] All three shared similar stories of origin that trace their descendants to the courts of Warangal and Vijayanagar. Interestingly, size did not always yield prestige or respect. For instance, of the remaining samasthans, Paloncha had a vast area of 3000 square miles, nearly three times the size of the "little kingdom" Pudukkottai, and one-third larger than Ramnad.[75] Yet, because of its dense forests and poor irrigation, Paloncha ranked fifth among the samasthans.

The *paigah* estates formed the second private landholding group within Hyderabad State. Unlike the samasthans, the *paigah* estates were of more recent origins. *Paigah* is Persian meaning "foot" or "stable." The term came to be applied to those who supplied cavalry. The *paigahs* were also sometimes called *jamiat jagirs* (a landholder who provided troops). The Qutb Shahs had granted their lands, and their territories were generally noncontiguous and scattered over a large area, making their control difficult. In Hyderabad, there were three major *paigah* estates. All of them were held by descendants of the same family, founded by Mulla Jalal ud Din in the time of the Mughal Emperor Akbar. These were the Asman Jah, Kurshid Jah, and Vikar ul Umra families. Following Mughal practice at Hyderabad, the Asaf Jahs had later continued grants to these men in return for military support. For example, under Nizam Ali Khan, the *paigahs* provided the Nizam's private Household Troops, and if necessary could raise as many as 100,000 additional troops.[76] Their lands formed, "over 150 islands of *paigah* territory scattered about the state."[77] In total, they maintained twenty-four *taluks*. These covered 4,134 square miles with an assessed revenue of 40 lakhs (a lakh is 100,000). The *paigah* holders, like other private landholders, were exempt from *dewani* control and maintained their own internal administrations, "though the efficiency of these was often absurdly low."[78]

The third group of private landholders were the *ilaqadars* and *jagirdars*. The *ilaqas* were the premier group of *jagirs*. *Ilaqa* refers to a property or estate. These landholdings, like the *paigahs*, were spread out over vast areas making their administration difficult. Further, their scattered political geography invited abuses between the *ilaqadar* and the *ryot* (cultivator, subject). The *ilaqas* included the estates of Salar Jung, Kishen Pershad, Khan Khanan, and Fakhr ul Mulk. The largest *ilaqa* in Hyderabad was that held by Salar Jung. He and his family had, at one time under Salabut Jung, maintained 7,000 horses and 7,000 footmen for the Nizam's use. Salar Jung's estate, like that of the *paigahs* and other *jagirs*, was scattered throughout the state. It covered over 1,486 square miles in six *taluks* and had an annual revenue of 8.2 lakhs.[79] Beneath the *ilaqas* in rank were the *jagirs*. A *jagir* was a grant of land made for military support, or as a personal honor bestowed by the ruler upon a subordinate. They could be held in one of three ways: for the life of the recipient, for a predetermined amount of time, or permanently by being made hereditary. The last type of holding was most common. By 1948 there were roughly 1500 *jagirs* in the Nizam's dominions. In theory, the Nizam owned all *jagirs* and he could reclaim them at will. In practice, through giving *nazrs*, families could keep their *jagirs* for generations. Only when an heir was not available, when succession was in dispute, or when some other misfortune occurred, did the Nizam have occasion to reclaim a *jagir*.[80] Of the *jagirs* A.M. Khurso has written:

> Steeped in the habits of a by-gone feudal age, receiving generally nazars, gifts in cash and kind and other parasitical incomes without simultaneous exertion, many a *jagirdar* had become negligent of the affairs of his *jagir* and indulged in a good deal of extravagance, pomp and ceremony.[81]

Other types of *jagirs* and smaller landholdings could also be found within the Hyderabad dominions. *Al-Tamgha jagirs* were made as special favors, and were revenue-free, permanent, perpetual, and hereditary. *Zat jagirs* were given for the maintenance of the grantee. Grants given for the maintenance of some service (military, religious, etc.) were *mashrooti jagirs* (not unlike *devasthanams*—grants for the maintenance of a temple). *Madad mash jagirs* were for the maintenance of the recipient, or could be given in conjunction with other grants. *Tankha jagirs*, like *paigahs* were granted as a salary for those who rendered some service. Other *jagirs* included *mokassa jagirs*, whereby the grant was for a special purpose or individual who remitted one-fourth or one-third of the revenue. Finally, *inams* were granted in favor of an individual or institution, and the donor relinquished all, or most of its claims to the income from the grant.[82] As table 2 demonstrates, the *jagirs* formed the largest block of landholding in the state, followed by the Nizam's personal lands (*sarf-i-khas*), then the samasthans, followed by the *paigahs* and *ilaqas*.

Table 2 Estates of Hyderabad State

Estate	*Area (Miles)*	*Villages*	*Annual income (Rs.)*
Sarf-i-khas	5,682	1,374	
Paigahs	4,352	1,194	7,597,750
Ilaqas	2,836	1,243	7,614,814
Samasthans	5,030	497	5,536,999
Jagirs	11,619	3,122	14,251,437

Conclusion

Hyderabad State thus provides a picture of a multitiered, multiethnic state similar to, yet different from other comparable states in nineteenth- and twentieth-century India. Unique to the state's polity were the samasthan rajas and their domains, leftovers from the Kakatiya and Vijayanagar empires, and embedded within new Muslim regimes. Yet, as subordinate rulers within the state, they were not alone, often competing with and fighting against a host of newer landholders as well as a variety of more free floating ethnic communities who served a variety of purposes. However, scholarship has largely failed to move beyond examinations of the dominant power of Hyderabad in the form of the Nizams and their British counterparts. Using the samasthans as a case study, in the following chapters, this work argues for a revisioning of the state as one where power was negotiated over and across a multiethnic and composite milieu. Chapter 1 examines how the samasthans emerged in the medieval Deccan from the ruins of the Kakatiya and Vijayanagar empires. The histories of those empires make frequent mention of nobles who held territory at their edge. As empires fractured and reformed, some rajas who settled south of the Tungabhadra river emerged as independent kingdoms and bear names familiar to us, for instance Ramnad and Pudukkottai.[83] Those rajas north of the river became the samasthans of Hyderabad. The samasthans thus provide a bridge to the period that followed, and a continuity between those empires and the new ones established at Golconda and Hyderabad.

The rulers of Golconda and Hyderabad called upon these rajas to provide troops for battle. In return, they were allowed to maintain troops in their own capitals, and deduct the cost of this maintenance from the tribute they paid. Chapter 2 examines the twilight of this medieval era and the dawn of the colonial period. For Golconda, John Richards has shown how some of the samasthan rajas served as able revenue farmers for large tracts of land, thus relieving the Golconda sultans from even greater administrative responsibility.[84] This military service relationship lasted well into the nineteenth century, and we find certain samasthan rajas maintaining enough armed force to warrant precautions by the Company. Critical to the Company and Hyderabad's security was safe passage through the countryside.[85] Bandits made frequent attacks on travelers, and the samasthan rajas were called upon to suppress these outlaws. Also functioning within Hyderabad and at the samasthan capitals were large populations of Arabs, Africans, and Afghans. Indeed, Hyderabad of the eighteenth and nineteenth century had not only religious (Hindu, Muslim, and Christian) but also ethnic diversity, each seeking out their own place within the state's composite social geography. Frequently incorporated into the armed forces of local and regional armies, these ethnic groups often turned from armed service to armed resistance, taking hostages and providing a threat to law and order. Again, the rajas were key participants in this wider net of ethnic and military activity. By the mid-nineteenth century, opportunities to maintain rank and honor through military service were rapidly dwindling When armed forces no longer carried adequate prestige, ceremony and pomp rose to fill the vacuum.

Critical to the maintenance of the samasthan rajas' power was the right to hold ceremonial durbars, as well as participating in those of the Nizam. These events allowed for individuals to be ritually incorporated into the spheres of their superiors. Chapter 3 examines the multitiered ceremonial integration played out in the durbar and other select sites. Durbars held in the samasthan capitals allowed for the rajas to receive and present *nazr* from nobles who served under them. At the regional level, the durbar of the Nizam allowed him to symbolically incorporate the samasthan rajas and other nobles into his realm.[86] At the highest level were the imperial durbars created by the British. Thus, processes of incorporation spanned from the smallest states to the breadth of empire. Beyond durbars, the authority to mint coins and hunt (especially tigers) in one's territory were key components in maintaining the samasthan rajas' honor. Caught between their own sense of honor and duty to the Nizam, the rajas devised a multitude of responses to shifting patterns of loyalty.

The personal and sometimes whimsical nature of the Nizams, combined with increasing pressure for Western style reforms coming from the Residency, led to administrative change within Hyderabad. Putting the state on legal and modern footing was not easy, and institutions brought to Hyderabad were inevitably tainted by its autocratic ethos. Among these was the Court of Wards. This Court, an "institutional shelter," was responsible for handling child heirs as well as settling succession disputes.[87] Almost all of the samasthans came under the Court's care, and Chapter 4 is devoted to examining the Court of Wards in Hyderabad, and the management of its charge. Under the Nizam's touch, however, the Court sometimes shifted from being a benevolent baby sitter to a bank robber, returning impoverished estates to heirs. While child heirs were educated both at European and Indian schools, the Court and its largely British chief administrators did not always act in the best interest of their wards. On at least one occasion the Court trumped a mother's wishes for her son, and at other times, interfered (for better and for worse) in the Nizam's demands for gifts from the Court's charges.

The 1920s were an especially trying time for the families at Gadwal, Wanaparthi, and Jatprole. In this decade, each family witnessed the death of a raja, and struggled to find heirs. Chapter 5 examines these events, highlighting the ways in which each family survived the transition from one ruler to the next. Chronologically, these successions are the penultimate events in the samasthans and Hyderabad before their demise two decades later. However, far from being "typical" succession cases (where a son followed his father to the throne), these cases were wrought with peculiarities. At Wanaparthi, a sudden death pitted the raja's young son against his uncle. This dispute landed in the Hyderabad court system where the very nature and definition of a samasthan came under inquiry. At Gadwal, the raja's death brought with it unprecedented interference by the Nizam. Osman Ali Khan sought to place Gadwal within the Court of Wards where its finances could more easily be tapped for his own projects. However, leading Gadwal was its widow, Rani Adi Lakshmi, who challenged the Nizam, both in an armed showdown and in the courtroom. The one samasthan noticeably absent from the Court's records is Jatprole, for then Raja Lakshma Rao, aware of the difficulty experienced at Wanaparthi and Gadwal, adequately prepared for his own succession by making his wife Regent of their young adopted son.

At India's independence in 1947, three princely states held out from joining either India or Pakistan. These were Kashmir, Junagadh, and Hyderabad. Diplomatic efforts to bring Hyderabad into the Indian Union moved slowly forward from 1947 to 1948. However, losing patience, Deputy Prime Minister Sardar Patel, with the permission of Prime Minister Nehru, ordered a "police action" against Hyderabad that forcibly integrated the state with the rest of India. The rajas and their states were caught up in this drama. The Conclusion explores the ways in which these men signed over their samasthans to the new Hyderabad and Indian governments, and how even at the very end, the presence of their pasts came to bear on their final moments in power.

Of course, a study of the samasthan rajas and their domains inevitably must include a discussion of the Nizams they served under, and the capital city of Hyderabad. Yet, the attempt here is to begin with the samasthans: to see Hyderabad, the British Raj, and a good part of the nineteenth and twentieth century through their eyes, to see both the challenges they faced and the successes they enjoyed. The samasthans demonstrate a continuity with those empires of the Deccan long past, and at the same time—as states within Hyderabad—they came to embody a resilient compositeness that included Hindu, Muslim, and European practices. As states within Hyderabad, having long historical lineages, the samasthans were crucial members of the Deccan's composite political structure. As valued local rulers, their position allowed them a greater degree of freedom of choice about social and political practices. As seen in the statue of Lakshma Rao, whether it was the dress of their Muslim overlords, the language of their own people, or the administrative reforms of British India, the samasthan leaders came to embody a compositeness, that while finally succumbing to India's nascent nation state, nevertheless successfully managed tensions within their own territories, with their overlords, and with the British Raj.

CHAPTER 1

At the Edge of Empire

In September of 1857, as the mutiny against the Company spread in north India, samasthan Raja Rameshwar Rao of Wanaparthi penned a letter to the governor general, Charles Canning, at Fort William, Calcutta. His letter demonstrated loyalty to the Queen and Company, and animosity rhetorically expressed against the mutineers.

> With the deepest anxiety and horror have I heard and read of the barbarous and atrocious conduct of the Mutineers of the Bengal Presidency, and their coldblooded and deliberate proceedings are of such a nature, as to stamp them with imfamy [*sic*], and brutality, unknown in the Histories of the most savage and uncivilized nations. Hence my sympathies towards the British have been roused . . . [illegible], and my wrath against the rebels has been kindled, so that if the offer herein made is accepted, I am resolved to avenge the atrocities committed on the subjects of the Crown of England, with an unsparing hand.[1]

The mutiny, rebellion, or war of independence, was an opportunity for nobles like Rameshwar Rao to offer their military services either to the Company, or to the mutineers.[2] The raja of Gadwal, Rambhupal II, might have offered his services to the Company, but was unable to do so. His samasthan was under Company and Crown control from 1853 to 1860. The Raichur *doab* along with Berar had been leased to the British Government. Already under the political umbrella of the British Raj, Rambhupal did not participate in the events of 1857. To the east at Jatprole, Raja Jagannath Rao seemed unlikely to take up arms against the Company. He was known for his fondness of sport, and frequently raced horses at Madras and Bangalore. He even founded the "Jatprole Cup"—which still exists. He too was able to weather events without commitment. Taking a different stance, the young raja of nearby Shorapur,

Venkatappa Nayak, fought against the British. However, his revolt did not last long and he was soon captured by among others, Rameshwar Rao.[3] In accordance with his natal astrological prediction, Nayak died in custody at the young age of 24 under mysterious circumstances. His territory of Shorapur was first annexed in 1858 by the Crown, then given over to Hyderabad State for management.

These roles as local participants in the larger regional conflicts of the day had long antecedents. The progenitors of the samasthans established themselves at the edges of the great Deccan empires. Deriving power and support from the Kakatiya and Vijayanagar kings, warrior chiefs suppressed local tribal inhabitants who were either forced elsewhere, or used for labor and land clearing. These emerging rajas cleared forests and brought land under the plow that generated commensurate revenue and provided a degree of financial stability—used in part to pay for their small armed forces. For the Kakatiya period, as Cynthia Talbot has argued, subordinate lords or chieftains collaborated and advanced through military participation.[4] When called upon, individual leaders appeared at the Kakatiya and Vijayanagar courts to demonstrate loyalty and receive honors. Their names are found in the rosters of nobles attending events at the Kakatiya capital of Warangal and at Vijayanagar's capital of Hampi. By the peak of Vijayanagar rule, influence from those regimes north of the Krishna river can be found at its court. Dress and titles used by those rulers bear witness to a process of Islamicization.[5] Samasthan rajas mimicked this process and continued to develop Indo-Muslim practices evident well into the twentieth century, embodying continuity with the past, and a composite of Hindu and Muslim ritual and political norms. With the arrival of Muslim rule in the Deccan, the samasthan chiefs shifted their support to these new regimes, clearly defying any notions of civilizational or religious allegiance. Over time, they found patronage and recognition by the new Bahmani, Qutb Shah, and Asaf Jah regimes.

This chapter locates the samasthans in the fluid political landscape of the medieval Deccan. The participation of the samasthan rajas was vital to empire building, and their territories were the largest political entities to survive the transition to Muslim rule centered at Golconda and Hyderabad, as well as that of the Company. By the eighteenth century, the Company's emerging supremacy and influence in Hyderabad began to be considered by the samasthan rajas who would have to consider this new power in their own political strategizing. Throughout, they maintained a balance of pleasing their overlords, while at the same time taking steps to assure the continuance of their own power. The Company and Crown's role in Hyderabad indirectly affected the samasthan families as they were sheltered from direct Company interference by the Nizam. The British Resident generally could only offer advice to the Nizam concerning the samasthan rajas, but was not in a position to take direct action.

A "Warlike Class"

In his offer to the Company during the mutiny, Rameshwar Rao located his samasthan's place in Deccan history. "It may be irrelevant here to inform your Lordship, that the country of Wunpurthy and its dependencies in the Hyderabad Deccan, was held by ancestral and hereditary right and succession for nearly six centuries."[6] In Rameshwar Rao's eyes, the samasthan was no less than a country unto itself. He identified himself and the samasthan not as a subordinate of the Nizam, but a free-standing entity, ready to independently give support to the Company. Two days after Rameshwar Rao submitted his offer, the British Resident at Hyderabad, Cuthbert Davidson, added his own opinion before forwarding both correspondences to Calcutta. Davidson recognized Rameshwar Rao's sincerity, but cast some doubt on his claims.

> The Rajah has been at Hyderabad for some months and has been most anxious to make himself useful to me. He has had to a certain extent an English education, and he is, I feel certain, loyal and sincere in his offers. He is much respected by his own people, who are of a predatory and war-like class, he would have no difficulty at any time in collecting around him a considerable body of armed followers, ready to do his biding in any way, although I imagine he considerably over-estimates his powers when he talks of a complete Brigade of Cavalry Infantry and guns, as he has no means of paying and supporting them.[7]

Davidson's comment foreshadowed later feelings that India's princes were the "natural leaders" of the country. He then duly passed on Rameshwar Rao's letter to the governor general, Charles Canning, in Calcutta.

Rameshwar Rao was the sixteenth head of the Wanaparthi samasthan. His family history and that of many "little kingdoms" share certain common features. How these families crafted their origin stories shares much with other kingdoms throughout south India. Susan Bayly, in summarizing the work and collections of such histories as gathered by Colin Mackenzie, provides an account of royal origins for the *nayaka* families (leader or chief) found south of the Krishna river. "His realm [that of an aspiring Raja] is born out of war, conflict and blood-letting: most of the texts begin with a great feat of arms for which the chief or clan head receives marks of royal rank and honour from a much greater ruler, usually from one of the nayakas or from one of the fourteenth—or fifteenth—century warrior dynasts of Vijayanagar."[8] Wanaparthi's history follows this very pattern. The progenitor of the family, Veer Krishna Reddy, was a commander within the Kakatiya army.[9] Through his efforts this shadowy military figure in the mid-fourteenth century marked out what would become the Wanaparthi samasthan. This territory was on the southern edge of the Kakatiya realm. While little more is known of Veer Krishna Reddy, details of the Jatprole samasthan's progenitor share similar epic and real qualities.

Unlike the Reddys of Wanaparthi, the Jatprole family were members of the Velama caste.[10] They saw themselves, and were generally acknowledged to be of higher social rank than the Reddys. Also, Jatprole was linked to families with antecedents and connections throughout south India. Such relationships later played heavily into issues of adoption and succession.

While the Jatprole family traced its origins to the thirteenth century, the name Jatprole or Jataprolu has an even earlier epic origin. In the *Ramayana* when Sita was carried south by the demon king Ravana, the latter was attacked by Jatayu, the vulture king. Ravana mortally wounded him, and he fell to the ground. Searching for Sita, Rama came to the place where Jatayu had fallen, and learned what had happened to his wife. With that, Jatayu died. On the spot Rama erected a temple in his honor. This place, that of Jatayu, has become Jatprole. A different explanation for the name comes from Lord Shiva's matted hair, "jetta." Devoted to Shiva, the town bore the name Jettaprolu, or place of Shiva.[11]

These early rulers were frequently incorporated into the larger empires of the day as subordinate power holders. The third Kakatiya ruler, Ganapatideva, rewarded the Jatprole samasthan founder, Chevi Reddy. Chevi Reddy was the progenitor not only of Jatprole, but also other Velama samasthan families at Bobbili, Venkatagiri, Pithapuram, and Mailavaram (in the Madras Presidency).[12] He was a local chief in southern Telangana and his rise to power is told and retold to this day.[13] Chevi Reddy was moving through the territory near Pillalamarri (in modern Mahbubnagar district), when he and his men came across a farmer whose plow was stuck in the earth. Reddy ordered his men to assist the cultivator. Unable to move the plow, Reddy himself dismounted and began to assist in the effort. At this point a local deity appeared, Bethala *deva*. Bethala was protector of a great fortune buried in the ground that the plow had snagged. Fortuitously, the treasure had long ago been buried there by a distant descendant of Reddy named Hemadri Naidu.[14] Since Reddy had shown great courage before the deity, Bethala agreed to hand over the treasure to Reddy if he would perform a human sacrifice. In Reddy's party was a Mala (the Telugu equivalent of an outcaste) named Rechan. Rechan was "prepared to die cheerfully" for his master, but only on certain conditions. He asked that his name be forever perpetuated within Reddy's family by taking his name as part of their own. Also, henceforth, the Chevi Reddy family would always perform a marriage in Rechan's family before performing one in their own home, thus guaranteeing Rechan's bloodline. Chevi Reddy agreed, the sacrifice was made, and he inherited a great amount of wealth. In recognition for facing Bethala, Ganapatideva bestowed land on Chevi Reddy, and thus came the new name of Pillallamari Bethala Naidu.[15]

At Warangal, Ganapatideva's daughter followed him in succession. She ruled for thirty-four years before her grandson, Prataparudra, succeeded her and embarked on an agenda to revitalize the domain. He appears in both the Gadwal and Jatprole samasthan histories as an important benefactor in their growth, giving land grants to clear forests and further settle the region.[16] For the Gadwal samasthan, Prataparudra gave the administration of the *doab* to three families—the Gona, Malaya, and Viryala. The Gona family, headed by Immadi Reddy, was responsible for the eastern section of the *doab* where the Gadwal samasthan became established.[17] A local warrior in the area named Pedda Veera Reddy (also known as Budda Reddy) assisted Immadi Reddy in land clearing. Immadi commended him for rewards to the Kakatiya king.[18] In 1290, Prataparudra awarded Pedda Veera Reddy the *nagagoud* (authority to administer and rule lands) for districts in the lands between the Krishna and Tungabhadra rivers. In return for this grant, Reddy and his descendents provided military service to the Kakatiyas and secured land for generating revenue at the Kakatiya frontier.

Contemporary with Pedda Veera Reddy was Dacha Naidu, then head of the Jatprole family. Prataparudra deployed Dacha Naidu and his forces against the Pandyan rulers in the south. Dacha Naidu was known as the "Kanchi Gate Breaker" for having destroyed Kanchipuram's magnificent gate. Kanchipuram, known as Conjeeveram during the Raj, was once the headquarters of the Pallava dynasty, and then the Cholas before passing into Muslim rule after 1310, and finally to the kings of Vijayanagar. Kakatiya rule was dramatically weakened by the armies of Sultan Khilji who imposed a heavy indemnity. Even with the help of men like Pedda Veera Reddy and Dacha Naidu, Prataparudra was not able to hold power, and in 1323 Warangal was sacked. At the fall of Warangal, the rulers of Gadwal realigned their forces with the Bahmani kingdom at Gulburga. As the Bahmanis split into smaller sultanates, Gadwal rulers again shifted allegiance to the Bijapur sultans.

By 1336, the Vijayanagar empire had begun to take root. Taking advantage of the natural barrier that the Tungabhadra river provided, two brothers, Bukka and Harihara established themselves on the river's south bank at what is now Hampi. They fled across the river from the town of Anagundi (also a samasthan) when Mohammad ibn Tugluk's army reached the area. Anagundi (in Telugu, literally "elephant pit") was where the Vijayanagar rajas kept their elephants. The family that came to rule the samasthan claimed lineal descent from the Vijayanagar rulers.[19] Vijayanagar reached its pinnacle in the early sixteenth century under the rule of Krishnadevaraya. At that time, the city of Vijayanagar covered nearly twenty-five square miles, and its domain reached to Orissa in the east, to Kanara in the west, and to Cape Comerin in the south. Within the polity were samasthan rulers as well as countless lesser chiefs.

Under Vijayanagar rule, kingship reached a pinnacle and landholding within the empire began to take on royal trappings. For the Vijayanagar kings, a stable of subordinates helped settle frontier agricultural zones, collect revenue, and serve as buttresses to their own rule. For local elites, recognition by, and access to, the Vijayanagar rulers gave them a degree of legitimacy in their own territories.[20] The conglomeration of chiefs and lords under the umbrella of Vijayanagar is what Burton Stein has referred to as a "segmentary" state.[21] Those who survived the fall of the Vijayanagar empire have been called "successor states," but this term, along with *nayaka* and *poligar* (leader or chief), is best applied to those states south of Vijayanagar. As Susan Bayly has explored, when some of the Deccani chiefs shifted south during the sixteenth and seventeenth centuries, they formed their own "little kingdoms" in Tamil lands around Madurai, Tirchy, and Tanjore.[22] These early domains were the *nayaka* states. They were succeeded by two groups: the first being the kingdoms centered at Travancore, Cochin, and Tanjore, and the second being the *poligar* states that included Pudukkottai, Ramnad, Sivagangai, and others.[23] Those states that were north of the Tunghabhadra river and became embedded within the Muslim dynasties of the time were in fact the samasthans.[24]

Within Vijayanagar's realm were men like Veer Krishna Reddy, then head of the Wanaparthi samasthan. This raja bears the same name as the progenitor of the samasthan; it is not uncommon to see names of important family figures employed again by later members of the dynasty, thus establishing important links to the past. Around 1510, Reddy came to Patapally, a village near the Krishna river and not far from the village of Sugur. The inhabitants of this area were tribals whom Reddy initially suppressed, thus securing for himself a portion of land and the attention of the Vijayanagar rulers. Thus, for a time the samasthan went by the name of Sugur.[25] In the Wanaparthi territories was a fort at Pangal (in Mahbubnagar district) that then ruler of Vijayanagar Krishnadevaraya visited in the 1520s. With the visit, he conferred authority on Reddy to administer the surrounding area.

Vijayanagar rule was also a critical period for the Jatprole leaders. Late in the fifteenth century two brothers, Madha Naidu and Yachama Naidu, marked out the domains of the Jatprole and Venkatagiri samasthans. Members from Venkatagiri would later establish other samasthans throughout coastal Andhra. At this time Madha Naidu came to Jatprole, at the confluence of the Krishna and Tungabhadra, and began to fortify it.[26] Three generations later Mulla Bhupati Naidu received a *sanaa* (royal letter, decree) from the rulers of Vijayanagar in 1507 confirming his authority over the samasthan. It is likely that it was Mulla Bhupati Naidu who attended the coronation of Krishnadevaraya as "chief of Velugodu," the Velamas.[27] The Vijayanagar and Kakatiya empires provided the samasthan rajas with land grants to raise funds for troops, then as those empires fell, these leaders were agile enough to survive and square their position with newer forces in the Deccan.

Shifting Alliances

Long before 1857, the Warangal and Vijayanagar empires had succumbed to newer dynasties. As early as the fifteenth century, the samasthan rajas found themselves allied with Muslim sultans who were making the Deccan their home. Faced with possible destruction, these rajas crossed religious lines and struck deals with the new rulers. By the nineteenth century, they were firmly embedded within Hyderabad State. Four dynasties mark the time from the late thirteenth century to the mid twentieth century: Ala ud Din Khilji and his descendents, the Bahmanis, the Qutb Shahis of Golconda, and the Asaf Jahs of Hyderabad.

While Islam came to the subcontinent in the early eighth century, Muslim rulers were kept busy establishing themselves in north India before eying the Deccan and the south for expansion. The first Muslim ruler to settle in the Deccan was Ala ud Din, a Turk and nephew and son-in-law to the sultan at Delhi, Jalal ud Din Khilji. His dynasty included repeated battles with the kings of Warangal. By the mid-fourteenth century, internal revolts by provincial leaders against the rule of Muhammad ibn Tughluk occurred at Gulbarga (1339), Warangal (1345–1346), and within Daulautabad (1347) leading to the foundation of the Bahmani empire.

The head of the Bahmanis was Ala ud Din Bahman Shah né Hassan, a descendant of the Persian hero Bahman. He and his descendants repeatedly engaged the rajas of Vijayanagar in battle. The bone of contention between the two empires was the "hotly contested" Raichur *doab*.[28] Not only known for its natural resources, the *doab* also had several strong forts including ones at Mudgal and Raichur. One such confrontation in the *doab* occurred in 1404 when the Vijayanagar armies advanced to Mudgal, just west of Gadwal. In an alliance that crossed Hindu-Muslim lines, and following a practice more common than not, Gadwal's forces joined the Bahmanis to defeat the invading Vijayanagar army. Cooperation such as this was a portent of the "criss-cross" and composite alliances and agreements made later between the samasthan rajas and their Muslim overlords at Hyderabad.[29] The final Bahmani ruler was Mahmud Shah who took the throne in 1482. It was during Mahmud's time that the Bahmani political fabric began to fray. First, the province of Bijapur led by Yusuf Adil Khan revolted and declared independence from the Bahmani yoke. Then, in 1512, the Qutb Shahs under the leadership of Sultan Quli Qutb ul Mulk declared independence.[30] By the fifteenth century, the Bahmani domains had splintered into five smaller regional regimes: Bidar, Berar, Bijapur, Ahmednagar, and Golconda. It is the latter with which we are centrally concerned.

In 1512, Qutb Quli—of Turkic origin—established the Golconda sultanate. Under his reign, the rulers of Golconda continued their struggle with the Vijayanagar kings. Early the next year in preparation for battle against his Turkish northern neighbors, Krishnadevaraya summoned his nobles—including Velugoti Yachama Naidu of Jatprole—to inquire as to their troop strength.[31] The battleground was the Raichur *doab*, exactly where the samasthan rajas held power. At Pangal in 1513 the Qutb Shahs defeated the advancing Vijayanagar armies. In victory, Quli advanced further west into the *doab* and took the forts at Raichur and Mudgal.[32] Sultan Quli lived to the age of 90 before being assassinated. He was followed by his heirs Jamshid (in 1543), and Subhan Quli (in 1550). After Subhan Quli, Ibrahim Quli took the reins of power. Under Ibrahim in 1564, the Gol'conda and Vijayanagar forces met at Talikota in the central *doab*. In what has been dubbed the "war of the goldsmith's daughter," they fought for supremacy in the Deccan.[33] Ibrahim emerged victorious and the area from Golconda south to the Krishna river came under Golconda's rule.

For the samasthan rajas survival now meant accommodating themselves to these new rulers. Within both Hindu and Muslim political and military practice, valiant foes were generally replaced to their positions of power, although without armed forces to support any further revolt. The samasthan rajas chose this possible accommodation over confrontation, and soon found places within the structure of the Qutb Shah regime. The process did not take long to begin. Ibrahim's grandson, Abdullah, recognized the military support given to him by Raja Immadi Venkat Reddy of Wanaparthi who had captured the fort at Udaigiri in the name of the sultan. Immadi was followed by Gopal Rao. He was also known by his nickname, *Ashta Basha* (eight language) Gopal Rao because as a warrior-pundit he is said to have known eight languages. For the sultan, this raja maintained a force of 2,000 infantry and 2,000 cavalry. In return for this, the sultan awarded Gopal Rao the additional title of *bahiri* (eagle), a hereditary title used throughout the family's history. Gopal Rao was followed by his child son Kumara Bahiri Gopal Rao. This child heir was protected by his mother, Rani Janamma, who sided with the Golconda sultans and resisted Mughal Emperor Aurangzeb's repeated attacks against the last sultan, Tana Shah. She held the forts at Ghanpur and Pangal against those who had sided with the Mughals. Wanaparthi relations with the rulers of Golconda seemed to have fluctuated. At one time, the rulers of that family were called upon to escort Maratha ruler Shivaji (1627–1680) to the town of Srisailam. This was done at the request of Akkanna and Madanna, the Brahman brothers then serving the sultans of Golconda.[34] Yet, at another time, it appears that Janamma was arrested by officials at Hyderabad. In revenge, she ordered her people to round up the relatives of Akkanna and Madanna who were traveling near Wanaparthi.[35] Tana Shah also had the support of the Jatprole family who ruled according to the wishes of the Bhagnagar rulers, a different name for Hyderabad.[36]

By 1687, the Golconda sultans, having challenged Mughal authority now faced the consequences. In 1688, Aurangzeb sacked Golconda. In the process he recognized those samasthan families that had provided valuable assistance in his efforts, specifically honoring Shorapur and Paloncha.[37] These families had sided with the Mughals while others had sided with Golconda. In victory, however, Aurangzeb did not crush the rebellious samasthan rajas, but instead began—through his newly appointed governor—to weave them into the political fabric of the territory.

From this point forth, the samasthan rajas witnessed increased autonomy and royal status. Jatprole was among the first to be brought into the new political order of this administration. John Richards has shown how the Jatprole family—then headed by Gopal Rao—was able to consolidate its grip on the region from Jatprole in the south to Pangal and Yeljal in the north.[38] To accomplish this, the Mughals adopted a "decentralized" administrative style that granted considerable autonomy to nobles like Gopal Rao. In return for this, he managed a large territory for them while paying heavily to the Golconda coffers. Under Mughal ascendancy, Gopal Rao and his three sons were responsible for the district capitals of Pangal and Kotha Kota as well as for Jatprole.[39] Yet, their position within the Mughal polity was not easily defined. As Richards explains,

> More important than an ordinary deshmukh dominant in a single pargana [district, province], Gopal Rao was not a prince who possessed the autonomy implied by the payment of straightforward tribute (like Annand Rao of Paloncha [another samasthan in the region]). He occupied, instead, an intermediate status somewhere between the two. The ambiguity of the Valama raja's position reflects the flexibility of the Golconda agrarian system.[40]

A year later, Gopal Rao and his sons renegotiated their contract with the Mughals for even greater holdings. As a result, their revenue increased dramatically. In one strategic move, the family acquired lands with a larger revenue promise, as well as jurisdiction over policing, markets, roads, and towns. Furthermore, the family expected to receive *inam* lands for themselves. In return, the Mughals brought into the fold a large and powerful ally, while at the same time being relieved of the burden of revenue collection.[41] Yet, the fragile agreement between the old and established Jatprole family and the newly established Mughal and Asaf Jah regime at Hyderabad did not last long.

In 1694, Narsingh Rao revolted against the Mughals. He committed offences including the capture of the Mughal mace bearer, and submitted demands including control over Ganjikota (ninety miles south of Jatprole) and Srikakulum (along the Bay of Bengal). To pacify him, his requests were granted and his powers enlarged.[42] Richards explains this desire for administrative powers over nearby Ganjikota as reasonable for an ambitious landholder. However, seeking powers over Srikakulum is less understandable. Richards has suggested the Mughals would have benefited from Narsingh's presence in Srikakulum because he would have been an outsider in the area, yet still bound to their rule, thus offering them an outpost of stability far from Hyderabad. An alternative explanation exists for Narsingh's requests. As we know, the Jatprole, Bobbili, Venkatagiri, and Pithapuram samasthans all shared a common ancestry. On the Venkatagiri side, the family had split, and Raja Pedda Rayadu established the Bobbili samasthan. He had come with

Sher Muhammad Khan to the Bobbili area in 1652. Bobbili and Srikakulam are only seventy miles apart. It was only forty-five years later that Narsingh attempted to extend his jurisdiction over territory nearer to his relative at Bobbili. Perhaps a familial reason prompted Narsingh to make his request. While this explanation is only speculative, it fits with a history of visits, exchanges, and adoptions between these Velama families.

Also caught in the struggle for supremacy was the ruler of Gadwal, Somanna. In honor of his service, Aurangzeb awarded him the title of *raja* in 1696. Eight years later in further recognition of his assistance, Aurangzeb awarded the raja an area of six *mahals* (districts) including territory in the Kurnool region and also west into Raichur. Gadwal levied tribute from Kurnool until the latter's merger with British India in 1800.

In 1713, Aurangzeb's second successor, Farruksiyar, appointed Qamar ud din as governor of the Deccan, better known by his title of Nizam ul Mulk Asaf Jah I. Under the Nizams, the local chiefs and rajas of the Deccan formed new alliances and received new rewards for their assistance. For instance, in 1715, Farruksiyar sent Lingamma, the rani of Gadwal a *firman* (imperial order, edict) that bestowed authority on her to rule the samasthan until her son came of age.[43] Gadwal was not only incorporated into the regional fabric of the Deccan, but was clearly recognized by the Emperor at Delhi as a valuable constituent of his polity. Gadwal's territory was expanded from six to fifteen *mahals* in and around the *doab*. While the Mughals clearly valued the support of Gadwal, when the first Nizam declared his independence in 1723, Gadwal's rulers shifted their allegiance to the local house of Asaf Jah.

The samasthan rajas continued a checkerboard pattern of alternate loyalty followed by brief periods of revolt. For instance, in 1714 Raja Venkat Reddy of Wanaparthi revolted against the local Mughal officer, Mubariz Khan. Reddy found himself under siege by Khan within the fort at Changapettah. He was outnumbered and died in defense of the location. Changapettah was subsequently renamed to Farrukhnagar in honor of the Emperor.[44] Venkat Reddy's son, however, was raised in a time when the Asaf Jahs were already rulers in the Deccan, and he caused no difficulties for the royal house at Hyderabad. At other times, assistance between the rajas and their overlords sometimes took the form of one raja keeping another in check. Such was the case when Nizam ul Mulk called upon the raja of Wanaparthi, Gopal Rao, to subdue the head of the Jatprole family, likely Chinna Madhava Rao. This accomplished, he wrote in 1734:

> The most excellent Zanampally Raja Bahiri Gopal Rao Deshmukh Sar Deshmukh Perguna Sugur Kothakota Haveli Sircar Pangal is hereby informed that under the orders of the Government you have supressed the

> rebels and captures [*sic*] the zamindar of Jetpole at great risk. It is the result of your good will and sacrifice. Well done, a hundred times, well done. You with your troops bring the said zamindar to our presence with great care.[45]

While it is unclear exactly what misdeed Chinna Madhava Rao had committed, it is likely that this episode concerned failure to pay *peshkush*, military insubordination, or both. Later, the Nizam again called on Gopal Rao in 1743 to guard the city of Hyderabad while he was away fighting in the Carnatic. At Jatprole, within a generation the samasthan came under the new leadership of Bari Gadupala Rao who received new boons from the Nizam.[46] After the death of Nizam ul Mulk, Nasir Jung (1748–1750), Muzaffar Jung (1750), and Salabut Jung (1751–1762) succeeded him. Under the second Asaf Jah, Nizam Ali Khan (1762–1803), Gadupala Rao received a *sanad* in 1771 along with the title of *raja bahadur*, thus putting he and the samasthan on royal footing. This did not end the skirmishes between Jatprole and Wanaparthi. For instance, in 1799, Raja Jagannath Rao of Jatprole failed to pay *peshkush*, and Wanaparthi's Rani Janamma (junior) and Raja Ram Krishna Rao were sent to capture him.[47] They accomplished this and brought Jagannath Rao to Hyderabad where he faced punishment.[48]

By the late eighteenth century, Maratha power in the Deccan was approaching its apogee, and the Gadwal samasthan had come under both Maratha and Hyderabad's fiscal umbrella. It appears that Nizam ul Mulk was not yet strong enough to keep the Maratha powers from levying *chauth* on the Gadwal samasthan. This amounted to Rs. 60,000 annually, and records suggest that Gadwal continued to pay to the Maratha powers until their defeat in 1822.[49] However, the Gadwal rajas, far from paying tribute to both the Hyderabad and Pune coffers, played the two powers off of each other, and occasionally paid tribute to neither. This refusal to pay is mentioned in the treaty of 1800 between the British and Nizam (explored later). If the raja refused payment, the subsidiary force in Hyderabad might be called upon to ensure compliance. From 1807 to 1840, Gadwal was under the rule of Sita Rambhupal I, his accession being granted by both Hyderabad and Pune. By this time, Maratha powers in the Deccan were defeated, and Gadwal's head was obliged to return the regular payment of *peshkush* to only Hyderabad. At his death, Sita Rambhupal's wife, Venkatalakshmiama, succeeded him. The heir, Sombhupal II, was later adopted into the family, and recognized by officials at Hyderabad.

Sombhupal II was not Gadwal's finest leader. He indulged in "drinking and debauchery," and payment to support the samasthan troops fell behind.[50] Tensions rose between Sombhupal and his adopted mother. Each sought military assistance: Sombhupal sought help from mercenaries in nearby Shorapur, and Venkatalakshmiama had the support of Gadwal's own troops. On 26 September 1844, in a chain of events still unclear, the raja was shot in his own durbar. Meadows Taylor, then serving the Nizam in Shorapur, noted the events at Gadwal with some alarm. Taylor had been commissioned as a lieutenant in the Nizam's army, and was promoted to political agent at Shorapur from 1841 to 1853, and finally placed in charge of Berar until his retirement in 1860. He describes that the raja, his brother, and father had all been killed and their bodies "cast out of town."[51] Again, Rani Venkatalakshmiama held the reins of power until 23 November 1845, when Rambhupal II was placed on the *gaddi*.

From 1853 to 1860 the Raichur *doab* section of the Hyderabad dominions was under Company and Crown administration. At the beginning of the decade, with Nizam Nasir ud Daula increasingly in debt, several districts were annexed by the Company for payment. Among these were those districts between the Krishna and Tungabhadra rivers, along with swaths of Berar.[52] During this interim administration, the Company sought to implement change. In one instance, the Company tried to impose its own police force in Gadwal. On 11 September 1856, then Resident George Bushby wrote to the Government of India defending the rights of the Gadwal family. Having discussed the matter with Edward Maltby (who later served as acting governor of Madras 1863–1864), Bushby wrote:

> [W]e find much reason to doubt the propriety of placing Gudwal in the same category as the Surfi Khas and other Jagheer Estates . . . I cannot discover any *sunnuds* [sanad] which would very clearly determine the position of the Raja of Gudwal with respect to the Nizam, but the records of my office show that he has always been regarded by my predecessors as superior and more independent than ordinary jagheerdars or Zamindars.[53]

Bushby's intervention on behalf of the samasthan succeeded, leaving the raja to manage law and order within the samasthan free from interference. The next year, while Rameshwar Rao offered his services to the Company and Crown, and while Raja Venkatappa Nayak in Shorapur revolted, Rambhupal II remained loyal if not indifferent to the mutineers' cause. Some hint of his actions comes from eminent Hyderabad chronicler Krishna Swami Mudiraj. "[A]nd though the Raja was young, it is due to the wise administration of Rani Venkatlakshamamma that

Gadwal did not imitate the bad example set by Shorapur which ended so disastrously to that Samasthan."[54] Nearly eighty years before the mutiny and the "disastrous" fortunes of Shorapur, members of the Company established themselves in Hyderabad, thus marking the arrival of a new group of participants in the state's multiethnic and multitiered political structure.

Company and Crown

That Rameshwar Rao addressed his letter during the mutiny of 1857 directly to the governor general of the Company is indicative of its growing power in the subcontinent. Rao recognized that it was the Company, not the Nizams of Hyderabad or any other princely house, that had become a major force, if not *the* major force in south India and the Deccan. In continuation of the long-held practice of supporting the larger regional power of the time, Rao offered troops to help suppress the mutineers, and concluded with a rhetorical flourish of passion and sympathy for the Company and Crown.

> I beg to assure your Lordship in Council of my loyalty, affection, and attachment to the British Government; to whose kind and patronal [*sic*] protection I owe my life, my liberty, my safety, and my all; and it would be disloyal in me, not to tender my services at this painful crisis, to aid in quelling the disturbances, and in destroying and dispelling the Mutineers.[55]

On 21 October 1857, the secretary to the governor general in Council responded to Rameshwar Rao.

> In reply I am directed to acquaint you that His Lordship Hon'ble feels assured that your Highness' troops would, if called into the field, do excellent service. But the retaking of Delhee, and the arrangements that have been made for finishing the mutineers in all other directions, renders it unnecessary for the Govt. to accept the aid of your troops.[56]

In the years after 1857, the Crown sought to reward those who had remained loyal during the mutiny (especially in the princely states). Lord Canning bestowed ceremonial rewards at durbars held throughout India. On 5 October 1861, Rameshwar Rao was given such honors by the Government of India as well as from the Nizam's government. He received a *khilat*; an English double-barreled rifle; a sword and belt with inscriptions; and a pair of revolvers.[57] At the event Hastings Fraser (son of James Stuart Fraser, Resident at Hyderabad) noted that Rameshwar Rao was, "dresse[d] in the English costume, and command[ed] a considerable body of troops in the Nizam's service."[58] By now these troops and the samasthans' role as a military buttress to the Nizam's forces and the British was nearing its end.

The governor general's local representative in Hyderabad was the Resident. As the Company expanded direct control over parts of India, other regions were under indirect control by the "native chiefs" and "native states." The "native states" or princely states were 562 in number. Some like Hyderabad and Kashmir were vast states with considerable wealth and critical geographic positions. Relations with these and other powerful states were handled by the central government in Calcutta, and later at New Delhi through the Resident. Others states were not much larger than the garden surrounding the prince's palace, and their relationships via the Resident were handled by the provincial governments.

The first Resident in Hyderabad was John Holland who assumed his duties in the spring of 1779.[59] Depending on his personality and that of the Nizams, the relationship between the Resident and the head of India's largest princely state was either warm and congenial, or at times veered toward acrimony. As the nineteenth century dawned, relations between the Resident and the Nizam were particularly strong, largely in part to the personality of then Resident James Achilles Kirkpatrick (1764–1805). Kirkpatrick was not only responsible for building the Palladian style Residency building in Hyderabad, but enmeshed himself in Hyderabadi nobility when he married a young woman, Khair un Nissa. Their relationship largely marked an end to the liberal and libertine eighteenth century in India, and heralded the rise of the more conservative Victorian nineteenth century. William Dalrymple demonstrated that Kirkpatrick's comfort with Indian dress, language, and customs made him a favorite of the Nizam. However, his marriage to Khair un Nissa drew considerable attention and consternation from Company officials at Madras.[60] His successor, Henry Russell, and all those that followed up to the last Resident, Charles Herbert, took a decidedly more conservative view of their position and relations with Hyderabad.

The Residency system served as a form of "indirect rule" in India. In Hyderabad, it merely offered advice to the Nizam while on other occasions its influence had more tangible outcomes. For instance, as Michael Fisher has explored, in the 1820s interference in the Nizam's court by the Residency reached new heights. In efforts to counterbalance this trend, the fifth Nizam, Afzal ud Daula, forbade nobles from establishing direct contact with the Residents. The Residents, in turn, sought to expand contacts and influence with nobles in order to gain further influence with the Nizam.[61] When Afzal ud Daula died in 1869, the child Nizam, Mahbub Ali Khan, was only three years old. The change in power provided the Residency with a prime opportunity to further shape and influence the Hyderabad court. With the young Nizam unable to speak for himself, Salar Jung was amenable to suggestions made by the Residency. Salar Jung and Nawab Shams ul Umara served as coregents for the young Nizam.

To help oversee many of these changes, Salar Jung regularly employed Europeans in Hyderabad State's bureaucracy. They served as bureaucrats, military commanders, and advisors. By the early years of the twentieth century, the Nizam's government consistently employed several Britons. They served as heads of important administrative branches such as the Court of Wards. Yet, while their pay came from the Nizam's treasury, their loyalty seems to have ultimately been with the colonial administration. While in other arenas this might have given rise to strife, in Hyderabad a long tradition of generally warm relations between the Nizams and British officials in the state held sway. Two individuals in particular loom large in the internal affairs of Hyderabad State, and have particular importance to the samasthans.

Richard Chenevix-Trench, born in 1876, came to India through the army, but then spent the remainder of his career in the Indian Political Service. He served in Kashmir, Baluchistan and other sites in the northwest before coming to Hyderabad in 1927. From that year to his retirement in 1935, he served as Revenue member of the Nizam's Executive Council. Trench died in London in 1954. As we shall see, as Revenue member he was called upon to give his opinion on several succession cases involving one or more samasthans. Trench was aided by a second officer on loan from the Government of India, Theodore Tasker. Tasker was born in 1884 and entered the Indian Civil Service (ICS) in 1908. He served at Madras, Bangalore, and Coorg before arriving in Hyderabad in 1927. From 1927 to 1935 he served as director general of Revenue and Revenue secretary, and from 1942 to 1944 was a member of the Nizam's Council. Tasker died in 1981. Like Trench, Tasker's position within the Hyderabad government brought him into contact with several of the samasthan families.

Tasker's position as a member of the ICS while employed by the Nizam's government put him in a delicate position. He was an employee of the Nizam and hired to work for the best interests of Hyderabad. Yet, he also retained his ICS position and was a Briton whose loyalty ultimately rested elsewhere. Tasker explains:

> The Notes [from Tasker to the Resident], for which Sir Richard Trench or myself were responsible, were written at intervals for the information of the Resident at a time when the Viceroy and the Nizam were to meet. We were, of course, the Nizam's servants, and did not seek, or take, orders from the Resident, but in the last resort we were answerable to the Government of India for conducting ourselves in the spirit of the intervention, and it was a responsibility of a Resident to keep an eye on us. It was therefore traditional for the lent officers to see the Resident from time to time, and to let him know how things were going. The Nizam never objected to this. It was in this tradition that these very occasional Notes were written.[62]

The Nizam seemed not to object to Tasker and Trench's divided loyalties. Perhaps in the administration of Hyderabad State, their position and "intervention" was aligned with the Nizam's own intentions. Thus, British officials became integrated and integral to the internal functions of Hyderabad State, adding one more group of participants in an already crowded political milieu. From the Kakatiya period, many of these participants were at times drawn together by an interest in the valuable geographic assets that the Deccan contained. Geography and specific geographic locations served as magnets for Hyderabad's multiethnic participants. Fortuitously, among the most valuable assets in the Deccan were (literally) in the samasthan rajas' backyards.

Geographic Assets

In the Deccan, the samasthan rajas constructed forts atop buttes, controlled ferries to regulate river crossings, and mined diamonds and other precious minerals used for trade.[63] Large hill systems marked off the Deccan from the rest of the subcontinent, and within the region, buttes rose from the vast Deccan plateau. These smaller geologic formations made excellent locations to construct forts, or join together large rock outcroppings to create defensible positions. Traveling an imaginary road from Warangal to Hampi, one crosses feeder rivers that flow south into the Krishna river. The Krishna is joined by the Tungabhadra river east of Gadwal forming the Raichur *doab*. This area extended from the fort town of Mudgal in the west, to the rivers' confluence in the east, about 100 miles in length.[64] The *doab* was important for its physical attributes as well as fiscal resources. Rich cotton fields and a vast wildlife population were attractive to nobles and villagers alike. The region also contained mineral wealth in the form of diamonds, precious stones, and iron ore. The Krishna and Tungabhadra passed through deep chasms as well as broad fordable areas. The former made it difficult to harness the rivers for irrigation purposes, while the latter provided strategic points to cross the rivers in the dry season (March–May).[65] During the rainy season (June–September), the swollen rivers served as barriers that held marauding armies at bay.

Buttes

The village and fort of Pangal serve as an example of the interplay between geography and political-military strategizing of the day. This small village is eighty miles south-southwest of Hyderabad city. It lies roughly equidistant from the towns of Wanaparthi and Kollapur. A large butte, capped with a decaying fort dominates the village. The fort was one-mile long and one and a half miles wide. It had seven sides with seven towers. These walls and towers gave its defenders, along with the elevated position of the fort, an excellent strategic position from which to defend themselves. Within the fort's confines was a citadel for its royalty and commanders to reside in. Ascending the hill one can see out across the semiarid landscape. While goats, buffalos, and buses now traverse the surrounding plain, the scene was once very different. Pangal was at the fault-line between both the aforementioned samasthans, and political and military borders of the Vijayanagar and Bahmani empires. From the fifteenth century, Pangal saw action both in the wars between empires, and in the smaller skirmishes between the samasthans. Less than twenty miles south of Pangal, the Krishna river makes a large "U" shaped bend to the south before resuming its eastward flow. Thus, the fort was among the first defensible positions on the north side of the Krishna river.

Among the earliest mentions of Pangal comes from the year 1417. In this year Firoz Shah Bahmani decided to demolish the fort. In Deccan warfare, this might have included filling in a moat, leveling defensive strongholds, or dismantling gates. The Vijayanagar king, Devaraya, had taken it two years earlier. This gave the Vijayanagar forces a stronghold on the north side of the Krishna river, too close for Firoz Shah's liking. At that time, the large Vijayanagar army was ill-equipped to fight the more agile cavalry employed by the Bahmanis, and Devaraya had to retreat. He left a force behind at Pangal that did remarkably well, but over a year later, disease broke out within the ranks of the Bahmani troops thus forcing their retreat. Devaraya seized the opportunity and recrossed the Krishna with a larger force. Under his leadership, the army had begun to incorporate cavalry, horses from Persia, and archers. These improvements were the difference when the two armies met again. The Bahmanis lost the battle and the Vijayanagar forces, in the shadow of Pangal, "in a frenzy of triumph and religious rage erected a great platform with their [Bahmani] heads on the battlefield."[66]

The fort at Pangal repeatedly changed hands. In 1513, the Vijayanagar and Qutb Shah armies met. During this encounter, Quli Qutb Shah had defeated the Velamas at Devarakonda. Where once had stood temples and palaces, Quli Qutb Shah ordered them destroyed and erected mosques in their place. Across the river, angered, the great Vijayanagar king Krishnadevaraya opted to march against the Qutb Shah leader. He came with 30,000 horses and 3,000 foot soldiers.[67] Quli Qutb responded, and the two armies met at Pangal where the Vijayanagar army had encamped. In battle, the Golconda forces were successful, forcing the retreat of Krishnadevaraya who left behind a small force to defend the fort. The fort occupants held out for nearly two months before capitulating to the besieging Qutb Shah forces. Pangal had other noble guests: in 1604 the fort was home to the Golconda sultan's mother along with the *qiladar* (fort commander) Khairat Khan, and in 1786–1789 the fort played host to Nizam Ali Khan himself. By the early eighteenth century, under the Asaf Jahs, Pangal had become a district capital with 125 villages within its bounds, and staffed with 500 infantry. This force was stationed at Pangal to check the periodic rebellions of samasthan rajas and other landlords in the region.[68]

Rivers

While hilltop locations provided one geographic advantage, rivers provided another. The Krishna and Tungabhadra rivers not only formed the outline of the Raichur *doab*, but also served important military functions. Where the rivers were fordable, forts dotted the landscape. In the bend of the Krishna river, an area administered by the Jatprole rajas, there were no less than four forts within a few miles of each other. These were: Jatprole, Velaturu, Chinnamauru, and across the river at Utakuru. Here, the river and its banks were shallow and sloped to the water's edge, making it an ideal place to ford the river. Control of this bottleneck was achieved through the construction of forts. Those who could control the forts could control movement across the river.

Where the river and its banks were shallow and fordable, regular ferry services developed.[69] These were *puttis* (basket boats), under the control of local rajas who could demand payment for this service. Anagundi, Gadwal, Jatprole, Wanaparthi, Amarchinta, and Paloncha samasthans all bordered on rivers and provided ferry services—a source of income and leverage. These basket boats have been in use since at least the time of the Vijayanagar kings, and one can still see them today. Firoz Shah Bahmani used these boats in 1398 to cross the Krishna river and disrupt the camp of Krishnadevaraya.[70] The Portuguese traveler Domingo Paes—in about 1520—provided a detailed description of the boats and their use. He described the town of Anagundi, across the river from Vijayanagar.

> A captain lives in this city for the king. People cross to this place by boats which are round like baskets; inside they are made of cane, and outside are covered with leather; they are able to carry fifteen or twenty persons, and even horses and oxen can cross in them if necessary, but for the most part these animals swim across. Men row them with a sort of paddle, and the boats are always turning round, as they cannot go straight like others; in all the kingdom where there are streams there are no other boats but these.[71]

Near Jatprole at Sangameswaram in 1590, Muhammad Qutb Quli crossed the Krishna river to reach Musalimadugu, then famous for diamonds.[72] Among other crossing points were further to the west near Pedda Marur, and at Vyaparla; the latter was under the control of the Wanaparthi samasthan. Periodically the rivers flooded and military leaders had to take this into consideration. In 1570, Tirumala crossed the Krishna river into Qutb Shahi territory and seized the fort at Penukonda.[73] Muhammad Qutb Quli Shah marched south against the insurgent Vijayanagar force and laid siege to the fort. However, with the rains approaching, the sultan knew that the river would "cut off all communication with the Golconda territory" and retreated.[74]

Diamonds

The rajas of samasthans, the sultans of Golconda and the Nizams of Hyderabad all benefited from the *doab*'s rich mineral resources. Diamonds, gold, ore, and coal were located in valleys between the mountains and the rivers. Diamonds were mined in an area along the Krishna river extending north through Jatprole and south to Ramallakota; coal in the Godavari basin near Singareni; and gold near Lingasur. Richards has called the Golconda mines, "one of the richest prizes to be found in the Deccan."[75] These became sources of wealth, the objectives of entrepreneurial travelers and traders, and targets of military action.[76]

Diamonds were a particularly coveted resource for their value and beauty, thus attracting the attention of the Deccani rulers as well as international visitors. Their mine sites attracted many of the Deccan and Hyderabad's diverse ethnic communities. Not only were Hindus and Muslims present at the mines or visitors to them, but also non-*mulkis* (outsiders; *mulki* being a son of the soil) from other parts of India, as well as the ultimate non-*mulkis*, Europeans. How diamonds were first discovered is not fully known. One story suggests that a shepherd found a shiny stone and brought it to Hyderabad.[77] When cut and polished, word rapidly spread that the stone was in fact a diamond. As early as 1425, under Ahmad Shah Bahmani, diamonds and their mines are mentioned. In that year, while suppressing a rebellious zamindar, Ahmad Shah came into possession of a diamond mine at "Kullum," or Kulur, on the Krishna river, near Jatprole.[78] Later, Muhammad Qutb Quli Shah, while campaigning south of the Krishna river, came upon another diamond mine at "Moosulmooroo." This was the town of Musalimadugu about fifteen miles east of Jatprole. By the eighteenth century, Jatprole Raja Venkat Lakshma Rao was known as *hira raja*, or "diamond king," for his results from the mines.[79]

European visitors to these mines called their organizers "governors," "chiefs," or "captains," when they were likely samasthan rajas, as only they could muster large enough numbers of laborers to work the mines. At the time, the rajas were the major local political figures in this region, and they were best suited to mobilize the labor needed. These operations required staggering numbers of men at a site: 20,000 or more might have been involved in the larger mines.[80] Mines were either exposed (in the form of pits), or caves dug into the sides of hills. An early but unverifiable account comes from Nicolo Conti who reveals one method for collecting diamonds. Having driven oxen to the top of a hill next to another hill where diamonds were found, locals killed the oxen and threw their flesh onto the adjoining hill. "The diamonds stick to these pieces of flesh. Then come vultures and eagles flying to the spot, which, seizing the meat for their food, fly away with it to places where they may be safe from the serpents." Locals then raided the nests and retrieved the diamonds. Conti was followed by the Russian, Athanasius Nikitin who describes some 300 diamond dealers residing at "Kooroola," likely Kulur.[81] A later account of the mines comes from the Portuguese traveler Fernao Nuniz who visited Vijayanagar in 1535. He describes how stones of a certain weight or more were sent to the kings at Vijayanagar.

> He [a chief or captain] pays to the King every year four thousand *pardaos*, with the condition that all diamonds which exceed twenty *mangelins* in weight shall be given to the King for his Treasury. He serves with eight thousand foot [soldiers] and eight hundred horse[s] and thirty elephants, and pays the King every year one hundred thousand *pardaos*.[82]

A further account presented by the Earl of Marlbal illuminates the management of the mines. A governor lived at the "Melwillee" mine, in order to deal with merchants and traders who came to purchase stones.

> He [the governor] (to draw the Adventurers and Merchants near him, that he may be better informed of the actions and advantages, and how the better how to fleece them, the general practice of Governours in these parts;) has very lately forbid their [mines at some distance to the governor] use. [83]

From the report, "The Miners, those that employ them, and the Merchants that buy the Stones of them, are generally Ethnicks; not a Mussleman, that ever I heard of, followed the employment."[84] Interestingly, here the use of the word "ethnicks" seems to refer to indigenous Indians of the region as opposed to the Muslims who formed their own ethnic group. That Muslims did not take much, if any role in the direct supervision of the mines can perhaps be explained by the unsettled nature of the area. Samasthans were already in place, but *jagirs* and *paigah* lands (those granted by the Asaf Jahs) had not yet been established in this area. Regardless of their administrators, according to one author, the miners themselves possessed somewhat unusual talents. "The miners had become so expert in their art that they could trace out diamonds by means of the nature, *smell* and colour of the mound."[85]

Precious gems and metals secured from the samasthan rajas and their mines increased the value of the samasthans in the eyes of their Hyderabad lords. Gems and metals worn as ornaments were not only fashionable, but generated an entire industry in the city. One entire quadrant of Hyderabad was devoted to jewelers. It is not surprising that the "most important industry of those times was jewellery."[86] As mineral wealth went from the mines to the jewelers, the process merged with the Hyderabadi culture of gift giving between nobles. Thus, the mineral wealth of the state, in part, fed the cultural demand for gifts.[87]

By the mid-nineteenth century, gift giving and other ceremonial exchanges would begin to eclipse the skirmishes of earlier centuries. Up to that time, the samasthan rajas—born of the larger medieval empires—carved out territory where revenue could be collected and troops maintained. These in turn were called upon by those larger empires of the day. Northern armies brought the collapse of the Kakatiya and Vijayanagar empires, but for the samasthan rajas, far from participating in a 'clash" with new Muslim overlords, accommodated and supported these new empires—with an eye toward their own survival. As the British established their presence in the Deccan and at Hyderabad, the rajas of the samasthans recognized the presence of this new and growing authority. Thus, when an opportunity to provide support arose in 1857, Rameshwar Rao followed a practice long in establishment by his predecessors. However, the 1850s were the penultimate decade in which to provide military support. Across south India armed force was in decline, and lavish ceremonialism was on the rise.[88] While armed forces were still necessary, their importance had already begun to fade. It is this process that we explore next.

CHAPTER 2

Soldiers, Mercenaries, and Moneylenders

In 1934 William Barton published a historical survey of the princes of India. Barton had ample experience with the princes, and with Hyderabad, serving among other positions as that state's Resident from 1925 to 1930. In recounting Hyderabad's history, Barton described the time a century earlier when "[t]he country was overrun by disbanded mercenaries, Arabs, Pathans, Rohillas. The Hindu feudatories, of whom there were several of importance, were everywhere in revolt."[1] The Hindu feudatories that Barton refers to were among others, the Gadwal, Wanaparthi, and Shorapur samasthans. Barton's comments highlight Hyderabad's multiethnic composition that included not only the state's Hindu and Muslim nobility, but also communities of Arabs and Africans as well as Pathans, Rohillas, and Sikhs. The revolts taking place in the countryside included skirmishing between these different groups, as well as robbery and banditry. Larger scale skirmishes were aided by the ready supply of mercenaries for hire, in particular members of the Arab and African communities. Together with the armed forces maintained by the samasthan rajas, Hyderabad's mid-nineteenth century was marked by both ethnic diversity and petty crime.[2] This array of participants formed "alliances of expediency" throughout the countryside.[3] This chapter examines the samasthan rajas as one component in Hyderabad's multiethnic mix that participated in various types of illicit activities. At the same time, this lengthy period of military skirmishing in Hyderabad's history was beginning to draw to a close. Under British influence and the personal direction of Hyderabad's minister Salar Jung, diplomacy gradually replaced armed confrontation. The late nineteenth century was a time of transition from the medium of armed force to other more symbolic and ceremonial means.[4]

The Nineteenth-Century Dawns

Hyderabad, its rajas, and their domains underwent rapid change throughout the nineteenth century. First, the samasthan territories began to be consolidated. Roads were laid, armies reformed, revenue expectations fixed, and each samasthan family became linked not only with their principal fort or town, but also with a specific geographic territory. For instance, Gadwal was not only the royal family, but also the samasthan capital. This had a twofold effect. First, if the family line was broken, an argument could be made for annexing the samasthan territory identified with the family, a process explored later. At the same time, as Hyderabad's elites acquired further royal trappings, if a family line faltered, the physical and administrative infrastructure of roads, forts, and contracts were in place to maintain the family's integrity. The Gadwal palace, schools, and roads were part of the samasthan infrastructure and survived regardless of whether the family managed a smooth succession.

A second change to occur was the integration of ethnic groups—in particular Arabs and Rohillas, non-*mulkis*—who had once comprised a less structured but nonetheless powerful social order dispersed throughout the state. During the nineteenth century, the role of different ethnic and outsider groups began to be formalized. Africans, Rohillas, Arabs, Sikhs, and Afghans who had comprised much of the military milieu of the day either chose to revolt as their position in the state diminished, or found themselves increasingly incorporated into the state's newer administrative forms.

As different communities within Hyderabad State jostled for power in the nineteenth century, their military interdependence had earlier precedents. Throughout the eighteenth century, the Nizams regularly required military assistance from members of the Hyderabad milieu. When the first Nizam came to power in 1724, his position of authority in the Deccan was far from secure. He required a regular supply of troops, some maintained in Hyderabad and others sent from the countryside. One such relationship formed between the Nizam and the rulers of Gadwal. That samasthan would be later woven into the larger treaties of the day between the Nizam and British forces over concerns about its possible revolt. Yet, in the early decades of the eighteenth century, cooperation, not revolt, marked the relationship. During the first decade of his rule, two women, Rani Ammakka and Rani Lingamma, co-administered affairs at Gadwal until their adopted heir came of age. These women commanded the army and ruled the samasthan. A series of requests made by Nizam ul Mulk to the women clearly indicates that they controlled Gadwal's armed forces. Further, the exchange is that of a Muslim ruler requesting the help of two Hindu women—perhaps remarkable in today's world—but less shocking in a more fluid eighteenth century. On 3 September 1727, the Nizam wrote: "An earnest requisition has already been made to you requesting you to come with your army. Please reach Gulburga at once and await (our army). Please treat this matter as urgent."[5] The Nizam sent further entreaties throughout 1727 and 1728. However, by early 1729 no troops from Gadwal seem to have arrived. A stronger request was sent: "It is hereby written that the winter season is over; the season for marching has come. Last year, in spite of repeated requests, you did not send your army . . . This was not proper. Please send as early as possible your army in the charge of a trustworthy officer. Please treat this as urgent."[6] To this the women acquiesced.

The forces at Gadwal had likely not been sent earlier as they were needed to protect their own local interests; if sent to fight with the Nizam, the samasthan had to cover the cost, but received little concrete benefit. However, as part of the Hyderabad political system, providing military support was integral to Gadwal's role within the state's emerging composite structure. As the Gadwal force was considered strong enough to pose some threat, Nizam ul Mulk chose diplomatic entreaties rather than a confrontation with the Gadwal women.

The Gadwal forces were busy a few decades later in 1752. They engaged in months of skirmishes with Munawar Khan and his forces that numbered about 2,000 strong. Khan was a nobleman from the Kurnool area who was returning from Arcot to claim his ancestral lands.[7] We can assume that the Gadwal forces were roughly equal to Khan's in size. While the Nizam and other nobles like Munawar Khan were well aware of Gadwal's power, so too was the Company increasingly interested in the "zamindars" within Nizam Ali Khan's domain. A report from the1780s describes these forces as such:

> There are many zamindars tributary to Nizam ally whose followers variously armed with matchlocks, swords, pikes, bows and arrows are very numerous, but they cannot otherwise be considered a part of his military force than as auxiliaries that regarding him as their feudal Lord, they are more bound to obey than other troops of that denomination, for their attendance in the field is only required where his operations lie on their vicinity, and then, it is usual for him to allow batta or subsistence to such of them as are employed in his service.

> It may therefore be of . . . consequence to know the number of his zamindars adherents than the situation and description of their several countries the revenue they draw from their stipulations with the Nizams or other points that marks their degree of importance . . .[8]

By the late eighteenth century, Gadwal posed enough threat to warrant specific mention in a treaty signed between Nizam Ali Khan and the Company.

In 1798, to end the French presence in the Deccan, the Nizam proposed that he would release the French troops under his employ. In return, the British would rent units of their own troops (a "subsidiary force") to the Nizam.[9] The man responsible for disbanding the large French force, and the installation of Company sepoys was John Malcolm, a masterful diplomat. The role of the subsidiary force was sorted out in a series of inquiries between Governor General Wellesley and James Achilles Kirkpatrick. At stake was a tripartite concern over the Nizam, the Marathas, and the "tributaries" subject to both royal houses.[10] Below, Kirkpatrick outlines the relationship between Company troops, and the *poligars* of Hyderabad and the Maratha State.

> Besides, though these restrictions were properly enough established by us, yet they are considered, and not entirely without reason, as great hardships by the Court of Hyderabad, between which and the Government of Poona there subsists a sort of tacit convention, whereby the forces of his Highness have not only occasionally passed through the other's territories, but even acted against the Polygars tributary to both states (as those of Shorepoor and Gudwaul), without any visible objection on the part of the Mahrattas. We certainly could not now relax from the rigidness of our practice in these particulars, without giving offence and furnishing a just ground of complaint to the Government of Poona; but, on the other hand, the peculiar nature of the case would appear to warrant a hope that the difficulty might be surmounted by means of a suitable representation to the Court of Poona, made in concert with that of Hyderabad.[11]

Thus, a treaty of "defensive alliance" between the Nizam and the Company was drafted in 1800. Bharati Ray has emphasized, "In the history of Nizam-British relations the importance of this treaty cannot be exaggerated."[12] This treaty would guarantee the use of the subsidiary force and British reinforcements should the Nizam's territory come under threat. Further, for the first time, two of the samasthans were specifically mentioned in the treaty thus entering them into the larger discourse of rebellion and stability within the state and expanding Company control.

Why were Gadwal and Shorapur singled out? Gadwal lay just across the river from Kurnool, and it was thus Hyderabad's first line of defense from territory administered by the Company. At the same time, as the nearest polity to Company territory, a means of ensuring Gadwal's peaceful neighborly relations with the Company was critical to its own interest. The samasthan also commanded enough military power and revenue to warrant its specific mention for possible rebellion. Shorapur served a similar purpose vis-à-vis the Marathas, lying due west of Hyderabad and buffering that state from any Maratha incursions.[13] For Gadwal and Shorapur, having to pay tribute to both Hyderabad and Poona was anathema, so the rajas—benefiting from the larger political storm above them—at times withheld payment completely, knowing that neither side was likely to take action with the risk of greater war at hand.[14] The treaty assured the Nizam use of the subsidiary force should his domestic or regional peace come under threat.

> [I]t is therefore hereby agreed that if in future the Shorapore or Gudwall zemindars, or any other subjects or dependents of His highness's government should withhold the payment of the Circar's just claims upon them, or excite rebellion or disturbance, the subsidiary force, or such proportion thereof as may be requisite, after the reality of the offence shall be duly ascertained, shall be ready, in concert with His Highness's own troops, to reduce all such offenders to obedience.[15]

However, payment for the subsidiary force fell in arrears, and future Residents were reluctant to send it to quell rebellions in the countryside. The Nizam was thus in no position to compel payment from Gadwal and Shorapur.[16] Rebellion in Hyderabad's countryside frequently included a powerful mix of landed nobility (the samasthan rajas) as well as other members of the state's multiethnic mix, including Africans and Arabs—both communities frequently offered their services as mercenaries, or were employed as elite bodyguards.

Africans, Arabs, and Afghans

As capital of the Nizam's dominions, Hyderabad city served as a major trade center not only for weapons, diamonds, and pearls, but also mercenaries and slaves. For samasthan families, the maintenance of an African or Arab bodyguard not only echoed earlier military practice, but was more immediately an imitation of the same practice in Islamic states. Africans had come to the subcontinent as slaves with earlier empires. Two groups, the Abyssinians and Ethiopians, were called *habshi* or *habashi* (Ethiopian), a general term for all those who were of African descent.[17] Those slaves, once freed and converted to Islam, called themselves *sayyads* or *siddis* (descendants of Muhammad). *Siddis* participated as soldiers in campaigns in the northwest, in Bengal, and in the Deccan. The Deccan's most famous *siddi* was Malak Ambar. He served under the Bijapur and Golconda regimes before establishing his own forces at Ahmednagar in battle against the Mughals.[18]

Amongst the samasthans, the rajas at Wanaparthi seem to have most widely participated in Hyderabad's multiethnic armed milieu. The genesis of Wanaparthi's African force can be traced to Raja Ram Krishna Rao II, who was granted a private bodyguard by then minister of Hyderabad, Chandu Lal, on Christmas Day, 1817. The force included 25 *sawars* (riders, horsemen), 175 footmen, and one elephant. Elephants were used as a kind of mobile platform for weapons (archers and gunners) and were supported by more agile cavalry units. Infantry was the largest body within an army. Javelin or spear holders, archers or bowman, ordinary soldiers, and general laborers were all employed in battle.[19] At that time Ram Krishna Rao II also purchased *siddis* at Hyderabad to expand his personal forces, so the family maintained two bodies of armed forces.[20] While the African Bodyguard served the raja and his immediate family, the second group of men were kept on notice, to be called up by the Nizam or offered by the raja to the British government (such as in the Crimean War of 1855 and the mutiny of 1857). To cover the expense of these troops, Wanaparthi deducted Rs. 16,000 from its tribute payment to Hyderabad.[21]

While the Africans in Wanaparthi were part of that samasthan's armed forces, the larger community of Arabs and Afghans within the region had a more checkered role in the state. Arabs, generally mercenaries for hire, had come to the Deccan either from north India in service to the Mughals, or by sea from north Africa or west Asia. The Afghans and their tribal members, the Pathans, Rohillas, and Yuzufzays, comprised another ethnic group in the region. They came from the northwest, now Afghanistan. In Hyderabad's *mufassal* Arabs and Rohillas, as well as disgruntled landholders, carried out a variety of raids and crimes. In Hyderabad city, the Arabs maintained their own jails, law courts, officers, and of course, armed forces, comprising in effect a "military republic superimposed on the Hyderabad administration."[22] The Arab and the Rohilla communities, while not highly centralized, created a web of legal, financial, and military power that was used to advance their own positions, and to respond to those who maligned them. While Arabs were a major force in Hyderabad's armed milieu, they were not used in its official armed forces. Military officials avoided their recruitment into the Hyderabad Contingent, the Arabs being "too difficult to discipline and the Rohillas too truculent for enlistment in our army."[23] However, they were feared when met in battle. Not only were Arabs excellent marksmen and extremely agile on horseback, they were also fiercely loyal to their commanders. "There are," wrote Reginald Burton,

> perhaps no troops in the world that will make a stouter or more determined stand to their posts than the Arabs. They are entirely unacquainted with military evolution and undisciplined; but every Arab has a pride and heart of his own that never forsakes him as long as he has legs to stand on . . . Nothing can exceed the horror and alarm with which some of our native troops view the Arabs.[24]

While Arab forces may not have found employment in the Hyderabad Contingent, due to the fear and respect they evoked, they found ready welcome in other sectors of Hyderabad's armed milieu. Attempts to curb their activity often resulted in violence. If threatened or attacked in the city, Arab soldiers retaliated in the country.[25] "Those stationed in the country were employed more frequently as the instruments of oppression than as the preservers of the peace or protectors of the people. The Arabs and Rohillas were the terror of the whole country, and the Minister could not disband or reduce them without the risk of serious disturbance."[26] These groups by no means consistently worked together; reports of skirmishes between Arabs and Sikhs, for instance, were not unheard of.[27] In part, the Sikh presence in Hyderabad can be accredited to Chandu Lal who retained a large number of Sikhs for his own personal protection.[28] Trouble with these different groups extended into neighboring territories. For instance, Meadows Taylor indicated that Arabs from Hyderabad who were hoping to recruit men for an uprising had to be repulsed at the border between Hyderabad and his Shorapur territory.[29]

Arab and Afghan militancy spurred the Residency and the Nizam's government to action in a sort of "cleansing." In May of 1849, the Resident, James Stuart Fraser, wrote to Lord Dalhousie: "I am assisting the Nizam's Government to get rid of some troublesome Rohillas, or, to speak more properly, Afghans, from this country."[30] Dalhousie did not agree with Fraser's plan, but said in his reply that the removal of Rohillas *could* be considered on the grounds that, "if there is to be an expulsion at all, it certainly should be those who are entirely foreigners."[31] By "foreigner,"

Dalhousie likely meant those who were outsiders, that is, not native to the Deccan, or non-*mulkis*. But when Fraser's revised plan called for transporting the Rohillas to one of the neighboring provinces of British India, Dalhousie protested, "But I really cannot recognise any sort of obligation, or any reason, for carrying the complaisance of the British Government so far as to undertake the conveyance of the collective vagabondism of the Nizam's Kingdom in order to deposit it in one of our own Provinces."[32] Thus, in the end the plan was scrapped.

Arabs in Hyderabad were also involved in moneylending. Pooling their earnings they made loans—at high interest rates—to those who required funding. The *jamadar* (local commander) of a particular group negotiated these transactions and acted as broker between the Arab troops and the borrower. If a transaction failed, they easily shifted from moneylender to soldier, thus better to secure their investments. If the borrower defaulted, "A landed estate or a district was occupied in force, and the Jemadar in possession collected the rent or the revenue for the benefit of his band."[33] An occupation is exactly what befell Rameshwar Rao at Wanaparthi.[34]

Giving Money, Taking Money

Two incidents from the mid-nineteenth century illuminate how the various participants in Hyderabad's multiethnic mix negotiated their relations. The first involved a robbery at the village of Janampet, the result of which entangled the raja of Wanaparthi, the Nizam Nasir ud Daula, and the Resident, James Stuart Fraser. Here, the event moved up the echelons of power. A second event that occurred three years later involved (again) the raja of Wanaparthi, but this time ensnared an Arab moneylender, Abdullah bin Ali as well as the Nizam and Resident. Moneylending was a personal matter between the raja and Abdullah bin Ali, and would have remained so had the raja not defaulted and fled to Hyderabad for protection. This event explicates the role of the Arab moneylending community in Hyderabad, and shows how easily that role morphed into one of armed enforcers.

In March 1846, merchants of Janampet (a village 15 miles north of Wanaparthi) deposited Rs. 24,580 there for safe keeping and posted guards. At night a group of 300 armed men came to the village, opened fire on the guards, killing five, and stole the money. Agents of the affected merchants petitioned Rameshwar Rao for help because Janampet fell within his jurisdiction. But he neither aided them nor reported the incident to the Hyderabad *majlis* (board or court). The

Nizam's government had created such a board to coordinate forces in the countryside to punish wrongdoers.[35] The board, however, came to know of the theft through other channels and wrote to the raja: "You have neither attended to the matter yourself nor have you reported it to the Government for action to be taken. If it is not announced in the State that the case has been stolen and if arrangement is not made by the Government to recover it, the business of all the merchants would be affected." The letter informed him, "in a purely friendly spirit," that the thieves were reported to be hiding "without fear" in Wanaparthi territory. The board instructed Rameshwar Rao to search them out, return the money, and send a full report.[36]

Rameshwar Rao responded to the accusations five days later in a letter to Raja Ram Baksh, nephew of Chandu Lal, and Hyderabad's *peshkar* (minister's assistant). First, he claimed that he had in fact submitted a report detailing events of the case. Second, he complicated his own role in the matter by suggesting that "enemies" had fabricated many of the facts. "Out of spite my enemies put the blame for this theft on me. . . . This humble servant has always been obedient to the Government therefore you must not believe the stories made up by my enemies."[37] In a second letter on the same day he further elaborated on the events at Janampet. After rushing to the spot, he learned that the dacoits were hiding in the village of Baswapally; he then directed the heads of that village to search out the culprits within twenty days. By way of concluding his report, he flatteringly asked, "Kindly do due justice to me as you are the master of the samasthan and your ancestors are known for courteousness and a sense of justice."[38]

By early June, the thieves had been traced to a village a dozen miles west of Wanaparthi. This area was under the control of Raja Som Bhupal of Gadwal, and it appears that Rameshwar Rao all but placed the matter in the former's lap. By April the affair had caught the attention of the press. While the correspondence between the board and Rameshwar Rao mentioned no suspects, the editor of the *Madras Spectator* was more brazen and directed blame at Rameshwar Rao as well as the rajas of the Narayanpet and Gurmatkal estates, located just northwest of Wanaparthi.

> Our Hyderabad accounts inform us that the disorders of the Nizam's unhappy kingdom are increasing daily, and the force of impunity, combined with example, will doubtless continue to hasten the progression. The Zemindars of Nareinpet, of Goormutkal and Wunpurtee, all powerful persons, are plundering the country—by way, it is probable, of retaliation for

> past injures sustained. These parties, we may notice, reside in the south of the Hyderabad dominion . . . The Nizam's Government, it is understood, have apprised the Resident of their intention to send troops, of which Arabs will constitute the larger portion, to quell the outbreak of the refractory Zemindars in the south.[39]

Meanwhile, the Nizam did not send Arab troops to quell the trouble, but instead requested that the Hyderabad Contingent be sent. The Contingent's pay was months in arrears; and Fraser refused to dispatch them unless they were fully paid. It was in this climate of dacoitry, claims and counterclaims, that Rameshwar Rao found himself summoned to Hyderabad by Fraser in late June 1846. Fraser's intent was to seek a non-military solution to the crisis. To guarantee Rameshwar Rao's attendance, he issued a notice to landholders and government servants stating that Rameshwar Rao had been called to Hyderabad, and that he should be allowed to pass without interference.[40] That the summons came from the Residency was indicative of its growing involvement in affairs of the state.

Rameshwar Rao and others met with Fraser and "made a peaceable submission" before him.[41] Fraser, who had referred to these nobles as "refractory zemindars," reprimanded the men and sent them home.[42] With that, the unsolved affair came to a close. On 21 September 1846, another notice came from the Residency to the "amils, taluqdars, zamindars, chaukidars and the guards of the roads and highways of the Hyderabad Dominion" stating that Rameshwar Rao was returning to Wanaparthi, and should be allowed to pass unhampered.[43] Fraser understood the importance of the safe return of a powerful noble. If Rameshwar Rao had been involved in the robberies, as the newspaper had suggested, he would have been unsafe outside of his own domains. Conversely, if he was innocent, his status made him a tempting target for kidnapping or extortion—not uncommon activities at the time.

The second event occurred in 1849. In that year Rameshwar Rao became involved with the Arab moneylender, Abdullah bin Ali. The raja, short of funds, mortgaged part of the samasthan, but unable to repay the debt, the matter turned ugly. Raja Ram Baksh summoned Rameshwar Rao to his office and duplicitously handed him over to his secretary, who in turn handed him over to his Arab creditors. It seems that the Arabs then put Rameshwar Rao into one of their jails. But the raja was not in the jail for long. His father's death anniversary fell about this time, and Rameshwar Rao asked the Nizam, Nasir ud Daula, to intervene and allow him to perform the necessary ceremonies. The Nizam agreed—in accordance with the respect paid to such a noble—and during the day on

9 December 1849, the raja, a Brahman priest, and some servants entered a temple to perform the service and closed its gate. Guards stood by outside, their job made more pleasant by the liquor and food provided, courtesy of the raja's men. They could hear the tinkling of the bell involved in the ceremony, and none grew suspicious until several hours had passed and the gate still remained closed. Finally, sensing something was amiss, the guards forced open the temple doors and found inside only a cat with a bell tied to its neck. The raja and his men had dug a small tunnel under the temple wall and were met with fast horses on the other side.[44] Within twelve hours they arrived safely in Wanaparthi territory, temporarily beyond the law's grasp.[45]

However, retaliation was imminent. In the spring of 1851, Abdullah bin Ali ordered his troops to seize Wanaparthi under a commander named Bamdaz. Hyderabad *kotwal* (police chief) Talib ud Daula advised Rameshwar Rao who had escaped to Hyderabad to "raise troops" and fight the Arabs.[46] Implicit in this advice was the message that the Nizam's government was not willing to get militarily involved in Rameshwar Rao's problem. Under Abdullah bin Ali's orders, 300 Arabs seized the Wanaparthi palace and Rameshwar Rao's family, as well as some children of the samasthan whom they abused. At this point the Resident, "with an humanity which gives grace to his office," reprimanded the Nizam for allowing innocent people (especially children) to be abused. The Nizam summoned Abdullah bin Ali to the court and chastised him for the way events were unfolding. Ali pleaded that his men were mercenaries and could not be completely controlled.[47] Throughout April the occupation at Wanaparthi continued, while the Arabs continued to demand payment of the debt owed to them. The Nizam's attempt at mediation had failed, and he was forced—under pressure from the Resident—to pay part of the debt.[48] In May the Arabs still occupied the palace and fort but had released the children. From Hyderabad, Rameshwar Rao then gathered his troops and attacked. By November, Wanaparthi forces took a prized cannon, and by January of 1852 the incident was all but over, and Rameshwar Rao emerged victorious. Bamdaz, who had fought at Wanaparthi seems (in revenge) to have turned his men against Talib ud Daula. In this subsequent dispute, the Nizam sided with Talib ud Daula, and Bamdaz was forced to back down.[49]

These two incidents centered around the affairs of Raja Rameshwar Rao. The first—the robbery at Janampet—because of its law and order implications, drew the attention of the Nizam and the Resident. Protection of roads and monies was critical to the welfare of the state.

The second incident—a loan gone bad between the raja and Abdullah bin Ali—drew in the powerful Arab moneylending community. This time, due to abuses occurring at Wanaparthi itself, the Nizam and Resident (perhaps spurred on by unfavorable newspaper coverage of the event) became involved.

Hero and Villain

In the short time from Rameshwar Rao's victory over the Arabs at Wanaparthi, to his offer of assistance during the mutiny of 1857, his reputation wildly fluctuated. His career is indicative of the fluid nature of power and positions at the time. To begin, the Nizam's government had promoted him within its military structure: he became brigadier of the state's forces, inspector general of the cavalry, then inspector general of the Nizam's army. Further cementing his role as a supporter of the Nizam's government and the British Raj, in 1855 he made his services and troops available to the British in the Crimean War. As Penderel Moon has noted, "Educated Indians were now sufficiently awake to the outside world to follow with close interest this European war in which their masters were engaged."[50] Rameshwar Rao offered himself and 1,000 Arab troops; this force consisted of hired troops (the Arabs) and his own African guard. In response to his offer, George F. Edmonstone, foreign secretary, wrote that "the Governor General is gratified by the indication he has given of his good-will towards the British government but that—circumstances do not render it necessary that his Lordship should avail himself of the offer."[51] In any case, by the end of November Sebastopol had fallen and Rameshwar Rao's offer was outdated even before it had reached Calcutta.

Only months later, the Wanaparthi raja found himself under a darkening cloud of suspicion. The Resident, George Alexander Bushby, summoned him to Hyderabad to face criminal charges; two for highway robbery, one for the seizure of the Gopalpet samasthan (formerly part of Wanaparthi and governed by a relative), and the last for coining impure currency at his mint in Sugur.[52] Rameshwar Rao came to Hyderabad and faced a committee that included two British officers, Major Briggs and Captain Barrow as well as a *maulvi* (Muslim legal scholar). By the summer's end, the committee had finished its work and convicted the raja of all four crimes. He was sentenced to four years in jail.[53] His sentence likely took the form of house arrest. This punishment, however, did not prevent Rameshwar Rao from corresponding with the outside world, or from having servants and visitors. It appears unlikely that Rao served all of this sentence as the correspondence surrounding his offer of troops in 1857 makes no mention of the raja's imprisonment, and by 1859 he was once again free and in command of his own forces.[54] In sum, the punishment seems to have been largely symbolic rather than punitive.

As Rameshwar Rao came to play a larger role in the mainstream of Hyderabad's military affairs, records of his forces and activities become more abundant. From 1859 to 1865 details of Rao's forces momentarily come into sharp focus in the Receipt Books and Military Dispatch logs that survive for several of these years. These records provide an almost daily account of the force's doings, either from his reports sent to Hyderabad, or from the Hyderabad reports sent to him. We find a multiethnic force under the raja's command being deployed for a variety of reasons: to suppress bandits, to clear roads, to offer service to the Company, and the like. The force comprised both Hindus and Muslims, *mulkis* and non-*mulkis*, men native to India, and those whose ancestors were in Africa or Afghanistan. For instance, an expense report for the month of January 1862 details the variety of age, origins, "caste," pay, and position of two groups: the Abyssinians and the *Habshis*. Their ages ranged from 16 to 60, and their places of origin spanned from Ellichipore, Aurungabad, Bijapur and Bedar, to as far away as Delhi. The first group of Abyssinians were fifteen in number, at a monthly salary of Rs. 27 each. The second group, *Habshis*, included a *jamadar* (Rs. 15), two staff bearers (Rs. 9), two *naiks* (Rs. 8), twelve "old" gunners and eight new gunners (Rs. 7), as well as bullocks, camels, and other supporting staff.[55] Further records detail the First Regiment of the Wanaparthi Lancers where *sawars* are listed by name, caste, place or country, age, and size and health of their horses. Thirty-four men are listed in this regiment; almost all were Muslim. Their "caste" names included '*syed*," "*sakh*" (shaikh), "Mogul," and Yusufzai, a Pathan tribe.[56] These troops later became the Golconda Lancers. The report is not only a testament to Hyderabad's ethnic diversity, but as all of the different groups were fitted into the category of "caste" (typically reserved for Hindus), a composite force takes shape: each ethnic group clearly visible, but combined under a single heading to forge a larger body.

Because maintaining the African guard was costly to Rameshwar Rao, he seems to have used it for illicit purposes while he served the Nizam. His great-great grandson commented, "Raja Rameshwar Rao's army of African slaves cost him a lot of money and to meet this expenditure he helped himself to funds from the Nizam's territory."[57] In 1859 while pursuing Rohillas for the government, the raja came under censure from zamindars and *talukdars* near Wanaparthi who accused him of wrongfully acquiring booty from places he visited on official business. Rameshwar Rao countered that the zamindars and *talukdars* were themselves in collusion and in fact giving assistance to Rohillas.[58] Eventually, the charges were dropped and Rameshwar Rao emerged from the affair with his popularity renewed. It seems that his perceived loyalty in 1857 found him allies within the British community. The *Englishman*, a voice of British opinion, reported that "He is seen by us to be our friend, and at no period of the disturbances [1857] has he been any other."[59] And, if an inquiry were held into the charges by the zamindars and *talukdars*, Rameshwar Rao would "never receive justice in a City Court" because being a Hindu, and the zamindars and *talukdars* being Muslim, the latter would have had undue influence in the Hyderabad court system.[60] An element of communalism had crept into the newspaper account, which came from a British source, yet no evidence of communal tension between Rameshwar Rao and the Muslim majority Hyderabad court or government seems evident.

One way in which Rameshwar Rao helped solidify his position as an ally to both the Hyderabad government and to British officials was to preserve law and order along the roads that traversed his samasthan. Roads became the responsibility of certain states and persons, and as revenue and military traffic increased, they became a frequent venue for robbery and plunder. Stewart Gordon has described the reasons for needing a safe and clear road as follows: safe movement of land revenue (usually in cash), communication between the center and periphery, movement of armies, import of goods to the center, revenue from tolls, and merit from water tank building.[61] These connective threads wound through the interests of the samasthan rajas, the Nizams, and the Residents. For the Residency, roads were a vital link (militarily and financially) to the Madras Presidency. For the Hyderabad government, roads fostered trade as well as communications with subordinates at the periphery of the state; for the samasthans like Wanaparthi, they were all of the above. In addition the roads were a source of income for the samasthan administration as local rulers collected tolls and taxes and provided supplies to travelers.

From Hyderabad, major trunk roads fanned out in all directions, some of which British forces had constructed for military purposes, others dating to antiquity.[62] The road to Kurnool wound south from Hyderabad for 136 miles by way of the Wanaparthi and Jatprole samasthans, and continued past the Krishna river to Kurnool, Bangalore, and Madras. Side roads led to the Krishna river, the military outpost at Makhtal, and onward south to Gadwal. During the earlier Qutb Shah era, this route led to the diamond mines along, and just beyond, the

Krishna river. At that time the road extended from Hyderabad to Golconda, Khanapur, "Cohenol," Kovilkonda, Jatprole, Alampur, and then into the Adil Shahi territory to Kurnool and Rammallakota.[63] As the road to Kurnool passed through Wanaparthi, Hyderabad officials and the Resident called on Rameshwar Rao to help maintain it. Correspondence between Hyderabad officials and Rameshwar Rao reveals the problems faced by those using the state's road network.[64] In 1862, a letter to Rameshwar Rao complained that a *maniwar* (hereditary police official) in the samasthan had failed in his duties, and this failure had led to "thieves and plunderers looting and torturing travelers." The letter emphasized that "English people" used the road and that special care was required to provide for their safe passage.[65] Throughout the correspondence, Hyderabad officials stressed the Resident's comments and instructions, with special emphasis placed on Europeans' safe passage through Wanaparthi territory. Safe passage also depended on the roads being clear. The most common cause of obstruction was over-filled irrigation tanks that flooded the roads and forced travelers to either postpone their trip or find alternate routes. In later years, flooding also threatened the poles used to support telegraph wires. For instance, in October 1868 orders came from the Resident forbidding flooding that blocked the main road in Wanaparthi. "This means the owners of the holdings have stored much water and thus constrained travelers . . . On this highway such hindrances may not be put, as it is the only route of Communication between Hyderabad and Calcutta."[66] Rameshwar Rao further had to report any outbreak of disease in his region. During the mid-nineteenth century cholera and famine outbreaks were common. As roads, transportation, and communication improved, an outbreak in one region posed a serious threat to travelers and to people in other areas. Reports throughout the period are peppered with news of cholera outbreaks and their victims.[67]

British troops frequently traveled by way of Wanaparthi, and Rameshwar Rao was obligated to supply them with provisions when they entered the samasthan. Sometimes these requests were large. On one occasion, the raja had to feed a contingent of 350 horses along with 400 men. The request came with a warning from Hyderabad officials: "precautions must be taken to see that no complaint of any kind in this regard comes to the Government."[68] In another instance, in September and October of 1861, a series of orders requested assistance for a British military captain wanting bullocks, carts, and even cannons.[69] While Rameshwar Rao was paid for these services, they must have represented a constant and considerable drain on samasthan resources.

The Wanaparthi samasthan did not carry the burden of law enforcement in the countryside alone, it was shared by the other samasthan families as well. Further, it was not always to the raja of the samasthan that orders were addressed, at Gadwal during several interludes, the rani of the samasthan was asked to assist in matters of law and order. For instance, in August of 1845 a request came from Raja Ram Baksh to Rani Venkatlakshmi. She had succeeded Raja Sombhupal II, and held power at Gadwal no less than four different times.[70] In his letter, he indicates that the Residency had notified him of a stolen bull, taken from the Bellary district, and supposedly now held in "the Gadwal State." "It appears that during the investigation into the matter it has been ascertained that the said bull is now with one, Guruvayya, an inhabitant of Faridpur, in the Gadwal State and that the said Guruvayya does not surrender the bull in spite of being asked to do so."[71] While the fate of Guruvayya and the bull remain unknown, the correspondence between officials at Hyderabad, in the samasthans, the Residency, and officials in the Madras Presidency are indicative of the larger network of communication, and law and order concerns that flowed across political lines both within Hyderabad State, and between Hyderabad and the Madras Presidency.

Nagappa

Robbing travelers on the roads of Hyderabad was a common activity for the state's disaffected landholders. Rameshwar Rao was called upon to capture these criminals, and in one particular case, he cemented a positive reputation for himself by capturing and killing a particular goonda, Modena Nagappa. According to the General Defensive Alliance of 1800, banditti (like Nagappa) were important contributors to disruptions in the Nizam's dominions, especially in Berar.[72] The activities of Rameshwar Rao, Nagappa, and the band of Rohilla followers fit into a pattern of banditry that had been visible at least a century earlier. For instance, in the 1700s, the bandit Papadu gathered a large force of men and commenced a decade-long spree of plundering in the Deccan. Both Papadu and Nagappa exercised forms of "dual rebellion." These men challenged the suzerain on one hand, and on the other, threatened the local zamindar community from which they themselves had emerged.[73] Nagappa began his career as *ilaqadar* (property or estate holder) of Madnapally. While Papadu's story has survived in the folk tradition, Nagappa became historically visible through military records and newspaper accounts.[74] Both Papadu and Nagappa seem to have chosen a path of banditry, spurred by economic hardship and aided by the ready availability of mercenaries. While the Mughals eventually caught Papadu and his core supporters, Nagappa fell victim to Rameshwar Rao's forces.

When Nagappa was raiding the territory in and around Wanaparthi, Rameshwar Rao acted both as a commander within the Nizam's forces, and a concerned landholder. As a bandit, Nagappa gathered around himself a group of at least 100 Rohillas and 100 additional followers. The Military Board of Control wrote to Rameshwar Rao requesting that he take action and, if Nagappa and his men put up a fight, 'destroy them."[75] It would be almost a year before Nagappa was caught. In the interim, Hyderabad officials received reports in late 1859 of a large band of Rohillas plundering the countryside and sent Rameshwar Rao to investigate.

It is not clear if the Rohillas and Nagappa's band were the same. The Rohilla band had 100 horsemen and 300 foot soldiers, and while camped near Chincholi they were "giving much annoyance to the Ryots."[76] Chincholi is in the Gulbarga district, west of Hyderabad city, and northwest of Wanaparthi. Two weeks later, the band seems to have been 300 Rohillas strong; and, three days later 400 Rohillas were reported moving from Hanamkonda toward Koilkonda.[77] Hanamkonda was in Warangal district, east of Hyderabad City, while Koilkonda was just northwest of Mahbubnagar town, not far from Wanaparthi. Given the imprecision of the reports, and the geographic proximity, it is likely that these bands of bandits were one and the same.

By February of 1862, the government ordered Rameshwar Rao to pursue Nagappa.

> [T]he past month there is a report of the trouble maker Nagappa Ilaqadar of Madnapally and that he gave asylum to some Rohillas and is encouraging and helping the rebels [*sic*] such information is also received often by the Government from different sources. Moreover since the last few months, dacoities [*sic*] and robberies have been increased.[78]

However, before Rameshwar Rao could leave in pursuit of Nagappa, he was ordered to pursue Rohillas who had stolen horses from the village of Kamalapur, near Gulbarga. Thus, it was Rameshwar Rao's commander who pursued and finally captured Nagappa in 1863.[79] The Military Board wrote to the captain-in-charge asking that Nagappa be brought in chains, but the rebel needed no chains—he was already dead. The captain and his men had surprised Nagappa and the Rohillas in the jungle. After a short battle, a few of the Rohillas had been caught. One of these had turned out to be Nagappa in disguise. Wounded, he died not long after being taken captive.[80] Nagappa's death was important enough to bring praise from Meadows Taylor. Taylor was busy in Hyderabad preparing to leave for England, but took time to write to Rameshwar Rao:[81]

> I can safely say that during the last two years your Field Forces has rendered very essential service in checking predatory combinations north of the Bheema. You prevented the band of which Nagappa was at the head, making advances into the Sholapore country, plundering the Nizam's districts . . . and had he not been checked, the Rohillas with him, and Bedars of that part of Sholapore would have done a great deal of harm. No one attempted to check disorder but you, and the Naibs & Tulookhdars of districts north of the Bheerur were both in league with these rebels or afraid of them.[82]

Taylor was no stranger to the inner-workings of a samasthan and well understood the dangers of taking up arms against fellow elites in rebellion, thus for Rameshwar Rao his praise carried the highest value.

Incorporation

After Rameshwar Rao's death in 1866, the expense of maintaining his African Bodyguard put the samasthan in debt. In a move both fiscal and ceremonial, Rameshwar Rao's widow, Rani Shankaramma, presented the bodyguard to the Nizam as *nazr*. This relieved the samasthan of its expense and generously fulfilled part of the ceremonialism of the day.[83] Once incorporated into the Nizam's army, the African troops periodically marched in parades or other public events. On parade, Temple noted that the 275 Wanaparthi Lancers had been merged into the Reformed Troops.[84] Although now part of the Nizam's forces, because of their African element, the Wanaparthi forces retained their name. The Reformed Troops represented forces from many nobles of the state. The men on parade this particular day included one squadron of African cavalry and two squadrons of Lancers who served under European commanders. The Lancers would be assigned to Makhtal, Shorapur, and other areas in the southern portion of the Nizam's dominions.

At the same time the rani diplomatically courted then Resident, Richard Temple. Not only did Rani Shankaramma recognize the older relationship between the samasthan and the Nizam, but she simultaneously acknowledged the power of the Resident, and he in turn recognized her own position within the state. His letter to her of 3 January

1867 compliments her on her son's succession:

> I have also seen the Khillut presented to the young Rajah by the Nizam's Government . . . I now congratulate you on your son's succession. I hope he will imitate the example of loyalty and fidelity set by the late Rajah. And I trust that the Wonpurthy territory may always enjoy the advantage of the good system of management which has been established in it.[85]

This was only the beginning of Rani Shankaramma's engagement with British officials at Hyderabad. Later in the year, she sought out the help of one Lieutenant Rennick of the Royal Artillery. Rani Shankaramma was engaged in a dispute with another rani of the samasthan, and the affair landed in Hyderabad's courts. To possibly sway the outcome to her advantage, she had established contact with several Europeans, both in service to the British and to the Hyderabad government. Temple viewed this as a case of enlisting "European influence."[86] When confronted by Temple, Rennick revealed that "unbeknown to him" the rani had left him some £20–30,000. Temple concluded, "Regard this as a [illegible word] matter touching British honour."[87] It appears that Rennick's connection with Rani Shankaramma came to an end, and that "British honour" was maintained. As we have seen, Rani Shankaramma's actions were neither out of place for the head of a samasthan, nor for her as a woman. Both at Wanaparthi as well as within the Gadwal and Jatprole samasthans, women—from at least the early eighteenth century to the beginning of the twentieth century—played a critical role in maintaining the samasthans' existence, and were unreserved in their command of contingents like the African guard, or in their participation in Hyderabad's colonial and political circles.

Just as the African guard were incorporated into the Nizam's forces, so too did the Arab community of Hyderabad see its role diminish. By the 1880s, the role of Arabs at Wanaparthi had become largely symbolic. Being allowed to keep Arabs within the Wanaparthi forces (although ceremonial in function) was a mark of honor bestowed by the government to the samasthan dating from the eighteenth century. In a letter to the Nizam in 1884, the lawyer for the samasthan, Seshgir Rao, writes that "the zamindar of the above-mentioned samasthan may feel proud that the Government has shown its favour by the presence of the Arabs . . . Respected sir, this is an honour given by the Government a long time ago. Thus, if it is abolished now, the samasthan will be dishonoured among the zamindars."[88] How the Arab community became symbolically rather than practically important to the state is explored in the next chapter. Thus, the "military republic" that once constrained the state, ensnaring Rameshwar Rao and exasperating the Nizams and Residents, had weakened. Writing of Hyderabad in the late nineteenth century, Henry Briggs commented, "They [the Arabs] are now invariably nominal and may be considered to form a sort of Legion of Honour."[89] Hyderabad was no longer the Arab el Dorado.[90]

Well into the twentieth century, degrees of honor surrounding armed forces continued to be debated. In 1927, Nizam Osman Ali Khan ordered the convening of the Reilly Commission. Sir Henry D'Arcy Cornelius Reilly served in the Madras legal system for much of his career. The Nizam's government not only employed British ICS officers within its ranks, but called upon leading officials in Madras to convene particularly important commissions. This was likely done to avoid any accusation of bias possibly imparted by either a Hindu or Muslim convenor. The Reilly Commission's task was to further centralize and reform forces held by Hyderabad's nobles. It found that much honor was attached to their "personal" forces, and that disbanding these forces might damage that honor. Thus, a compromise was reached whereby some forces were left untouched, while others were disbanded. This arrangement worked to the advantage of the samasthans, which, unlike their *jagir* neighbors, held contiguous units, and were largely allowed to maintain their troops.[91]

In 1884, a call went out to Hyderabad's nobles to attend the coronation of the sixth Nizam, Mahbub Ali Khan. This event largely marked the end of a long era in which the samasthans had survived by providing military support to their overlords. Through the nineteenth century, borders and territorial assets began to be increasingly fixed, thereby solidifying the link between the samasthan families and the samasthan as a whole. Mercenary groups now found their positions jeopardized. Once the strong-arm of the state's nobles, they were now disbanded and incorporated into the state. Some remained visible such as the African core of the Wanaparthi armed forces, others blended in to Hyderabad society. Where swords, knives, and guns were once the norm, both the samasthan rajas and the formerly militarized ethnic groups now took their seats at increasingly ceremonial and ornamental events, and faced the new challenge of surviving this next evolution of Hyderabad's political culture. To those events we now turn.

CHAPTER 3

Turbans, Titles, and Tigers: Symbols of Rulership

By the late nineteenth century, the petty warring among Hyderabad's elites had subsided. As the samasthans had survived by the military support they could provide and the armed forces they controlled, what would now fill the vacuum created by a more peaceful Deccan? The answer to this predicament had already been in play for centuries, but now took on fresh importance. The samasthan families as well as other participants in Hyderabad's nobility capitalized on ceremony, pomp, and bluster. These ceremonial activities began to absorb the attention and wealth once expended on military adventures.[1] This occurred concomitant with the "high noon" of the Raj, which brought its own need for ceremony and imperial display. The ways in which these processes materialized was a form of "ornamentalism" or, "hierarchy made visible."[2] A composite court culture emerged that contained elements of Hindu, Muslim, and European practice. The samasthan families used a variety of strategies to take advantage of this increasingly ceremonial world. Recognizing status, reaffirming rank, exchanging gifts, and other negotiations over power were largely meted out in the durbars held at different levels of power in Hyderabad State, and in British India as well.

The rajas held durbars on numerous occasions throughout the year where in addition to distributing rewards and boons to their petty nobles, they accepted *nazr* and other gifts as well as appearing before their people dressed in their finest robes, jewels, and other royal paraphernalia. In their territories, the samasthan rajas performed certain other royal and ceremonial duties in expectation of their position. As Pamela Price has argued, kings dispersed wealth among constituent members of their kingdoms, as well as protecting them—first in war, and later in activities such as hunting—in an exercise of royal prerogative. These acts of largesse aided in the greater fulfillment of *rajadharma*. For this, the samasthan rajas were celebrated for their acts in poetry, family histories, by royal visits made by the Nizams, and official visits made by either the Residents or other British officials.[3] Ceremony became a new way of keeping order, where participants in the Deccan once exchanged canon shot or sword blows, they now more often exchanged gifts of gold coin, robes of honor, portraits, paintings, and other accoutrements of the time.

This increasingly important ceremonialism demanded participation of the samasthan rajas—and indeed, they wanted to participate—in higher ceremonial circles; first at the Nizam's durbar, and on occasion at the great all-India durbars held by the British at Delhi. At the Nizam's durbar, roles were reversed. The rajas were secondary to the rank of the Nizam, and they came offering their own praise and gifts to him, and in turn were rewarded with gifts according to their status. At times, the Nizams abused their position and demanded exorbitant *nazr* from their court members. As we shall see, this was endemic under the last Nizam. Added to this political fabric's weft was a warp: as the samasthans were embedded within Hyderabad State, so too was Hyderabad embedded within the Raj. Thrice India's nobility assembled in Delhi to participate in the durbars called by the suzerain authority. Here, the Nizams offered their own gifts and received rewards as well. The samasthan rajas saw themselves as ancient and royal families of the Deccan and participated (with varying degrees of success) in these imperial durbars. Their presence at home, in Hyderabad city, and in Delhi secured them a share of power in this highly ceremonial era.

One event within Hyderabad deeply affected these processes. In 1911, the sixth Nizam, Mahbub Ali Khan died, and his son, Osman Ali Khan, took the reins of power. Since Hyderabad was fundamentally an autocratic state, the atmosphere of its court politics directly reflected the personality of the Nizam. Mahbub Ali Khan was much beloved by his people and known for his generosity.[4] Thus, under his reign abuses at the durbar were generally rare. However, his son's reputation was almost a mirror opposite. Osman Ali Khan, while generous in his donations to Britain during the two World Wars, and generous in establishing Benares Hindu University and Osmania University, was however, particularly zealous in collecting inappropriately large *nazr*. The abuse of this practice drew the attention of the Resident as well as the displeasure of the samasthan families. In response to pressure from the Resident, and demands for change by the samasthan rajas, the Nizam found himself on the defensive, and forced to find less obvious methods of collecting *nazr*.

As ceremonialism grew, including delicate discussions of rank and power, it was colored by the character of the individuals involved in these negotiations. Such negotiations, however, began before nobles ever met face to face.

Coming to Hyderabad

By the late nineteenth century Hyderabad city was a place where military accoutrements were the norm, not because the city was violent, but because the display of weapons was part of demonstrating status. Knives, swords, and pistols accompanied displays of palanquins, robes, and bejeweled turbans. "[T]he dignity of the many nobles and petty chiefs that abound in the city of Hyderabad is maintained by their keeping up such a number of armed men as they consider necessary to make their rank and station as great as possible in the eyes of the public."[5] Ceremonial display reached one among several peaks in 1884 when a call went out to all landholders to attend the coronation of the sixth Nizam, Mahbub Ali Khan. By that time, the military presence in Hyderabad had changed from a collection of personal armies to a larger and more centralized state force. As nobles lost the prestige once measured in troops, they rushed to fill the vacuum with ceremonial gestures and displays.

Unlike sending troops, the Hyderabad durbar required the bodily presence of the state's nobles. For the samasthan rajas, their attendance at a durbar was an opportunity not only to indulge in copious gift giving and receiving, it also reminded the Nizam of their role as members of the state. In short, being present was critical. But the Hyderabad durbar was not simply an event of an hour or two; it involved a host of related issues of honor and ceremony. The trip to Hyderabad required a contingent of largely ceremonial armed escorts; the stay in the capital city meant that each samasthan had to maintain its own palace for such occasions; and the whole complex of obligations called for constant vigilance in maintaining one's honor in the eyes of the Nizam and compeers. In one case, before leaving Wanaparthi for the march to Hyderabad, Raja Ram Krishna Rao III (Rameshwar Rao's successor) wrote to the Nizam's government reminding it of the hierarchy that was to be maintained. Hyderabad's durbar had been admitting non-*mulkis* as the administrative system continued to grow. He wrote, "I do not know how some of the Rajas would behave because they neither know the old traditions nor the dignity of the rank . . . " The letter goes on to request that "at the time of distributing robes of honour whatever has been fixed for must not be exceeded."[6] Obliging the raja, Salar Jung sent gifts in accordance with his rank that included perfumes, sweets, grains, butter, meat, sugar, ghee, and 150 coins.[7]

Court culture included the protocol for the physical arrival of samasthan rajas in the city. Usually, these men were welcomed several miles in advance and escorted to their Hyderabad palaces.[8] Along with this welcome, they were provided a military escort for the duration of their stay, as well as a carriage and other necessary accoutrements. These obligations to the rajas were set strictly according to the rank of the individual. Once settled in their palaces, the rajas would send a note to the Nizam announcing their arrival and subsequent intention to attend durbar, or requesting a private interview. Thus, in 1895, when the raja of Anagundi came to Hyderabad and was not welcomed with the appropriate greeting, his *dewan* wrote to the Nizam's secretary:

> On a former occasion when the Rajah came here he received a gov't. carriage and five sowars. He has come again and only a carriage was sent to the station for him but no sowars were allowed, and so the Rajah won't leave his bungalow. The Jodpol [Jatprole] Rajah who is here has been allowed several sowars and surely the Anaigoondy family as representing the old Vijayanaga[r] Kingdom is entitles [*sic*] the honour also.[9]

The Anagundi family claimed lineal descent from the rulers of Vijayanagar. The Anagundi raja was aware of the treatment awarded the Jatprole raja (Lakshma Rao), and *izzat* (personal honor) demanded that he remind the Nizam's government of his own family's heritage and rank. Two days later the government acquiesced and he was given five guards to attend him. When Lakshma Rao arrived, he had come with a retinue of armed men. Since his palace was near the Residency, an application was needed to carry weapons. This required the consent of the Resident, the Nizam's secretary, and the police chief of the Residency bazaar. This allowed the raja's armed men to move about freely in the bazaar.[10] His entourage included twenty-one *sawars* with swords and lances, two Arabs with *jambias* (daggers) and guns, and twelve police *jawans* (soldiers). The entourage was certainly engaged more for pomp and display than any real military use.[11]

Negotiations over arrivals, accommodations, and seating frequently proved confusing to the parties involved, and even more so between Indians and Britons. British officials were quick to adapt and adopt the protocols of the durbar and formal visits, but not without occasionally causing a degree of confusion among their guests. For instance, Indian nobles found the more egalitarian British style of seating at times baffling. In 1799, John Malcolm, a military commander in the Company's army, was en route to Hyderabad and camped for the night in the countryside. A young Hindu raja of the Nizam's dominion visited him at camp.[12] Malcolm and his attendants sat down with the raja, his Brahman tutor, and their attendants. When the meeting concluded, the raja remarked to his tutor in Telugu, which Malcolm understood, "One gentleman sat on my right, another on my left. I am quite at a loss to discover which is the principal person of these two." Given the highly ordered space of the Indian durbar, we can imagine the thoughts of the young raja when all were seated in the tent with no man elevated, literally, to a higher and more authoritative position. A master of princely protocol and diplomacy, Malcolm responded in Telugu, "There is no principal person in the tent but the chief who has honored us with this visit."[13] With the negotiations for arrivals and accommodations successfully completed, nobles gathered for the durbar itself.

Durbar

Throughout India, and spanning both Hindu and Muslim political practice holding a durbar and receiving *nazr* ranked among the most important of the symbols of rulership. These events and practices allowed differently ranked nobles from a multitude of faiths and practices to engage with each other in the highly ordered space of the durbar. Earlier durbars were held in tents if the ruler was in camp, a practice that Muslim rulers borrowed from their central Asian predecessors. As nobility in South Asia became more settled and less mobile, durbars were held in specially constructed buildings such as Delhi's *dewan-i-am*, the public audience hall of the Red Fort. Formal durbar halls were large, supported by ornately carved pillars. Candles lit the room, but later in a nod to modernization, electric lights twinkled throughout. The floor of the hall was covered with carpets or mattresses, and then with pristine white cotton sheets. Nobles and visitors to the court left their footwear outside, and proceeded barefooted into the presence of the ruler.

In Hyderabad, durbars were generally held at three levels. First, at the local level, the samasthan rajas held durbars where they received petty nobles who served under them as well as guests passing through their territory, and occasionally a visit by the Resident or Nizam. One such example (explored later) is when a visitor came to the durbar of the Gadwal samasthan. At these events, the ruler sat at the side or the head of the hall, usually on a large *masnad* (throne) or *gaddi*, and might recline on ornate bolsters or cushions. In some courts rulers used a richly decorated chair as their throne.[14] A canopy crafted of the finest brocade often covered this throne. Court members sat to the left of the ruler bearing royal emblems that might include a fly-whisk, mace, and other symbolic paraphernalia, and family members to the right. Musicians played in the background, and the air was laden with scent. Attendees might present a variety of gifts, and at the close of events, *attar* (rose water) and *pan* (betel nut) would be distributed. Durbars were often organized around the personal life of the noble (birthdays, anniversaries, etc.) as well as the religious holidays of both the Hindu and Muslim faiths. Occasionally they were held on one-off events such as a visit by one ruler to another's territory. The rajas retained practices that dated from their ancestors' attendance at the great durbars of the Kakatiya and Vijayanagar kings. These included affiliating their rule with particular deities whom they propitiated. They also included practices borrowed from the Indo-Muslim-styled durbars of the Golconda and Asaf Jah regimes. For instance, the presentation of *khilats* (robes of honor) that further bolstered their own *rajadharma*. As British influence directly and indirectly crept into their kingdoms, they began to incorporate practices from their colonial neighbors. These included the assimilation of new technologies in India (automobiles, telegraphs, phones, electric lights, photographs) into the royal paraphernalia. The use of such technologies only added to the composite nature of the samasthans' practice.

At the second level, the Nizam's durbar marked the pinnacle of Hyderabad's political culture. Nobles would, after bowing deeply, present their *nazr*. Coins would be placed on a silken or cotton square of cloth, and held out—head bowed—with both hands. In some durbars, the Nizam simply touched the offering and returned it to the donor. At other times, he took the offering and in exchange gifted the donor with a *khilat* or *sar-o-pa* (complete outfit). In either case, "the offering was not meant to enrich the recipient or to impoverish the donor."[15] Another type of gift was the bestowing of a new title. For the Nizam's Silver Jubilee in 1905, Rameshwar Rao II of Wanaparthi and Lakshma Rao of Jatprole received new titles of *mahabhupal* and *nazim nawazwant bahadur* respectively.[16] These occasions marked the Nizam's birthday, religious holidays (Muharram and Eid), investitures, and other public or family events. The state's elites (and on many occasions the British Resident) attended the Nizam's durbar. These events were carefully orchestrated and reflected the political hierarchy of Hyderabad itself.[17] Nobles highest in rank sat closest to the Nizam, with successively lower ranked nobles seated further and further away. For a durbar in 1902 where the samasthan rajas were present, Mahbub Ali Khan used a specific seating arrangement. Gadwal and Wanaparthi, the two most prestigious samasthans, were seated closest to the Nizam. Jatprole and Domakonda came next, and the remaining samasthan holders followed them in descending rank. That Mahbub Ali Khan held a separate durbar for just the samasthan rajas indicates the pride of place they assumed within Hyderabad's polity. These proceedings were carefully choreographed in advance. For instance, by the early twentieth century, Mahbub Ali Khan was at the height of his reign and strictly regulated dress for the durbar. This seems indicative of the reforms and centralization occurring at the time. Further, meetings between the Resident and Nizam, as well as with other dignitaries visiting the court, required uniform dress. Thus, in anticipation of the viceroy's visit (Lord Curzon) to Hyderabad in 1902, the Nizam sanctioned the following plan for court dress.

> The undress coat will be of plain black *banat* as in the fulldress, (without any embroidery) and its buttons will be like those of the fulldress coat. The trousers, belt, sword and ankleboots will be of the same kind in both fulldress and undress, and the trousers will have a stripe of Ogalvie lace 2 inches wide. The pattern of belt has not yet been sanctioned by H.H. and until that time the old belt may be used. Photos of the uniform plans are available at Deen Dayal and sons.[18]

In recognition of the technology available at the time, the Hyderabad nobility utilized photographs to help them attain a uniform look in their dress. The use of such technology, which later came to include other "European" items such as cars, electric lights, telephones, cameras, and so on, forged within the samasthans a composite of Indian and European technologies. Coming from the periphery of the state, these durbars afforded the samasthan rajas an opportunity to "see and be seen," thus subtly reminding other members of the court of their presence.[19] Finally, at the third and grandest level were the great imperial durbars of 1877, 1903, and 1911, held by the British in Delhi. In attendance at the first two events was Mahbub Ali Khan and later his son, Osman Ali Khan attended in 1911, as well as India's many other recognized princes. Gifts were exchanged and honors bestowed, yet the levels of power made manifest by holding durbars existed not without challenge. As David Cannadine has argued, with the decline in real power comes a rise in the use of symbolic and ceremonial activity that carries with it new power relationships.[20]

The samasthan rajas were in some sense caught between two social orders, and constantly striving to maintain power and honor. On the one hand, they were among the premier nobles *within* Hyderabad State. On the other, once *out* of Hyderabad they had to compete (sometimes unsuccessfully) with the Nizams for recognition.[21] Two examples bear out this precarious position with respect to Gadwal. The young raja of Gadwal, Sita Rambhupal II, while still a minor under the Court of Wards, made every effort to attend the Delhi durbar of 1911. He intended to do this not as a vassal of Hyderabad, but as the head of one of India's oldest noble families. After the death of Rambhupal II on 31 March 1901, the Hyderabad government had placed Gadwal under the Court of Wards. The Court had been established only recently, and Gadwal was its largest estate at the time. Sita Rambhupal II, himself still a minor and under the supervision of the Court of Wards, began to take an active role in the affairs of the samasthan. In 1911, in advance of the Delhi durbar, Rambhupal II wrote to A.J. Dunlop, the Revenue member responsible for directing the Court of Wards, to request a seat at the great gathering. Dunlop in turn wrote to the Hyderabad political secretary.

> The Rajah of Gadwal (Rajah Sitaram Bhupal Bahadur) is going to Delhi, and I hope it may not be too late to include his name in those who will be invited to the public ceremonies at the Durbar. I may mention that Gadwal is the largest Samasthan in His Highness' Dominions, with an income of 4 1/2 lacs of rupees per annum.[22]

Dunlop felt it necessary to reiterate Gadwal's position within the dominions because of its size and importance. While no ticket was available for the raja, he went north nonetheless. Unable to get accommodation on the Hyderabad-Delhi train, he was forced to travel to Bombay in order to reach Delhi. Unfortunately no further mention of the raja and his Delhi journey can be found, and it seems unlikely that his efforts were successful. Thus, outside of Hyderabad, the raja and his samasthan were not recognized as having a (high enough) rank to warrant a seat at the durbar, however, Rambhupal clearly felt that his rank both inside and outside of Hyderabad warranted such recognition. The presence of the raja at such an event was deeply linked to his maintenance of his own sense of honor. This pride and the raja's importance within Hyderabad's polity is supported by a second event. When the young raja was in need of a tutor, no less than the Resident, Charles Stuart Bayley, and the Hyderabad Prime Minister, Kishen Pershad handled the affair.[23] That the matter was attended to by the Resident and prime minister, and not lower ranking officials, attests to the raja's importance within the state. While Sita Rambhupal did not attend the durbar, there was a precedence already established for a samasthan raja to accompany the Nizam to a

Delhi durbar. In 1903, the raja of Wanaparthi was a member of the Nizam's entourage. The list of nobles accompanying the Nizam was in fact a "who's who" of Hyderabad's polity. The Nizam's minister, Kishen Pershad, along with Colonel Afsur ud Daula headed the delegation.[24] When Lord Curzon commented on the simplicity of the Nizam's dress, Mahbub Ali Khan gestured to his nobles and replied that in fact his jewels were with him.[25]

A momentous change occurred within Hyderabad in 1911 when Osman Ali Khan took the reins of power.[26] The installation of a new Nizam warranted not only lavish durbars where nobles would attend, present *nazr*, and be incorporated into the new Nizam's realm, but also visits from other dignitaries of the Raj. When Osman Ali Khan took power on 18 September 1911, his inauguration durbar included the Resident, Alexander Pinhey, as well as the distinguished nobles of the state. Clearly visible in the photograph of the occasion is Raja Lakshma Rao of Jatprole. While the Nizam stands with hands clasped on a walking stick at the center of the photograph and flanked by durbar attendants, the third person on his left is Lakshma Rao. Dressed in his finest, the raja stands erect, his gaze fixed across the room. He wears a turban; a white tunic and pajama pants with English laced shoes. Around his neck a bejeweled *har* (neckwear). On his shoulders are epaulets and in addition to a sash and cummerbund, a sword hangs on his left side. In the photograph he carries on his body the symbols and accoutrements of power infused with the pride of his family and samasthan history[27] The next month, when the viceroy of India, Charles Hardinge, visited the newly installed Nizam, a photograph taken after lunch shows the Nizam and viceroy seated in the center of a large group of nobles. Flanking them on each side is one row seated and behind them another standing. Furthest to the Nizam's left, standing, is Raja Sita Rambhupal of Gadwal. Bespectacled, wearing a black tunic and disc-shaped turban (very different from the Hyderabad style turbans), Rambhupal stares directly into the camera.[28] His presence at a lunch with the viceroy reflects his premier rank amongst the samasthans. As the decade progressed, this standing would take on a cost, as Rambhual would become the favorite target of Osman Ali Khan's requests for *nazr*. Over a century earlier, Rambhupal's royal predecessor—also named Sita Rambhupal—was visited at his durbar by an official coming from the Madras Presidency.

Gadwal Durbar

Gadwal was among the oldest, largest, and wealthiest of the samasthans, and visitors occasionally attended its durbar. Given its strategic location at the intersection of Hyderabad, British, and Maratha territory, it is not surprising that in the early nineteenth century, Gadwal was politically incorporated into larger spheres of power beyond Hyderabad. One such occasion of this process occurred when Colin Mackenzie sent his assistant, Narrain Row to visit the Gadwal durbar in search of family documents. Mackenzie, a colonial official, was appointed to Hyderabad in 1792 to survey lands ceded by Tipu Sultan. In 1810 he was named surveyor general of Madras, and later from 1816 to 1821 served as surveyor general of India. Mackenzie died in 1821, leaving behind a tremendous collection of records gathered from across south India and the Deccan. Part of this corpus came from families in Hyderabad State, such as Gadwal.

The visit provides not only a rare first-hand account of a samasthan durbar, but also illuminates the delicate negotiations that took place between an outsider (Row) and his host (the raja). Helping to make this process easier, a variety of court officials were present, not only those who served the raja in different capacities, but also those whose proximity to the raja provide a further example of how power and rank in the durbar were made manifest. Further, the languages employed at the Gadwal court are indicative of Hyderabad's composite and multiethnic members. The samasthan occupied a critical position in the Raichur *doab*. It was physically separated from Hyderabad territory by the Tungabhadra river, and the Madras territory by the Krishna river. Yet, its liminal geographic position to Hyderabad State or the Madras Presidency did not prevent Mackenzie's efforts to gather information about the family and kingdom. According to Nicholas Dirks, in areas not under direct British rule, "Mackenzie's men had to use their wits."[29] In visiting Gadwal, Narrain Row did just this.

It was mid-October 1809 when Narrain Row visited Raja Sita Rambhupal at the Gadwal palace.[30] From Row's letter to Mackenzie, we can glean details of the visit and the Gadwal durbar at this time.[31] On the 15 October, Row found himself on the south side of the Raichur *doab* and the Tungabhadra river, wanting to cross to the north to reach Gadwal territory. In his possession, Row had a letter from Mackenzie to Sita Rambhupal asking for historical materials from the samasthan. Row "waited for the boat of Gudvole" and made his crossing.

Reaching the outskirts of Gadwal town, guards at the outermost gate detained Row while they called for Jeevaujey *naik*. Row identifies Jeevaujey as a Rajput in the service of the raja. After waiting several hours, Jeevaujey escorted Row past the gate and to a grove of trees where he was made to camp. Again Row waited several hours while Jeevaujey, having questioned him, went to see Sita Rambhupal. By the late afternoon, Jeevaujey returned and escorted Row to the raja's durbar.

Before entering the raja's presence, Row obeyed the etiquette of the court, removed his shoes, and entered barefoot. Seated around Sita Rambhupal were several courtiers; their relative proximity to him determined by their rank. Closest to the raja was his *dewan*, Venkat Rao. Next to the *dewan* sat an unnamed Muslim, and beyond him Enauyatkha (chief of the army) and the court *vakil*, Vaubkhan. Beyond them sat Chauvady Bheemarow the *serishtadar* (record keeper, accountant). Also present at the durbar were several Brahmans and other court attendants. Furthest from the raja sat Narrain Row.

Vaubkhan began by asking Row about his pedigree and employment. This was done in the "Masulmaney" language (Urdu). Then, Venkat Row came forward and read the letter from Mackenzie. The letter, in Persian, asked the raja to provide any information about his family history. As Venkat Row explained the letter to Sita Rambhupal, one of the courtiers commented that Mackenzie had in fact visited Gadwal before. Vaubkhan added that he had met Mackenzie at Hyderabad, to which Narrain Row added (in Telugu, the raja's native language) that Mackenzie was a friend to Sita Rambhupal's predecessor, Maharaja Sombhupal. From this brief exchange it is clear that Gadwal's court was already a linguistic composite—attendees shifting between Urdu, Telugu, and Persian as conversation demanded.

With introductions and some collaborative identification complete, Narrain Row was served betel nut and dismissed. Venkat Rao assured him that he would receive a letter from the raja. Narrain Row spent a rainy night camped in a grove. The following morning the raja sent him provisions as a courtesy. For the next three days, Row tried in vain to attain some better lodging. His initial entrée into the durbar, Jeevaujey, promised to help him but failed to deliver. Before his camp could find drier quarters, on the 21st Narrain Row was once again summoned to the durbar.

There he found the raja seated on a cot, accompanied by Venkat Row, Vaubkhan, Chauvady Bheemarow, and others. Vaubkhan began with questions about Narrain Row's destination after leaving Gadwal. Row was traveling next to Adoni district. Then, Row was asked how he would get the letter to his master. He replied that it would be sent by post. Satisfied, Vaubkhan informed Row that he would receive the information he wanted. Row was served betel nut and the interview seemed all but over. In whispered conversation, members of the durbar urged him to leave for "the country," but Row seemed to have something else in mind. He spoke directly to Sita Rambhupal, flattering him on the number of people the raja fed and housed, and how he hoped the raja would keep him in his favor. This elicited a nod from Sita Rambhupal, but no offer to house Narrain Row in a better location—the likely reason for the flattery. Wet and uncomfortable, but with letter in hand, Row left Gadwal the next day. Gadwal's history and the details of its rule were thus to be woven into Mackenzie's archival tapestry of south India. The visit between Rambhupal and Row saw the exchange of information as Row was at Gadwal on behalf of Mackenzie. Yet, more often than not, it was not information exchanged at durbars, but some physical exchange.

Articles of Honor

All of this pomp and circumstance associated with durbars was undergirded by the exchange of ritually symbolic items. These included *khilats, nazr*, portraits and photographs, and other items. Within this system of exchange, occasionally tensions arose over proper etiquette. These moments of disagreement bring to light the delicate negotiations over power and rank that took place between Indian rulers and their guests. A common point of friction began at the bottom, literally, with debates over the use of shoes when entering a durbar. Visitors to the durbar would first remove their footwear before stepping onto a floor covered with pristine white cotton cloth. This practice of removing ones shoes extended not only into the durbar, but was (and is) the custom throughout the subcontinent; shoes bringing polluting substances into the home. Yet, as the relationship between Britain and India gradually changed, so too did the policy concerning shoes. Tensions arose over who was to remove their shoes, and when. Bernard Cohn has written: "Indians were always forced to remove their shoes or sandals when entering what the British defined as their space—their offices and homes. On the other hand, the British always insisted on wearing shoes when entering Indian spaces, including mosques and temples."[32] Hyderabad was not spared this "shoe controversy."

Through the reign of Afzal ud Daula, it was the Nizam who retained the position of superior power vis-à-vis the British Resident, emphasized at the durbar by the Resident's removal of his shoes. Hyderabad's Residents were not entirely pleased with this, yet no change was immediately pressed for.[33] Prior to 1858, the Company's Resident had removed his boots before entering the Nizam's durbar out of respect for custom. Yet, Afzal ud Daula was not unaware of the Resident's discomfort surrounding this issue. He seems to have used court customs more amicable to the Resident for his own purpose. In 1850, he summoned James Fraser, Resident at Hyderabad from 1839 to 1852, to a private meeting that was held in a tent overlooking the Musi river. For the first time the Resident and Nizam both wore shoes and sat in chairs, and not on the floor. The break in custom was not without reason: the Nizam had invited Fraser to discuss the liquidation of the state's debt. He perhaps thought that having shoes and chairs might in some way benefit his case.[34] Following Fraser a few years later, Cuthbert Davidson, Resident from 1857 to 1862, struck a more paternal tone and felt that any change would only be embarrassing to the Nizam as the latter would be unfamiliar with the custom of wearing shoes.[35] George Yule, Resident from 1863 to 1867, said that the question of changing the shoe policy was more than any one Resident could handle. Given the larger issues to be dealt with at the time, he felt that the shoe question could wait.[36]

The shoe question was finally resolved at the death of Afzal ud Daula when the Residency (under Richard Temple and then Charles Saunders) gently pushed for changes in the custom.[37] Saunders wrote,

> This seemed a good opportunity of explaining to them [the Amirs of the court] that the old etiquette, according to which British officers were required to take off their shoes in approaching the Nizam, and seat themselves after His Highness's own fashion upon the ground, did not promote those terms of friendly intercourse with the Resident on which the satisfactory relationship existing between the two Governments so much depends.[38]

As Mahbub Ali Khan was only a child, Saunders suggested that if the custom was changed immediately, by the time the Nizam ascended the *masnad*, he would be accustomed to the wearing of shoes. The strategy worked, and when Mahbub Ali Khan was formally installed, shoes and chairs had become the norm at the Nizam's court. Saunders describes the durbar and the end of an "obsolete custom."

> [R]ows of chairs for the accommodation of the British visitors are arranged on the left of the *masnad*, which is elevated on a kind of dias, so as to place His Highness on a level with his visitors, while, upon the left, the Ameers continue to seat themselves in Oriental posture upon a similarly raised platform. And thus a usage which has excited must hostle criticism, and which was hardly consonant with the character belonging to the representatives of the paramount Government, has at last been quietly numbered with the other obsolete customs of former days.[39]

Once members of the court had begun to wear shoes, it was no longer suitable for them to sit on the floor. Thus, chairs also began to be used. With the advent of chairs in the durbar, the dress of the court also changed. The flowing gowns of the early nineteenth century were not so comfortable when seated in a chair, and a change was made to the more comfortable *sherwani* (knee length coat buttoned at the collar) and pajama pants. Thus, the greatest change came during the time of Mahbub Ali Khan's childhood when the accommodating minister, Salar Jung, and the child Nizam made it possible for the Residency to solidify its importance as a center of authority in Hyderabad.

Salar Jung maintained largely warm relations with the different Residents who served at Hyderabad. Not only was there cooperation and cordiality during a Resident's tenure, but the relationship seemed to extend even when individual Residents left Hyderabad for other postings. Critical to the relationship was the exchange of a gift. When Yule was preparing to leave his post as Hyderabad's Resident in the spring of 1867, Salar Jung wrote to him, wanting to give a gift.

> I trust you will not feel offended with what I am about to say, but I cannot let a friend like you leave this country without desiring you should retain some trifling memorial of our intercourse and friendship, if you will therefore kindly permit me I shall send a few articles to you to select from, so that yourself, Lady Yule and Miss Yule may each possess a small memento of our friendship. They will not be of any great value intrinsically I assure you, and I will only offer them on condition that you keep them with you to remind you sometimes of an absent friend, who will long remember with gratitude the kindness and friendship he has received from you.[40]

The minister was clearly aware of the difficulties and complexities of giving a British official a gift, lest implications of bribery or corruption should emerge. Thus, to ease the transaction, Salar Jung sends something not of "any great value," and to be kept only as a "trifling memorial" and "memento of our friendship." Thus, the tension over the use of gifts, shoes, chairs, and other items of the durbar was—over time—resolved through diplomatic channels. With the help of Salar Jung, the power of the Resident and his influence at court grew, but in other instances court practice either remained unchanged or became a composite of multiple practices.

Within the different levels of durbars lay the opportunity for objects to be exchanged between ruler and subordinate. This exchange ritually incorporated the latter into the former's realm. Among the most important gift was that of the *khilat*. F.W. Buckler and Bernard Cohn have both argued that *khilats* worn by the ruler were invested with power, and thus to give it to another was a move conveying authority.[41] The recipient was then incorporated into the donor's realm. He wore a physical item that had once touched his sovereign's body, and thus it was believed that part of that ruler's authority had now been conveyed upon him. However, Stewart Gordon has suggested that it was not only the giver who held a position of power in the relationship, but that the recipient of a robe had considerable agency in the process. For instance, rejection of a robe by a recipient could be an act of aggression, and even demand a military response.[42] Indeed, as Gordon points out, not all *khilats* were equal, and that recipients were aware of "gradations of fineness and value of robes."[43] Nobles frequently sent *khilats* to each other, however, as a simple exchange of gifts with no thought of incorporation. Gordon suggests that the exchange of *khilats* was "not an expression of a stable 'culture.' " Instead, he offers an alternative explanation that locates the exchange of *khilats* and other objects as part of a process of weaving together forms of governance.[44]

In addition to *khilats*, another important gift that was exchanged between ruler and ruled was *nazr*. *Nazr* was largely symbolic in nature, but at times was a real financial boon to the recipient. In Delhi, the great durbars of the Mughals and their predecessors, which shared much of the same court culture, provided the ultimate model for durbars held at Hyderabad. When the traveler Ibn Batutta had visited the court of Muhammad ibn Tughluq in 1334, no less than four court chamberlains preceded him into the durbar hall. They made "obeisance in three places" between the durbar entrance and the emperor's throne. In return the emperor might embrace the guest, accept their gifts, and give a robe and money.[45] Later, an Italian visitor to Delhi, Niccolao Manucci, commented on gift giving, "Any presents made to the king [Aurangzeb] are accepted in his capacity of sovereign—that is to say, he believes or makes out that these gifts are his by right, as homage rendered to his supreme majesty."[46] (Centuries later, Osman Ali Khan of Hyderabad would echo this sentiment, his "right" to receive *nazr*.) At the Vijayanagar court, the traveler Abd-er-Razzak presented horses and cloth to the king, and in return received gold and camphor.[47] *Nazr* at times was paid to ingratiate oneself to a more powerful ruler. Damaji Gaikwar of Baroda gave *nazr* to the Maratha Peshwa, Madhav Rao, and "atoned for his disloyalty" to the Maratha empire. *Nazr* was also given on the occasion of succession as well as for purely political reasons, when the donor expected no material gain in return but hoped to make a good impression on the recipient.[48]

For instance, in the south of Hyderabad, Venkatadry Naidu, the Great Vasireddy zamindar of Guntur district, gave *nazr* to Nizam Sikander Jah in the form of 100,000 pagodas while passing through Hyderabad. For this enormous sum, Naidu was given the honorific title of "Manur Sultan."[49]

British attitudes toward *nazr* changed over time. In the seventeenth and eighteenth centuries, the general understanding of *nazr* was that it was some form of payment at best, and a form of bribery at worse. In short, "[t]he British glossed the offering of *nazar* as bribery."[50] For Company officials in India, the giving and receiving of *nazr* was also an opportunity for increasing personal wealth, and thus seen by officials in London as a growing form of corruption. Thus in the summer of 1784, William Pitt presented to the parliament his India Bill that, among other things, officially made *nazr, khilats*, and *peshkush* recognized forms of bribery. At stake were two competing ideas of how the Company might be reformed and better managed: first was the idea that the Company could be managed by parliamentary commissioners who would oversee its doings, and second was Pitt's Bill that placed Company reform in the hands of royal control and crown appointments to India.[51] Among the first changes in the post-1784 era was the appointment of General Charles Cornwallis as governor general. He served in that position from 1785 to 1793 and returned to the Company a degree of "professional ethos."[52] Yet, Company officials could not altogether end or avoid the giving and receiving of *nazr*, thus a more refined understanding of the practice began to emerge in the late eighteenth and nineteenth centuries.

As Michael Fisher has demonstrated, when Company territories expanded, Residents at princely courts found themselves caught up in the giving and receiving of *nazr, khilats*, and *peshkush*.[53] By the nineteenth century this practice—to avoid the look of corruption—had become carefully monitored. Gifts received by a Resident were to be matched by gifts of equal value given to the Indian donor. Further, gifts received by the Resident or Company official became property of the Company and kept in the *toshakhana* (special treasury). Bernard Cohn argued that "[b]y converting what was a form of present-giving and prestation [*sic*] into a kind of 'economic exchange,' the relationship between British official and Indian subject or ruler became contractual."[54] Even with this understanding of *nazr* as "economic exchange," mistakes and offences still occurred. For instance, the acting Resident at Delhi from 1829 to 1830, Francis Hawkins, offended then Mughal Emperor Akbar Shah II by presenting *nazr* with only one hand. Protocol demanded that the donor present *nazr* with head bowed and holding the offering with both hands.[55] Clearly at times colonial officials misunderstood the local context and meaning behind such ceremonial exchanges.

Nazr in Hyderabad was usually presented in the form of *mohurs* (gold coins). *Mohurs,* also known as *ashrafis,* were used well into the twentieth century. The amount was specifically set according to the rank of the donor. Because most donors understood *nazr* to be deeply connected to rank and honor, they responded to opportunities to present these gifts to the ruler. As long as the ruler did not abuse the system, the donor considered presentation of *nazr* a privilege and not a burden. For aspiring government employees, or for a new Resident seeking the Nizam's approval, giving *nazr* was an opportunity to, albeit briefly, have the full and personal attention of the ruler. When nobles did not attend durbars, they were reprimanded for missing the opportunity and honor of presenting *nazr.* In a memo sent to the nobles of the state during Mahbub Ali Khan's reign, the Nizam's secretary outlined the reasons for attending the durbar

> Everybody is aware that in the course of a year only 3 or 4 Durbars are held in which an opportunity is given to kiss the feet of His Highness. I am greatly surprised as to why these people [nobles] do not avail themselves of such an opportunity . . . they should consider their presence on such occasions as their bounden duty.[56]

In the wake of decreased militarism and increased ceremonialism this "bounden duty" resulted in some unusual and costly expenses.

While presenting *nazr* was usually considered an honor, sometimes nobles protested. This was especially true under the rule of Osman Ali Khan. For instance, the raja of Anagundi wrote to the Nizam that the "peshkush imposed on my samasthan is hanging heavily upon me . . . you are also aware that an interview with my lord is the only chance towards the remission."[57] Ironically, to meet with the Nizam to settle the matter, the raja had first to pay a *nazr.* In the same vein, Raja Lakshma Rao of Jatprole, whenever possible, avoided coming to Hyderabad during Osman Ali Khan's reign because the Nizam and his officials would "pounce" on him for *nazr.* Thus, while it was often a matter of prestige to present *nazr,* by the time of the last Nizam, many nobles had come to dread it.

In 1920, Osman Ali Khan had been Nizam for nine years. He had periodically toured his domain as part of his royal activities and these tours allowed him to see and be seen by his citizens, to commemorate important events (such as the opening of a dam or other public works), and to visit his nobles who lived far from Hyderabad. That year he announced a tour of his dominion by train. Then raja of Gadwal, Sita Rambhupal, wrote to him offering *nazr* if he would visit the samasthan on his journey.[58] To reach Gadwal by train, the Nizam had to pass first through the station serving Wanaparthi (some miles from the town itself, called Wanaparthi Road). But if the Nizam visited Wanaparthi first, it would violate protocol since Gadwal was the higher-ranking samasthan. Knowing this and seeing a chance for profit, the Nizam began a bidding war between the two rajas to see who would offer a larger *nazr* for the honor of his visit first. Gadwal won the competition with a *nazr* of three lakhs, and Wanaparthi followed by giving two lakhs.[59]

Why should the rajas have engaged in such an expensive competition? Both Gadwal and Wanaparthi were distinguished members of Hyderabad's political system, and the two highest-ranking samasthans. Their rajas saw the acquisition of new titles and the opportunity to present *nazr* as part of their role. The Nizam's personal visit gave this particular instance added significance. To have the honor of receiving the Nizam in their own domains, and to receive commensurate titles on this occasion was doubly important to each raja. Add to this the personal character of Osman Ali Khan, and the scene was ripe for the bidding war that ensued.

The large *nazrs* given by Gadwal and Wanaparthi brought them certain benefits. For the *nazr* and the first visit, the Nizam bestowed the title of maharaja on the raja of Gadwal. The raja of Wanaparthi also received a visit and the title, but only *after* the visit to Gadwal. In addition, the raja of Wanaparthi secured for his two sons the title of raja. However, the Nizam was not satisfied with the *nazr* he had received. After returning from his visits to Gadwal and Wanaparthi, he wrote to Sita Rambhupal, playing on the raja's sense of honor:

> It is evident that the honour . . . that I conferred to-day was not merely on yourself but on the whole of your family. I know you will be able to realize it. The Nazar that you should have given on this occasion should either have been in consonance with my status or with your position . . . I am satisfied with your loyalty to my person. But in the eyes of the public your position will be degraded by reason of your Nazar of to-day. Please think of this.[60]

Under this pressure from the Nizam and the threat of shame—losing face in the eyes of "the public"—Sita Rambhupal added to the already exorbitant *nazr* he had given.

In the eyes of the Resident, Charles Russell, the whole affair reflected poorly on the Nizam. Osman Ali Khan defended himself to Russell and explained why he expected such large *nazrs* from Gadwal and Wanaparthi. First, he noted that the two samasthans were "senior to the others" in terms of income. He emphasized that his visit would "advance them in honour in the eyes of their compeers. Such a visit would count as a historic event and would be handed down as such in their families." The Nizam explained that large *nazr* had been given to reflect the honor of his visit, and the value received by the samasthans from such a visit.[61] Russell wrote:

> I asked [the minister] whether part of the feeling against the present Nizam was not due to his having substituted a regime of reasonable economy in the palace for the lavish extravagance of his father. He said that undoubtedly part of the feeling was due to this cause, but that it was very far from accounting for all. He added that he believed that the late Nizam could have taken from the Raja of Gadwal a *nazar* of Rs. 10 lakhs without exciting any special odium, partly because His late Highness enjoyed a general popularity or indeed devotion, and partly because whatever money he received he spent with an open hand, whereas everyone knew that the present Nizam did nothing but store the cash in his palace with no apparent object in view other than that of the mere possession of the silver and gold, which he seemed to regard solely with the instincts of a miser.[62]

But giving *nazr* was more than a financial matter, it held deep symbolic value for both the donor and recipient, and while the last Nizam somewhat abused this relationship, its complete abolition was unthinkable. Sir Terence Keyes, Resident at Hyderabad from 1930 to 1933, realized this. "The older families and those who are striving to acquire a similar status, far from resenting having to make these payments, would resent any attempt to do away with them."[63]

While the exchange of *nazr* and *khilats* continued through the nineteenth and twentieth century, other articles of exchange also came into the mix. At Hyderabad, the Nizams and other nobility made use of new technologies such as portrait photographs to create objects for exchange. As we have seen, for technical purposes, Mahbub Ali Khan used photographs to help his nobles dress appropriately for the durbar. For more ceremonial purposes, his son's installation was captured in a series of group portraits. A further extension of the use of photography came in the exchange of photographs as ceremonial gifts. This practice derived from an older one of exchanging portraits. This exchange, common in the

Deccan and in north India, expressed a recognition of rank manifested in overlords and suzerains. As photographs and photography became more widespread and less costly, they became an important new medium of exchange. Where nobles and friends might have once exchanged painted portraits, *nazr*, or *khilats*, by the late nineteenth and early twentieth century we see the exchange of photographs during and after visits. In her study of the material culture at the court of Pudukkottai, Joanne Punzo Waghorne suggests that "[t]he Victorian period, with its growing visual technologies, such as photography, may well have allowed greater opportunities for presentation of visual images than anytime previously."[64] For instance, Reginald Glancy, who served as finance minister of Hyderabad State from 1911 to 1921, visited Wanaparthi in January 1914. Upon his return to Hyderabad, he penned the following letter:

> I am writing to thank you both for your hospitality which we much enjoyed and for the opportunity you gave me of seeing your Samasthan, on the management of which I take the liberty of complimenting you in the warmest terms. I hope next year your fine tanks may be filled to their utmost capacity. I am sending you a copy of my photograph, and I hope you will honour me with one of your own.[65]

As the gift of a *khilat* once meant receiving a physical object associated with a ruler, now the exchange of photographs allowed individuals to have their rulers' or—in this case—friends' image with them in their homes. Thus, the exchange of articles of honor was a vital part of negotiating power relationships between different rulers. What the samasthan rajas or the British Resident offered to the Nizam was of deep significance both to the donor, and of course to the Nizam himself. What he in turn offered back to the donors completed the exchange. This ceremonialism extended from the highest echelons of power as seen at the Delhi durbars, down to the *mufassal* durbars of the samasthan rajas. This period of growing ceremonialism was not only negotiated in the durbar halls of Gadwal or Hyderabad, but also took other forms. The samasthan rajas and other Hyderabad nobility were granted certain rights and privileges that carried with them a recognition of their rank within the state, and granted to them certain special powers. Two of these rights among others were the right to mint coins, and the privilege of *shikar* (hunt).

Minting Coins, Hunting Tigers

Along with holding a durbar and receiving guests, the right to mint coins was also a valuable symbol of power. This privilege was granted to only a few members of Hyderabad State's political milieu, only to the samasthans: Gadwal, Wanaparthi, Shorapur, and Narayanpet.[66] The right to mint coins and having one's name read at Friday prayer (*khutba*) were the traditional markers of (Islamic) sovereignty. These practices were pivotal at moments of succession when questions could arise as to who was ruler. For instance, when the first Mughal ruler (Babur) died in 1530, with Mughal strongholds barely extending beyond Delhi and Agra, coins were immediately struck and prayers read in the name of his successor, Humayun.[67] The twin symbols of *khutba* and *sicca* (stamped coin) were also used to impress subordinate relationships between powers. A century after Humayun, his great-grandson Shah Jahan came to the Deccan and imposed tributary status on the Qutb Shah rulers at Golconda. This status was marked by coins cast from dies of the Mughal imperial mint, and having the name of the Mughal emperor read on Fridays, thus leaving a degree of Qutb Shah autonomy in place while at the same time signifying ultimate Mughal authority over Golconda.[68]

That the samasthans had enjoyed the right to mint currency from the eighteenth century demonstrates a composite conception of authority emanating from Hyderabad whereby other (non-Muslim) elites within the state had the right to mint coin in their own name. Currency within Hyderabad State was the *Hali Sicca*, or "current coin." The first mint opened in the city in 1803; it is likely that the samasthans were minting coins in their territories before this time. A variety of coins circulated in the state: those minted in Hyderabad, those minted by select samasthans, and those minted in British India. However, coins from Gadwal and Wanaparthi samasthans ran afoul of the Hyderabad government in the mid-nineteenth century when questions started to be raised about the purity of the coinage.[69] Debased coins were seen as a weakness in the administration of the samasthan. Saidul Haq Imadi has remarked that the *sahookars* (banker, merchant; but here samasthans) were allowed to mint coin, "in total disregard of the principle that coining was a reserved prerogative of the State."[70] Imadi's comment reflects a top-down, Nizam-centric view of Hyderabad. However, viewed from a different perspective, the right to mint coin had already been granted by the state to the samasthans as part of their power and prestige. It was only in the turbulent mid-nineteenth century that this practice came under scrutiny. At that time, Salar Jung began a series of reforms to root out such practices as diluting the purity of coins minted by the samasthan families.

As seen in chapter 5, Wanaparthi's raja Rameshwar Rao was a regular suspect in assorted nefarious activities. Again, in the middle decades of the nineteenth century, he was under a growing cloud of suspicion, and summoned to Hyderabad to face a series of charges, among them was minting degraded coin. Clearly, the power to mint coin tempted the less scrupulous to abuse this right. By debasing coin, the head of the mint (either under orders or acting independently) could extend their resources. The Wanaparthi mint at Sugur was in fact operated by a servant of the raja, who fearing an inquiry and possible violence, fled from Wanaparthi to Hyderabad, seeking shelter in the cantonment at Secunderabad. As he neared the city, he was apprehended along with his account books. These revealed to officials that "almost every sahoocar [*sahookar*]of note was concerned in the coinage of base money."[71] Implicated by the account books, Rameshwar Rao pleaded that he had been granted permission by past Hyderabad ministers to mint coin, and that no complaint had ever been made against the Sugur mint. However, the committee hearing the case, including notables Major Briggs, Captain Barrow, and Maulvi Ahmed, convicted the raja. His and other mints were summarily closed, an expression of the growing power of the Hyderabad government and the declining power of Rameshwar Rao.

As the Hyderabad government granted or withdrew the right to mint coins for certain of the samasthans, so too did it regulate another vital symbol of rulership: the hunt. In the first decades of the twentieth century, bridging the change in power from one Nizam to the next, the samasthan rajas, other nobles, visiting dignitaries, and the Nizams all participated in lavish and extensive hunts. Hyderabad State's diverse flora and fauna was home to a wide array of wildlife, none more prized than the tiger, but black buck, fowl, and deer were also hunted.

Photographs and photography, widely popular from the late nineteenth century on, capture the victories of the hunt. In Krishna Swami Mudiraj's *Pictorial Hyderabad*, a photograph shows the raja of Gadwal, Sita Rambhupal II with gun in hand standing over two slain tigers. The caption refers to him as a "Big Game Hunter." In another photo, the raja of Jatprole, Lakshma Rao, dressed in a khaki hunting vest replete with tie, sits amongst an impressive five slain tigers. The caption reads, "Raja Venkat Latchma Rao Bahadur's Magnificent Kill—Five Beasts Down In One Hunt." Yet another shows his adopted son, Jagannath Rao, standing with rifle in hand, and his pith hat on one of two large slain tigers.[72] All of these photos convey a sense of machismo and manliness commonly displayed amongst Indians and Britons alike who circulated in imperial circles.[73] Nizam Mahbub Ali Khan was fond of "bagging" prey as well. In one photo, he is shown sitting triumphantly on top of one slain tiger, boot resting on another, and rifle in his lap.[74] The Nizam was frequently joined by visiting dignitaries to the state. In 1891 the Emperor of Russia

Grand Duke Alexandar (1845–1894) enjoyed a hunt within the Nizam's dominions. He was followed by Lord Curzon in 1902, King George V in 1911, Lord Willingdon in 1915, and Lord Ratendone, son of Lord Willingdon, who in 1933 went on *shikar* but could bag no tiger.[75] Yet, for the samasthan rajas, hunting could pose problems of authority. Their desire to participate in an age-old sport, recognized as the prerogative of royalty, at times clashed with the state's desire to manage its wildlife. It often came down to what degree the state was willing to interfere in the hunting life of the rajas. In this regard, two samasthans not otherwise well represented in the archival record make an appearance: Domakonda and Paloncha.

In early 1902, the raja of Domakonda went hunting in his samasthan north of Hyderabad in Nizamabad district. While in camp, he was confronted by a district police officer who interrupted his hunt. At issue was whether the raja had the right to shoot in the villages that comprised his samasthan. Upon returning to his palace, the raja wrote to the minister's office and Sir Faridoon ul Mulk, the secretary to the minister. For the *jagirdars* of Hyderabad the game rules were clearly established: a *jagirdar* could hunt within his villages, and according to his wish, close them to public hunting if the limits were publicly posted. However, there was no clear statement on the rights of the samasthan holders and questions of the definition and nature of these estates again came to the fore. The minister's office consulted with the Revenue Department, and A.J. Dunlop responded in turn: "I have the honour to state that in my opinion, samasthans, for the purposes of the Game Rules, should be treated in the same way as Jagirs."[76] The minister's office wrote to the raja informing him that he was to enjoy all of the "privileges" of a *jagirdar*, but should he choose to close his villages to public hunting, a detailed list of those villages would have to be submitted.[77] At the same time, the inspector general of police, who had been informed of the matter, wrote to the district Police warning them not to interfere in the raja's hunting.[78] The matter seemed all but finished: the samasthan rajas would enjoy the same rights and privileges as their fellow *jagirdar* nobles.

However, two years later the raja again wrote to the government concerning his hunting rights. This time he had shot a tiger and caught three young cubs in his *makhta* (land held at a fixed rate) in Narsapur. Faridoon informed the raja that "you cannot shoot in makhtas as they are supposed to be khalsa lands."[79] *Khalsa* lands belonged to the state from which the Nizam directly collected revenue. The raja responded, bringing to the secretary's attention a clause in the morass of revenue laws that stated that *makhtadars* had no shooting privileges *unless* they were also large *jagirdars*, and the raja of Domakonda would be considered a large *jagirdar*. The matter was again forwarded to Dunlop who stated:

> In my opinion he should be for the purposes of the game laws be treated as a Jagirdar. A similar rule should, in my opinion, be extended to all Samasthans and only Makta villages belonging to small estates should be held to be under the Game Rules.[80]

Thus, the size of the estate seemed to be the determining factor in whether Domakonda was to be extended the same rights as a *jagirdar*. The raja won the right to shoot in Narsapur, but in his reply, Faridoon coolly added, "you will never be granted permission to shoot in open areas of the Government Preserves like others."[81] The matter might have ended there, but the raja seemed to desire the last word, and again wrote to the government on 20 August 1905. This time he included a list of 23 villages that he wished to have printed in a *jaridah* (official notice, publication) and closed to public hunting. The issue was again forwarded from the minister's office to the Revenue Department and then cleared with district officials in Medak and Nizamabad. It was not published, however, until 30 March 1908 by the Government Jail Press; at that point those villages were officially closed to public hunting.

The raja of Domakonda had maintained his right to hunt within his samasthan. The process of clarifying his position as a samasthan holder vis-à-vis other nobles, and the publication of his village list took time, but was eventually successful. The exact definition of a samasthan and the raja's rights (here even within its villages) remained an issue that was dealt with only as problems arose. It was in the Hyderabad government's interest to keep borders and definitions flexible so that should an issue arise where the government might benefit from a loose interpretation, no clear written order would stand in its way. Only through the raja's pursuit of his hunting rights were the villages of Domakonda made public and the exact domain of the samasthan recognized.

Another hunting episode that occurred a decade later tested the state's ability to interfere in the rights and privileges of local rulers. George Edward Campbell Wakefield served in the Nizam's government from 1900 to 1921 as irrigation settlement officer, deputy director general of Revenue, and director general of Commerce and Industries. While on tour in Warangal district and in the lands of the Paloncha samasthan, he came across a herd of bison. Paloncha had only seventy villages in its 3,090 square miles, and its dense forest made the samasthan rich in wildlife but poor in revenue. Wakefield wrote to Faridoon to suggest that the bison be preserved. His letter gives a glimpse of rural life at the time and implies his skepticism about the Paloncha raja's ability to manage his affairs.

> During my last tour through the Paloncha Taluka of the Warangal district I was delighted to find a most picturesque and fertile tract lying along the banks of the Godavari in which Bison are comparatively numerous and would very soon increase if they were protected. But unfortunately they have not been protected. The tract belongs to the Rajah Sahib of Paloncha and although the Game Laws provide that Bison shall not be shot in Jagirs and Samasthans, the Bison in Paloncha have been regularly killed, as witness photographs in my possession showing batches of Gonds dancing with bison horns (both bulls and cows) tied onto their heads. The Rajah Sahib's Motamid, who was in attendance on me during my tour, assured me that they had been unaware of the Game Laws and that he would see to it that no more bison were killed, but I would request that the Rajah Sahib of Paloncha should be written to and directed to fulfill the responsibility which the Game Laws impose upon him.[82]

Wakefield went on to suggest that this particular tract of land be taken over by the government, and a suitable one of the same size be granted to the raja. His tour and description follow well-established practices used by British military and civil servants employed throughout the Raj. The "tour" served to keep administrators in touch, or at least in contact with the administered. The camera Wakefield carried with him helped to document offences committed under the raja's jurisdiction, and the Gonds (a tribal group) dancing epitomized for him the "wild" and "savage" elements living in the Nizam's dominions. Yet Wakefield's view does not necessarily betray a civilizing mission, instead he notes that the inhabitants of this tract warrant protection based on their lifestyle and location. He continues:

> There is practically no habitation in the area I refer to, excepting isolated huts of a few people calling themselves "Reddis," who continue to live placidly in the midst of virgin forests, (full of tigers, panthers and bison,) and not in <u>villages</u> but in single isolated huts!—I would like to see the area in question (it is not large) exchanged and handed over to our Forest Department for protection of both forest and game.[83]

He was interested in preserving not only the area's wildlife, but also the "placid" inhabitants of the area. Faridoon had written to the raja concerning preservation of the bison, but Wakefield was not fully satisfied with how things were proceeding. He seems to have distrusted the raja's ability to protect the area. In a follow-up letter he stated:

> I feel sure that nothing but the taking over by Government of the bison area will save the bison. The Rajah Sahib's arrangements for protection of the bison are bound to fail in the long run, and the area in question is so exceptionally suited that it would be a thousand pities to allow them to be exterminated.[84]

The Game Laws, however, having been challenged and amended nearly a decade earlier to cover samasthans, clearly favored the raja's rights. They state, "[t]he Paigah Nobles, the owners of Samasthans and the Jagirdars, are entitled to grant or refuse permission for shooting in their respective Elakas."[85] In the end, government recognition of the rights of the samasthan holders precluded any interference, protection, or land-swapping of the sort Wakefield might have pursued. Hunting within one's own domain—whether samasthan, *jagir*, or *paigah*—was recognized as a fundamental right of Hyderabad's nobles, and remained deeply connected with their rule.

The "Gadwal" Dancing Hall

This chapter concludes with a vignette from the reign of Osman Ali Khan and raja of Gadwal, Sita Rambhupal. Here, the character of the Nizam and sense of honor held by the raja are played against each other. The Nizam was interested in learning to dance, and not having an appropriate space for dancing, saw an opportunity to use his authority over the Gadwal raja to extract funds. The Nizam had decided to build such a hall at his King Koti palace in 1921. The Prince of Wales' visit had inspired the idea a year earlier.[86] The dance hall was to be built over the tennis courts at the palace, and to fund this project the Nizam wrote to Sita Rambhupal.

Having earlier bilked the raja of Gadwal for two lakhs, the Nizam turned to him again for this project. However, in exchange Sita Rambhupal would not receive the Nizam at his own home, nor would he secure for himself much in the way of honor. Instead, the Nizam played on the raja's role as a member of Hyderabad's nobility and his being bound by honor to grant the Nizam his wish, however expensive. Two accounts of this exchange exist, one from the Resident, Charles Russell, and the other and more colorful rendition, from Edmund Hunt. Hunt served as surgeon in charge of staff of the Hyderabad State Railway and chief medical officer of the Railway Hospital, Secunderabad. While there are some discrepancies between these accounts, the avarice of Osman Ali Khan is clear in both of them. To begin, the Nizam asked the (now) maharaja for Rs. 40,000, although the estimate given by the Nizam's own engineer, Ahmed Ali, had been put at Rs. 38,000.[87] In return for the money, all taken as *nazr*, the dance hall would bear Gadwal's name. The Nizam first wrote in September 1922 asking for 30,000 rupees, then in February 1923 he wrote again stating, "You promised to pay Rs. 40,000 for the ball-room. Rs. 10,000 is the balance. Send Rs. 10,000 in B.G. [British Government] if you will, if not H.S. will do."[88] From Hunt we learn that the demands might have been even greater. In Hunt's account the Nizam had demanded Rs. 30,000, "half of what you promised" that if true would have made the maharaja's promise Rs. 60,000.[89] The Nizam explained: "Inasmuch as the rains are also full and as the crops are also good, there ought not to be any objection to your paying the amount especially when you have of your own free will and pleasure taken the responsibility notwithstanding my telling you not to do so. If not, Jatpole was ready to take it up."[90] Again, the Nizam deployed the threat of possible shame to ceremonially twist the raja's arm. At that time, Gadwal's economy could not easily handle such demands. Sita Rambhupal pleaded with the Nizam, "The crops this year in Gadwal have not at all been satisfactory and there is likely to be a great deficit even this year. Nevertheless I shall fulfill my promise."[91] It is unclear whether Jatprole, being the third largest samasthan, escaped payment. However, the Nizam's interest in the whole matter soon waned.

According to Hunt, while the hall was under construction, the Nizam had taken dancing lessons. Osman Ali Khan had soon "realised he could never learn to dance, and this is not surprising, as it is all he can do to walk." He ordered the construction stopped and the tennis courts rebuilt.[92] The contractor (Ram Gopal) demanded payment for his work. The Nizam countered that since things were the same as they had been, nothing should be paid. Hunt adds that the Nizam earned as much as Rs. 100,000 from the dance hall, which if it had been completed, might have had many names.

From the late nineteenth century, as rank determined by military power faded, rank determined by court culture—in all its composite manifestations—took on increasing importance. Symbolic and sometimes real exchanges continued to bind the Nizam with Hyderabad's nobles. Whether held by Hindu or Muslim, Indian or European, durbars both in the samasthan capitals and in Hyderabad became the arena where political and social power was meted out. Yet, the whims of the Nizams and the vagaries of gift giving did not make for consistent and reputable governance. Thus, under the reforms of Sir Salar Jung, and under pressure from the Residents, the Hyderabad government began to introduce codified legal systems to better regulate the state's nobles. First among these was the Court of Wards, the subject of the next chapter.

CHAPTER 4

The Court of Wards in Hyderabad

In 1882 under Salar Jung's guidance, the Hyderabad government adopted an administrative mechanism, the Court of Wards. The Court of Wards served as a kind of babysitter for young heirs, administrator for their estates, and shelter from the personal interests of the Nizams. For the heirs, it was literally *ma-bap* (mother-father). It was where legal practice settled many of the disputes rather than leaving them to the whims of the Nizam or armed conflict between family members. Implemented in much of India, the Court was a modified version of British law that allowed the Company and Crown to expand its control in the princely states. It foreshadowed India's secular democratic underpinnings, and in Hyderabad, had profound effects on the samasthans; it would remain the key to their survival well into the twentieth century.

As the new century dawned, three rajas continued to administer their samasthans: Rambhupal at Gadwal, Rameshwar Rao at Wanaparthi, and Lakshma Rao at Jatprole. Having survived as providers of military power to the rulers of Hyderabad, and having surmounted the challenges of court etiquette and ceremonial engagement, the samasthan families found in the Court of Wards an institution that directly concerned itself with their survival. It operated beyond the direct control of the Nizam, thus sheltering them from his occasional eccentricities, while its administrative ideology was aimed at improving both the health and welfare of the child wards, as well as their estates. The Court, a product of colonial rule, was present throughout much of the subcontinent. Thus, a "foreign" legal and colonial system deeply affected local and indigenous practices—serving both as a benevolent force concerned with the upbringing of young heirs and the successful management of their estates as well as at times being malevolent through its interference in private family matters. The Court's composition and administration in a princely state differed from those of British administered territories in that Hyderabad's Court of Wards was customized to suit the autocratic nature of the Nizam's rule.

Samasthan families rapidly changed the way they conducted their affairs with the introduction of the Court. First, they began to retain lawyers to plead their cases.[1] These men served as intermediaries between the families and their traditions, and the new legal spheres offered by court systems both in Hyderabad and in British India. Second, while not perfect, the Court marked a dramatic shift away from the personal management of the samasthan affairs toward a legally based system. In the *longue duree*, it would be a secular and responsive legal system that survived both the samasthans and the Raj, forming the underpinnings of independent India. As such, the Hyderabad Court of Wards provides a lens to more closely examine the samasthans, their continuity with the past, and evolving practices in the face of new legal systems and new challenges over authority in the region.

Originally devised for sixteenth-century England, the Court was well suited for Indian landholding tenures. India like England had countless landholders who ruled over areas ranging in size from garden plots to vast states. Difficulties arose when the landholder died and no heir existed to take his place, or when the heir was in some way unsuited to assume control. Many times the heir was a child, and further questions arose as to who was best suited to look after him (or her) and also properly guide the estate. The Court solved this point of tension by taking young heirs into its care while at the same time managing their estates. Ideally, upon the heir's reaching majority the Court returned his estate to him, a young man whom it had, hopefully, educated and prepared with the skills needed to manage his lands. However, the Court could exercise imperial or princely benevolence or malevolence, and in cases of the latter reduce an estate to penury. In short, the babysitter was sometimes also a bank robber. Within the dominions, the Hyderabad Court of Wards was responsible for heirs to the samasthans as well as *paigahs*, *jagirs*, and other landholders. Serving in this intermediate position, the Court also sometimes protected its wards from the advances of the Nizams.[2] The Nizams retained certain rights within the Court's structure but occasionally abused their position as sovereign. Nonetheless, the Court was guided by its own administrative ideology and could operate outside and even in opposition to these rulers' whims and demands.

First England, then India

The Court of Wards began in England under Henry VIII (c. 1540). The Crown granted land to tenants-in-chief who then paid dues to the royal coffer. If that tenant died, his or her land reverted back to the Crown. If an heir existed, he or she could take that property by paying a fee to the Crown. However, if the heir was under twenty-one (for boys) or under fourteen (for girls), then the land and its heir came under the Court's protection. The main function of the Court was to investigate heirs and see if the Crown could legitimately absorb their lands.[3] Further, the Court could also sell lands to settle debts that could not be recovered. Such processes often led to the complete loss of the property and were commonly felt to be an "odious practice."[4] At stake were the interests of the king, the heirs, and third parties interested in acquiring land. The Court served as a buffer between the king (interested in absorbing land), third parties (interested in purchasing lands from minor heirs), and the ward (interested in retaining his or her lands). The greatest threat came from the third parties. Through purchase these parties alienated property so it could not be returned to its legitimate heirs. Worse yet, third party members who purchased the rights to the land also assumed control over the fate of the ward, affecting their marriage, education, and other vital issues. Once the Court had assumed charge of wards, its administrators struggled to provide for them and improve their situation. They devised an educational plan—though it was not always implemented—that included training in law, military affairs, Latin and Greek, French, music and art, riding, vaulting, and weapons handling.[5] The Court also developed guidelines for handling "idiots." If a ward did not know his or her age, their father and mother's name, if he or she could not count to twenty, or have children, the ward was deemed not sane and denied the estate.[6] England's Court of Wards thus assumed a binary function: protecting its wards from external threats and at the same time nurturing them within its auspices. Although it was abolished in 1645–1646 as the civil war swept through England, this dual role would re-emerge with the Court's establishment in India in the late eighteenth century.

Long before the Court's arrival on Indian shores, Indian rulers practiced their own types of ward protection. For instance, when the Mughal ruler Humayun fled Delhi toward Persia, he stopped long enough to leave his infant son, Akbar, with his brother Askari.[7] While these Mughal brothers had an acrimonious relationship, older Timurid rules of conduct and respect ensured the protection of the infant. Akbar was lovingly cared for until his father's return. With the overlay of a British Court of Wards onto Indian traditions of child rearing and protection, the institution of the Court spread not only across British India, but was also adopted within its princely states.

The Court of Wards in India came into existence by an act of Sir John Shore, governor general in Council, on 28 August 1797. Earlier references to the establishment of the Court come from Philip Francis, appointed to the Bengal council in 1773. During his time in Bengal he pushed for the establishment of a Court of Wards in India, "for the care of estates, of which the incumbents are minors, idiots, or females; and to have the care of the education of minors, now usually committed to servants or relations, who have an obvious interest in bringing up the children in ignorance and stupidity."[8] Early on, men like Francis and Shore recognized the danger in allowing estates to go unattended. Minors, male and female, faced the possibility of being raised by corrupt or incompetent guardians and possibly denied their inheritance. When an estate holder became incapacitated, the Court was to oversee the conduct of heirs and the finances of the estate. At other times Court of Wards officials might choose different heirs, dissolve successions, and exert direct influence on the estates under its charge. At its most aggressive, the Court intervened on behalf of the state to preserve land holdings and revenue. After coming into force in Bengal, it was gradually implemented in much of India. Its appearance in Madras in 1804 represents its earliest implementation in south India.[9] Later, Courts of Wards were established in the Bombay Presidency and in the Central and United Provinces, Assam, Orissa, the Punjab, Sindh, and the northwest frontier Province. This institution was not only used at the Presidency or Provincial level, however. The raja of Gadwal, too, established his own Court of Wards to handle the many petty landholders within his samasthan.[10] By the twentieth century, Courts of Wards, in one form or another operated across much of the subcontinent.

The eighteenth century Court of Wards paved the way for the more invasive policies in the princely states. In the late eighteenth century, Lord Wellesley (governor general, 1798–1805) expanded the Company's practice of establishing subsidiary alliances with various princes. These arrangements required the prince to pay for Company troops to be stationed in the state. In return, those troops could be used to protect the prince's internal and external security. Further, the princes were granted promises of internal autonomy. To oversee these arrangements, the Company posted a Resident at the prince's court. Hyderabad, among others, participated in the subsidiary alliance system. By the early decades of the nineteenth century, imperial expansion once again commenced with increased pace. For the princely states, no policy had greater repercussions than Lord Dalhousie's "doctrine of lapse." As governor general (1848–1856) his doctrine was part of a tripartite policy of expansion that would bring more princely states under imperial control. A prince defeated in war; a prince who failed to produce a suitable heir (thus one who "lapsed" to British control); or a prince charged with misadministration was subject to annexation. The kingdom of Punjab suffered defeat in war and annexation; Satara, Jhansi, and Nagpur of the Maratha states were annexed due to "lapse," and (ominously for the events of 1857) the state of Awadh was annexed on the grounds of misadministration in 1856. The Court of Wards was deployed in those princely states that remained independent, such as Hyderabad, yet required some administrative system to handle internal succession disputes.

Like a *jinn* (ghost) who frequents an old palace, the Court of Wards makes fleeting appearances in histories covering the subcontinent. For instance, a short time after its establishment in the late eighteenth century, the Court assumed control of the Dinajpur zamindari in Bengal on the grounds of the ruler's "incapacity." Later, in another case from Bengal, the Court "stood ready to assume control" of the Burdwan estate in Bengal, which it did from 1838 to 1840 and again from 1885 to 1902.[11] The Court further became involved in sorting out mysterious circumstances surrounding the Bhawal estate. The young prince of Bhawal was thought to have died in the first decades of the twentieth century. His estate was placed under the Court's supervision for nearly a decade until, in 1921, an ash-covered sadhu appeared in Bhawal claiming to be the long-lost heir. The Court of Wards found itself adjudicating between the supposed heir, members of the royal family who did not believe him, and the peasantry who favored the new heir. Partha Chatterjee has explored this drama in full, explaining the difference between the administration of Bhawal by the family and by the Court.

> The rule of the zamindars . . . was in the traditional mode. It was oppressive, often arbitrary, but at the same time personal, capable of being paternal and caring. Tenants could be fined or punished for little reason, but they could also be rewarded by grand gestures of benevolence. . . . The regime of the Court of Wards was the exact opposite. It was cold, impersonal, ruthlessly efficient. There was no escape from its clutches.[12]

While the Court proved an efficient securer of revenue, it was less successful in the upbringing of its wards. For instance, far from Bengal, the Ramnad estate in the Madras Presidency also came under the supervision of the Court. The first period of this supervision occurred in the mid-nineteenth century, but it was the second spell that produced—or did not produce—a model zamindar. Ramnad entered the Court in 1872, and for some years its young heir, Baskara Setupati, was educated by Court officials. Baskara and his brother were sent to Madras where they studied under English tutors and pursued a largely English curriculum. This, combined with trips north and meetings with other respected princes and zamindars, all represented an effort to imbue the young Baskara with the skills needed to ably take charge of his estate. However, as Pamela Price has shown, "[t]he young Raja was not, however, a *tabula rasa* upon which the imperial government could write a code for the behaviour of the model zamindar."[13] He combined his ongoing education with elements chosen from his family's past, resulting in what Price calls a "mixed idiom."[14] To the north, the Court aimed to create a model Bihar zamindar in the late nineteenth century. The estates of Hathwa, Darbhanga, and Deo fell under its "institutional shelter," and the Court administration assured some individuals within these estates a privileged position in the management of the property, while others had to seek legal redress for adequate representation. As Anand Yang has argued, "[t]he Court of Wards enhanced their controlling position in local society."[15] In part this control meant ensuring payment of revenue, which would not be regular if landholding families were insecure or inept.[16] Some Bihari estate owners willingly accepted management by the Court of Wards. For the indebted, incompetent, or those enmeshed in dispute, shelter by the Court could save the estate from endless litigation and dismantling.

In Hyderabad

The Court of Wards in Hyderabad was somewhat different from its counterparts in British India. First, Hyderabad's Court was administered entirely within a princely state where the interests of the Nizam were critical to its functioning. While estates in British India were needed to generate revenue to support the government, estates in Hyderabad bolstered the Nizam's personal position as head of state. Second, samasthan rulers paid a fixed annual payment, so their land revenue was only a concern if it affected their ability to pay this amount. Finally, Hyderabad's autocratic structure allowed the personal involvement and interference of the Nizam on grounds of patrimonial interest both in the business of the Court and in the affairs of each samasthan.

Yet, the Hyderabad Court of Wards was not a static institution, it flexed and bent according to the changing needs of its wards and the necessity of reform over time. From 1882 to 1897, the minister of justice oversaw the Court. In 1898 the first Court of Wards Act came into effect, thus codifying the legal parameters of its jurisdiction. The Court was later transferred to the Judicial Secretariat, and in 1901–1902, it was placed under the Revenue Secretariat where it remained. While under the Revenue Secretariat, the Court was first put under the supervision of the director general of Revenue, and beneath him, the Superintendent of the Court and five divisional officers. This structure was modified so that the Court was administered by a director general and Revenue member, and beneath them the Court's *nazim* (chief administrator).[17] The divisional officer system was further restructured so that *talukdars* in the countryside administered most of the estates under the Court, and only a few remained under the direct control of Hyderabad. In 1894 the Court administered thirty-six estates, and the number steadily climbed to ninety-four by 1925. However, the numbers declined to fifty-two by 1940.[18] The Court employed a variety of professionals for the administration of the wards and their estates. These included engineers, doctors and nurses, lawyers, and teachers. At its height, the Court of Wards employed almost 900 people, with the average closer to 600, fluctuating with the rise and fall in the number of estates under the Court's charge.[19] In 1926 the Court began publishing its own annual reports. The first report stated, "This is a work the necessity of which was being felt for years and years together, but which for certain reasons could not be given a practical shape. It has at last begun and this report is now published after being perused by Government."[20]

The Court's jurisdiction covered the range of Hyderabad's estates: samasthans, *paigahs*, and *jagirs*. Estates in the Court of Wards were divided into four classes based on their income: first were those over one *lakh*; second, over one-half *lakh*; third, over Rs. 10,000; and finally, those under Rs. 10,000. *Paigahs* and *jagirs* regularly fell under the Court's care, as did the numerically fewer samasthans. Over the sixty-six years that the Court functioned within Hyderabad State (from 1882 to 1948), the Wanaparthi, Dubbak, Amarchinta, and Gurgunta samasthans spent nearly one-third of that time under the Court's supervision. Why? If a succession failed, the samasthan would revert to the Court. If an heir was a child, the samasthan could also revert to the Court. Producing a son who lived to be twenty-one (while his father still ruled) was not as easy or as common as the samasthan holders might have wished. Richard Trench referred to this situation as the "singular fatality" that plagued the samasthans.[21] Other samasthans were poorly managed or so encumbered by debt that they too were taken into the Court's supervision. However, not all of the samasthans found themselves within the Court; it was possible to prepare for a succession even if an heir was not yet present or of age. Absent from the list of wards is the Jatprole samasthan. Raja Lakshma Rao, having seen the difficulties experienced elsewhere, prepared adequately for his own succession: he ensured that his wife would be made Regent of the samasthan on his death, thus avoiding Jatprole's entrance into the Court of Wards.

Two leading officers of the Court were British (Trench and Theodore Tasker), and it is no surprise that the Court's direction leaned toward English norms. While the Court's highest officials were British, the remainder of the staff were Indians, both Hindu and Muslim. The Court frequently assigned a Muslim administrator to the samasthans. This occurred at Wanaparthi and Gadwal, where unlike the growing communal tensions in the rest of India, a civility and composite culture developed between nobles in Hyderabad where a Muslim Court of Wards administrators worked hand in hand with Hindu child heirs and frequently with their mothers as well. This compositeness, while it saw the successful return of Gadwal and Wanaparthi to their rightful heirs, did not always yield administrative success in Hyderabad.

Among the Court's failures was the construction and maintenance of a boarding house for its male wards.[22] This building, if successful, would have become the physical center of the Court's endeavors: a place where wards could be looked after as well as steeped in the Court's ideology. The earliest mention of a boarding house occurs in 1914 that states the boarding house is, "for the better supervision of the wards."[23] In the first few years the boarding house seems to have functioned quite well, and it was only after sometime that it faltered and failed. In the following year, 1915, the Court produced a somewhat glowing account of the improvements made through the boarding house system.

> A remarkable change for the better in the physique, morals, health, education and manners of the boys has resulted from the institution of a Boarding House managed on the best English lines . . . it includes the provision of riding horses, Motor-cars, board and lodging, physical training by a European Instructor, medical attendance and house-masters for home-work.[24]

The Court clearly intended itself to be more than an administrative wet-nurse, expanding to be mother, father, and teacher for the boys under its charge. Further, their upbringing was to be along "English lines," thus fulfilling Thomas Babington Macaulay's infamous wish for Indians to be "Indian in blood and colour, but English in taste, in opinions, in morals, and in intellect" from almost a century earlier. But the boarding house did not survive into the next decade. In 1921, without explanation, it was abolished. The expense of keeping the wards in one physical location most likely overwhelmed the Court's finances. From this point on, wards were cared for in a less physical sense, but as we will see, they were still closely monitored.

The scope of the Court's function expanded over time from primarily reclaiming indebted estates to a more direct involvement in estate affairs. The estate, its holder, the family, and of course any revenue all came under the purview of the Court. By 1940, we find how the Court's functions had grown.

> Originally intended as a security for the payment of revenue, the duties of the Court now extend to the management of estates in the interests of both proprietors and tenants, the support of the family of the proprietor, the education of young wards, paying off of debts, and spending the surplus in the improvement of property in the best attainable way.[25]

Further, the Court reported that "[g]overnment desires it to be regarded as one of the most important duties of the Court of Wards to maintain the closest personal contact with the progress of the wards in education, training and other matters."[26] In that year the state's administrative report listed a total of fifty-one estates under the Court's supervision, including two samasthans. Table 4.1 lists those samasthans under the

Table 4.1 Samasthans in the Hyderabad Court of Wards

Samasthan	*Year Placed in Court*	*Released from Court*	*Total Years in Court*
Amarchinta	1929	1933	4
Dubbak	1909	1928	19
Gadwal	1902	1912	10
Gadwal	1923	1928	5
Gopalpet	1923	1928	5
Gurgunta	1923	1933	10
Narayanpet[1]	1918	[1939]*	+21
Paloncha	1936	[1939]*	+3
Papanapet	1903	[1939]*	+36
Rajapet	1914	1928	14
Wanaparthi	1922	1945	23

1. Narayanpet is also sometimes referred to as a *jagir* estate. The classification within the Court of Wards records varied somewhat, and it is likely that Narayanpet was in fact a samasthan. This is supported by its mention in: Mirza Mehdy Khan, *Imperial Gazetteer of India Provincial Series Hyderabad State*, Reprint 1991 Atlantic Publishers, New Delhi ed. (Calcutta: Superintendent of Government Printing, 1909), p. 52.

*Bracketed release dates indicate that as of the last report, the estate was still in the Court.

Court's supervision. While the Court made improvements in the governance of local estates, such actions also benefited Hyderabad's larger political system. A financially healthy estate would likely ensure regular payment of tribute. Yet, heirs were reluctant to accept their income spent by the Court on public services. "Some of the estates are privileged by ancient Sanads to maintain their own law courts, police, jails and militia as adjuncts to their prestige and dignity. The estates jealously guard those ancient privileges and are not willing to incur large expenditure for the purpose of retaining them."[27] Resistance to the Court's mandates are examined later, but in most cases, the Court prevailed. An examination of the Court's ideology, as established by its governing Act, provides considerable insight on the direction and possible fate of its wards.

The Court of Wards Act

The Court of Wards adhered to an Act that outlined its operating parameters. This document was largely copied from those being used in British India, with some important differences. Most notable was that in Hyderabad the Nizam retained ultimate power. By his order, estates could be put into the Court or removed from it, thus circumventing official Court practice. As the twentieth century unfolded, Osman Ali Khan made changes to improve the Court's operation. In 1927, he decided that the Hyderabad Court of Wards Act should be changed and that of Uttar Pradesh adopted, "with necessary alterations."[28] Among the changes, estates once controlled by the central office were to be transferred to the control of district *talukdars* nearest to them. For instance, of forty-seven estates under the Court's control that year, all but eight were handed over to district officers.[29] The annual report of 1929 opens by stating that the year was "important" for the administrative machinery of the Court itself as the reorganization had occurred. Allowing district officers of the Court to manage estates meant a more responsive and local administration.

Critical to the Court's administrative reach were several conditions under which an estate and a presumptive heir could be brought under its supervision. The first was by order issued directly from the Nizam. Acting on solid grounds or sometimes on a whim, the Nizam could exercise autocratic power. Abuse of this power both undermined and damaged the position of Osman Ali Khan when, for instance, he wrongfully placed Gadwal into the Court of Wards, a point elaborated on later. The second condition under which an estate might be placed into the Court was when the heir was a minor under the age of twenty-one and not able to manage his or her affairs. Rarely, a Regent from within the family was appointed both to raise the heir and to manage the estate, as was the case with Jatprole. More often than not, the Nizam preferred to have estates put under the Court for administrative consistency although this occasionally resulted in the abuse of their funds. Third, if the heir was judged to be of "unsound mind and incapable of managing his property," or if the government decided that the ward suffered from physical or mental defect or was infirm, the estate and ward could be placed under the Court's supervision. Fourth, in many cases the sole legitimate heir to an estate was female, and if she was "declared by the Government to be incapable of managing her property," the estate might go to the Court. The Act did not forbid women from management, but instead suggested vague concepts of "capability" to be tested and applied to them.[30] Finally, if the heir was convicted of a nonbailable offense or was found to have indulged in extravagance and incurred insurmountable debt, the estate could be put into the Court.[31] Less common, an estate holder could apply to be placed in the Court. This occurred only if the estate and its holder would benefit from the Court's supervision. Not all applications were accepted, and the determining factor had to do with whether the Court could in fact provide better management.[32]

While the Court managed some estates from its central office in Hyderabad, it also employed local district *talukdars* to handle more sensitive matters. The Court of Wards Act gave these men broad power to intervene when an estate's leadership came into question or crisis. At times, the life of an heir might be in jeopardy given the violent nature of some succession disputes. The officer was in such cases invested with the power to protect the heir. "The Taluqdar may make suitable orders for the temporary custody and protection of such minor, and if the minor be a female, such direction shall be given with due regard to the custom and usage of the country."[33] Not only could he provide for female heirs, he could also search and confiscate any papers or documents that might be relevant to the estate. He had the authority to break into any house, room, box, or receptacle to collect information relating to the ward and the estate. In short, he was both the police and the administration. While the *talukdar* commanded these powers, there is little evidence that they were frequently exercised.[34] The Court of Wards Act further allowed for extensive involvement in the life of the ward. The Court could make decisions regarding custody, residence, education, and even marriage For instance, the Court oversaw the marriage of Varalakshmi, elder daughter to the late maharaja of Gadwal (Sita Rambhupal) in 1926 at a cost of Rs. 150,000.

Estates were not to be kept permanently under the Court's supervision. An estate could be turned back to the heir when he or she attained majority. Further, if there was some question as to the heir's mental stability, the estate could be returned when a civil court had declared, "that he is no more insane."[35] A *firman* from the Nizam could also release an estate from the Court, but this rarely occurred.[36] If the Court felt that the owner of the estate had somehow redeemed himself (financially or otherwise), it could return the estate.[37] When release was imminent, the Nizams used the opportunity to request *nazr*.

Since samasthan families had the longest lines of succession in Hyderabad, at the time of any individual succession, they paid *nazr* to the Nizam to gain approval for their continued family line. In return each received a *sanad* granting the succession, as well as a *khilat* or other gifts.[38] The amount of the *nazr* could vary depending on the whim of the Nizam, and could also be a point of contention. Yet, in the end, something had to be paid lest the succession should not be granted and the samasthan remain in the Court of Wards or be completely dismantled.[39] For instance, when the Gadwal family adopted Sita Rambhupal as raja, Mahbub Ali Khan demanded a *nazr* of seven lakhs. In return, the succession was granted and the young raja received the Nizam's blessing. However, this large request was felt to be out of proportion to the customary *nazr* of Rs. 75,000 given by Gadwal. The Nizam, known for his mild manner, consented to change his demand and the lesser amount was paid. However, his satisfaction was short-lived and he further requested that the samasthan pay the equivalent of one year's income as *nazr*. At the time the samasthan was under the Court of Wards, and the chief officer, A.J. Dunlop, eventually suggested a compromise with the Nizam and a reduced (but still sizable) *nazr* of Rs. 418,106. The entire affair dragged on until 1913, two years after Mahbub Ali Khan's death. Whether the Nizam demanded a large *nazr* because of Gadwal's wealth, or because the samasthan was under the Court of Wards (and thus more easily manipulated) is unclear. The struggles between these interests: the triumvirate formed by the samasthans, the Nizams, and the Court of Wards grew stronger as the century progressed, eventually seeing the Court and the rule of law emerge as *the* resource to resolve disputes.

Beneficence

Generally, the Court appears to have acted more as a benevolent babysitter. It provided an education for its wards, and the number of children attending school as well as the curriculum they followed allows us a glimpse into the Court's administration. It managed the estates' finances, and it participated in public works projects, from which we can get a sense of what the Court constructed for its wards and their estates. Physical improvements (building schools, paving roads, sinking wells) were part of the positive outcome of the Court's role in the samasthans, adding to the well-being of the samasthan citizens and the overall positive health of the estate.

Among the earliest references to the Court of Wards' active intervention in the welfare of a samasthan ward comes from Gadwal in 1904. At this time, the raja of Gadwal was a minor under the Court's supervision. The Court was itself administered by A.J. Dunlop, a colonial official on loan to Hyderabad's government. Events began with Dunlop approaching G. Tate, another European living in Hyderabad, to serve as the raja's tutor. Tate was Headmaster of the Madrassai-Aizza of Hyderabad. He accepted Dunlop's offer, but under Government of India policy, a European to be employed by a princely state had to be confirmed by the Residency and the Foreign Department. Thus Kishen Pershad was called upon to seek permission of the Resident for Tate's employment as tutor.[40] But a problem arose when Tate did not appear on the Foreign Department's list of Europeans employed in Hyderabad. Why was he not on the list? David Barr, Resident, explained that Tate had previously been on the appropriate list, but since the school he worked for was not officially part of the Nizam's school network, his name had been removed. For Barr it was an embarrassing error. "As a matter of fact, however, it would now appear that Mr. Tate is an European and ought not to have been employed in any capacity at Hyderabad without the sanction of the Government of India."[41] Two months passed and final approval arrived from Calcutta for Tate to assume his duties as the raja's tutor. Europeans were frequently employed in Hyderabad as tutors, and thus the decision to employ Tate was not surprising. However being employed through the Court of Wards added a layer of both bureaucracy and concern for the young raja's upbringing. Dunlop, as head of the Court, was responsible for the raja and sought the best qualified teacher possible. The Court of Wards, barely a decade old in Hyderabad, provided for the raja but found itself enmeshed in the politics and hierarchies of Hyderabad and the Raj. Laid bare is the Court's integrative role between the samasthans and the Hyderabad government.

Figures from the Court's records indicate that while a growing number of girls were being educated, the Court sought better educational opportunities for the boys under its charge. In 1915, eighty-five wards received education under the Court. Of these, three wards were listed as "insane," and only four of the total were girls. In 1926, there were 139 wards, 104 males, and 35 females. Of these, twelve of the males attended the Jagirdar's College, while twenty-five attended other educational institutions. Twenty-seven males and fifteen females attended private or religious educational institutions. Thirty-nine males and twenty females, 28 percent of the group, were in some way unfit to receive any education at all. For the year, a total of Rs. 923,209 was spent on the education and maintenance of these wards.[42] This was 22 percent of the Court's total income, which came from the revenue collected from the estates. The following year 145 wards came under the supervision of the Court. Of the boys attending high school in Hyderabad, several read for the Cambridge examination. Under instruction from the Nizam, the Court sent wealthier male heirs for further education in Europe. As its wards were educated either along "English lines," or at local Indian schools and colleges, the Court attempted to equip them with certain practical skills. For instance, the Court gave Rameshwar Rao III of Wanaparthi extensive administrative training pertinent to his becoming raja: he worked as a Patwari, Tehsildar, divisional officer, and then collector in the Revenue Department within the Madras Presidency. He also trained in the Home, Finance, and Judicial Departments.[43] That Rameshwar Rao was sent to the Madras Presidency for his training is indicative of the flow of ideas and information between the Presidency and the samasthans. This was aided by Tasker and Trench who both saw extensive service in the Presidencies. Thus, a preliminary judgment of the Court's endeavor to educate its wards is positive. Most wards seemed to have in fact received some education under the Court's guidance.

In addition to the education of heirs, the Court attempted to improve the samasthans' finances. This was perhaps the foremost mandate of the Court. "[I]t is the policy of the Court of Wards to reduce the cash balances as much as possible by investing the amounts in profitable concerns or spending them on public works."[44] Two options were available for investment. First, it could deposit any cash balances in financial accounts that would be available to the heir upon his or her taking charge. While this would immediately benefit the heir and their family, it could also invite abuses and lapses into lavishness that the Court had all along tried to curtail. The second option was to invest in public works projects. Here, Hyderabad's Court of Wards excelled. In Gadwal and Wanaparthi as well as in other samasthan capitals, numerous schools, rest houses, markets, roads, and bridges were constructed while their estates were under the Court. For instance, in 1927, the Court spent Rs. 25,000 on road construction in Gopalpet, and in 1939 spent Rs. 47,956 on building additions and alterations at Wanaparthi.[45] These projects benefited the samasthan families, the citizens of the samasthans, and as a by-product, the Nizam and Hyderabad as well. A healthier, fiscally sound samasthan was less likely to default on *peshkush* and be less of a burden on the state's police, courts, and other administrative offices. Not every estate, however, was returned with a balanced ledger book. When the Court released the Gadwal samasthan in 1928, its annual income had increased from Rs. 679,972 to Rs. 751,926.[46] At the time of its release, the samasthan had a cash balance of Rs. 101,284. Moreover, its debt from four years prior was gone. The excess funds were likely used by the family for its own needs.

Court administrators periodically assessed all the estates under its charge to see which of them might be ready for release. The largest single group of releases came in 1928. The year before, then Revenue Secretary Nawab Fasih Jung suggested that a committee be formed to examine and ultimately release those estates that no longer required the Court's supervision.[47] This was duly recommended and commanded by a *firman* of the Nizam, dated 5 May 1927. Among other questions, the *firman* queried, "Does every such proprietor, besides being capable and a major, possess such educational, moral and practical qualifications as would justify entrusting the management of his estate to him?"[48] The committee was headed by Tasker, Hashim Yar Jung, High Court justice, and Samad Yar Jung, military secretary. It convened and found that thirteen estates could be released, and sent this recommendation to the Nizam for approval.[49] Dubbak, Rajapet, and Gopalpet were three samasthans among thirteen. Gadwal was also among them, and arguably its release was most important, this event is taken up in the following chapter. While under the Court, each estate had made progress. Dubbak had entered the Court of Wards in 1907 when its holder, Uma Reddy, and his son had both died. "Grave differences" between the widows of these men had brought the estate under the Court. The Court having surveyed and settled the villages of Dubbak, arranged the marriages of four minor wards, and resolved the succession differences, released the samasthan to the new heir, also named Uma Reddy. On entering the Court, Dubbak had been encumbered with a debt of Rs. 131,181. By the time of its release, it had a cash balance of Rs. 49,382.

The raja of Rajapet, Rajeshar Rao, had died on 16 February 1914, leaving behind his widow, two daughters, Nainabai and Aitrabai, and a minor son, Jaswant Rao. The Court, having surveyed and settled the samasthan and lowered its tax rates, reduced the debt from Rs. 209,708 to Rs. 5,400. Still, Rajapet continued to be plagued by avoidable financial difficulties. The Court of Wards report states, "Repayment of debts, marriage of the ward, purchase of a motor car for him and many other extraordinary expenses of this kind prevented investments . . . or works of permanent improvement to be carried out in the estate."[50] The two daughters studied in the Wesleyan Mission Girls School.[51] To help with female heirs as a group, in 1915 the Court appointed the principal of Mahabubia Girls School, Miss Grace Mary Linnell to be "lady adviser." Perhaps the best known lady adviser in the Court of Wards system was Cornelia Sorabji who served in Bengal.[52] Linnell was responsible for visiting female wards and reporting to the Court on their education and health. She also appointed governesses and nurses to several of the estates, including Wanaparthi and Narayanpet.

At Gopalpet, after Raja Jagpal Rao's death on 9 March 1912, the rani, her adopted son, an ex-secretary, and some *ryots* quarreled over the succession. This multiheaded dispute yielded a large number of telegrams sent to the Nizam. He in turn ordered a committee to investigate the varying claims, and while this process was underway, had the samasthan placed in the Court of Wards.[53] The investigative report concluded that the rani was the rightful heir to the samasthan, but it would be released to her only under certain conditions: namely, she was to have a government official help administer it, and she was to have it surveyed and settled.[54] Upon release, the samasthan's income had risen from Rs. 130,613 to Rs. 157,632, leaving it with a cash balance of Rs. 364,823 and an invested balance of Rs. 25,000.[55] In its report of 1928, the Court boasted, "The estate was thus in a very flourishing condition at the time of release. The rani has been made free from all her worries and the committee has also decided that the estate which has been confirmed on her name, and will remain under her charge till her death, while the claim of her adopted son will commence only after her demise."[56]

In later years, two other samasthans benefited from the Court's maintenance. In 1933, the circumstances of the Amarchinta and Gurgunta samasthans had improved to the point where they became eligible for release. After inquiries, the Court had given Amarchinta to Rani Bhaggia Laxmamma. She had been given two officers to assist her in the samasthan's management, and together, several public works projects were completed, including the construction of a police station, a school, a rest house, and road improvements. At Gurgunta, Rani Gauramma Sherza had administered the samasthan until her death on 5 February 1914. She had left behind a widowed daughter and an adopted son, Jadi Somappa Naik. Somappa Naik, being a minor, was taken into the Court of Wards. The samasthan thus remained under the Court's supervision for two decades. Finally, it was handed over to Naik with all its debts cleared.[57] In April of 1930, Tasker visited the samasthan and in consultation with Naik, the decision was made to build a traveler's bungalow and a dispensary for public use.[58] Both the wards and their estates had been looked after, and upon release, many emerged in sound financial health.

A final glimpse of the Court's doings comes from a report by Muhammad Farooq, Hyderabad State's deputy director of Public Health. In April of 1941, Farooq toured the Wanaparthi samasthan and provided a first-hand account of projects undertaken by the Court and carried out by the Public Works Department. Arriving on the morning of April 17, Farooq noted that in the last decade under Court supervision, a number of new buildings had been constructed including a slaughterhouse, and a meat and vegetable market.[59] While these buildings were relatively new, he adds that "the town itself is still in a somewhat neglected condition." Though perhaps run-down, Wanaparthi town seems to have maintained a relatively healthy environment since Farooq notes that no epidemics had been reported. He suggested improvements to the water supply, drainage, latrines, and trenching grounds. The population of Wanaparthi town at this time was expanding. It included 6,800 residents with 1,574 houses. With population pressure rising, some residents petitioned to fill-in the palace moat and use that land for new construction. "The idea of closing the moat is excellent but I do not recommend any town extension in that locality." This was due to its low-lying elevation and problems with contaminated water. Farooq also toured the nearby temple and village of Rajanagar. Here, an annual *jatra* (fair, market) was held, and Farooq reprimanded the samasthan administrators responsible for the upkeep and sanitation of the grounds. "At the time of my inspection I found the temple area and its surroundings as filthy as could be imagined . . . Under such conditions it will not be surprising if cholera breaks out every year during the jatra." He suggested a series of improvements to be implemented.

This glimpse of the samasthan presents a somewhat mixed picture. On the one hand, the Court of Wards had successfully constructed new public buildings and facilities for the residents of Wanaparthi town, and Farooq, in reporting to the Court of Wards, lent his opinion and expertise to further improvements that could be made. Yet, on the other hand, conditions in the town and fair grounds indicate a lapse of responsibility. Some redemption can be found in the very fact that Farooq and the Public Health Department, as part of the Court of Wards administrative cohort, involved themselves in the samasthan's upkeep and improvement.

Inspection and intervention here, while not always generous, seems to have been done in a benevolent light, with the health and vibrancy of Wanaparthi foremost in the minds of Farooq and the Court of Wards.

By the twentieth century, many samasthans and their ceremonial use of armed forces came under the jurisdiction of the Court of Wards. For instance, the Court of Wards spent a total of Rs. 69,487 for armies held by Gadwal, Wanaparthi, Raja Rai Rayan, Surrya Jung, Durga Reddy, and Kalyani. By 1930, the Court gave the Wanaparthi forces a raise in salary; that year, the expense of maintaining Wanaparthi's troops was Rs. 18,103.[60] The Wanaparthi forces continued to train under the Court's supervision. For 1932, the expense had risen to Rs. 25,110, and the officers (the captain and *jamadar*) were sent for additional training with the Nizam's regular forces in Hyderabad; they returned to the samasthan the next year.[61] By 1939, the Court reports that Wanaparthi (as well as the Surayya Jung and Sheo Raj estates) maintained *fauj* (army) "as a token of dignity and honour for having rendered military services."[62]

Malevolence

At the local and personal level, one can see how the Court sometimes overstepped its bounds, and how its operations easily took on more malevolent tones. In one instance, in its desire to appoint a nurse for the young raja of Wanaparthi, Rameshwar Rao III, the Court simply exacerbated disagreements over care of the young raja. Further, the Court reprimanded Rameshwar Rao's mother, Rani Sarala Devi, for taking independent initiative in securing her son's education. While Sarala Devi remained "grateful" for the Court's interest in her son, she and her family had much reason to resent the Court's interference.

Sarala Devi and Rameshwar Rao visited Madras in February of 1931, a time when Hyderabad was suffering from an outbreak of plague. Fearing for her health, she wrote to the *nazim* of the Court (Syed Badruddin) requesting permission to remain in Madras. Sarala Devi added that a nurse assigned to her by the Court, a Miss Brawley, was also with them. The *nazim* granted her request.[63] Wards and their guardians were required to obtain permission from the Court to leave or to reside outside Hyderabad, understandable paternalism given the Court's responsibility for the health of both the ward and the estate. Thus, in a time of plague, the whereabouts and safety of each ward took on even greater importance.

By mid-March Sarala Devi again wrote to the *nazim*. This time her letter expressed considerable displeasure at the work of Brawley, whose attitude had become "markedly peculiar." Acrimony seems to have arisen from concerns about Rameshwar Rao's health. He had developed a fever, and Sarala Devi had called Dr. Narayana Rao, the family physician. Upon the doctor's arrival Brawley refused to allow him to examine the child. At the request of Court officials she called a European doctor, Colonel Hingston. Defiant, Sarala Devi told Brawley that she would put the child under the care of Dr. Rao, at which Brawley became upset. The following day she told Sarala Devi, "Don't interfere in my work . . . I have nothing to do with you." She made a scene and left the house.[64] Dr. Rao added that Miss Brawley, while "professing to be a nurse, does not seem to know the elementary rules of treatment."[65] Miss Brawley was dismissed by early April. The Court, in appointing Brawley and seeking Hingston's opinion, relied on the medical opinions of colonial officials. This is not surprising since the head of the Court, Tasker, was himself an officer of the British government. Rameshwar Rao recovered from his fever, and Brawley's "peculiar" behavior cost her the job. No other nurse was appointed to watch over the young raja. Issues surrounding child rearing and health care could be culturally specific and thus prone to misunderstandings and tensions.

Correspondence concerning Rameshwar Rao continued through the spring of 1931. First, a letter from the Court compelled him and his mother to return to Hyderabad on grounds that their allotted time in Madras had expired. Second, the Court inquired about the young raja's education. Sarala Devi responded that she did not want her son (nine years old at the time) put into a boarding school. Rather, she wanted to enroll him at a local school. She also wanted someone to teach him "colloquial Urdu and court manners." Diplomatically, she added, "I am very grateful to the Court of Wards in taking very keen interest in the welfare of my son."[66] A short time passed and the family secured a tutor, Gadepalli Suryaprakasa Rao, to teach Rameshwar Rao at home. However, upon hearing this, Tasker interfered. In a polite but firm letter, he informed Sarala Devi, "You seem to be under a misapprehension. I have never agreed that you should appoint particular persons to a post . . . particular appointments are subject to the approval of the Court of Wards, and nothing must be done in anticipation of that approval."[67] Tasker upheld Court policy, even though it meant going against family wishes. But Sarala Devi was a gifted diplomat. She responded, "I have merely selected the gentleman and settled terms with him and have intimated the matter to Nazim Sahib that he might, in consultation with you, approve my proposal."[68] With that, the matter ended. Suryaprakasa Rao was hired, and Rameshwar Rao went on to become one of Wanaparthi's finest rulers.

While the Court of Wards marked a significant step toward a legally based system of administration, older autocratic practices still periodically manifested themselves. Not surprisingly, under the rule of Osman Ali Khan, the practice of demanding *nazr* returned with vengeance. When the thirteen estates were released in 1928, the Revenue secretary had suggested that in return for being released their wards should offer *nazr* totaling five lakhs. This suggestion was somewhat unusual, and the Resident, William Barton, felt it was more than likely the Nizam's idea—crafted in an attempt to extract *nazr* from the estates before they left the Court. Barton added that the Nizam frequently "abused" the Court by dipping into its funds for *nazr*.[69] In the end, the estates paid a lesser sum and were released.

At this time, the Nizam would send a cart of mangoes (likely given to him as a *nazr*) to the Court along with a note demanding payment for the fruit. Officers of the Court sold fruit from their desks, and on similar occasions frequently deducted the expense from the samasthan accounts to cover the Nizam's requests.[70] At the same time, the Nizam sent a list of estates that were to help furnish his newly constructed palace in Delhi, "Hyderabad House." Many of these estates—some of them still in debt—were asked to make sizable contributions to the Nizam's various projects and satisfy his monetary whims.[71] As table 4.2 indicates, contributions by the samasthan holders made the Nizam's "Hyderabad House" in part a gift of the samasthans.[72]

Table 4.2 Contributions by the Samasthans to the Nizam's Delhi Palace

Samasthan	*Rs.*
Gadwal	10,000
Gopalpet	10,000
Narayanpet	5,000
Papanapet	7,000
Rajapet	1,000
Gurgunta	7,000
Wanaparthi	10,000

Litigation

The broader shift toward a secular and responsive legal system both within Hyderabad and British India through institutions like the Court of Wards was not uniformly embraced. The ability to retain a lawyer and enter into litigation was, on the one hand, a clear step away from the customary high-handed and autocratic legal practice, and on the other, a weight on the litigants that often, when pursued to extremes, brought bankruptcy and ruin.[73] Among those who urged India's aristocracy to avoid litigation and seek arbitration was the maharaja of Bobbili, Venkata Swetachalapati Ranga Rao. He and his brothers, including Lakshma Rao of Jatprole, formed a "great generation" (examined in the next chapter) that fully recognized the boons and pitfalls of litigation. The maharaja in his 1905 *Advice to The Indian Aristocracy* writes at length about the need to avoid litigation. He calls the process "very ruinous," even more so than war. Circulating in an Indian and English milieu, Rao was befriended by the well-known statesman of the day, Raja T. Madhava Rao, of Travancore and Baroda fame. Madhava Rao gave to the Bobbili maharaja a small card with a cartoon drawn on it. On the top of the card is the title "Litigation" in bold letters. Centered in the picture is a cow replete with garland. Pulling on the cow's horns and tail are two men, one labeled "Plaintiff" and the other "Defendant." Neither makes any progress in moving the cow in their directions. Behind the cow and kneeling in front of it are two more men, the *vakil* for the defendant and the plaintiff. These two are clearly in the process of milking the cow, while the defendant and plaintiff struggle in vain. Ranga Rao comments, "You may thus see, my dear friends, that both the parties are losers and the only persons benefited by litigation are the lawyers and the vakils."[74] While litigation brought ruin to some estates, in Hyderabad it was largely carried out under the administrative umbrella of the Court of Wards, thus restricting the breadth of any particular case and allowing the samasthan holders to pursue legal remedies to the challenges they faced.

The Court of Wards served as a temporary guardian for many of Hyderabad's samasthan holders and their estates, as well as other landholders. The Court, largely benevolent toward its wards and their estates, did its best to provide a sound upbringing for their heirs and at the same time to make physical improvements in their capitals and villages. Yet, functioning as it did under an autocrat, the Court could not always shelter its wards from the rapacity of the Nizam. Moreover, in some cases the wishes of a ward's family were ignored as the Court flexed its administrative muscle. Thus, when a suitable heir could not be found, putting an estate under the Court's supervision was not terminal to the family or their estate. Yet, even while under the Court, or while threatened with its intervention, estates also faced threats from a variety of other contenders. It is to these kinds of struggles that we now turn.

CHAPTER 5

The Death of Kings, the Birth of a Nation

The six years from 1922 to 1928 witnessed the death of kings at Wanaparthi, Gadwal, and Jatprole. With the help of the Court of Wards, or though their own arrangements, each family ensured the succession of rulers. The process of succession was vital to the survival of a samasthan. Various issues plagued Hyderabad's samasthans in the early twentieth century. Having an heir meant the continued survival of the family and the samasthan itself. If the raja produced no heir, they frequently adopted a relative from a village that had special connections to the ruling house. In Wanaparthi difference of opinion within the family raised questions about the very nature of the samasthan and the applicability of Hindu or Muslim law in the succession process. Further, this case brought to light the production and use of the samasthan's history itself to facilitate reaching a settlement. At Gadwal, a dispute between its rani and Osman Ali Khan shed light on the interference by the Nizam and Residency in such matters, and placed Gadwal within the larger fray of the emerging "Hindu" India. The Gadwal dispute further illuminated the Court of Wards' enduring role in the samasthan's future. Finally, the case of Jatprole serves as the exception in that it never came under the Court of Wards or suffered from the Nizam's interference. It illuminates issues of intrafamily bonds forged during a "great generation," and the product of those familial and generational bonds in the person of Raja Venkat Lakshma Rao. It provides an important example of the success of intrafamily adopting to sustain a long and successful reign.

The process of succession has surprisingly been little touched by historians. Most have taken notice of particularly nasty or eventful successions, but few have taken the process up in its own right. As

John McLeod has noted, succession "signifies a critical junction in any political system, but particularly one in which (as in the Indian states) the ruler is a personal, autocratic monarch."[1] Several successions have received scholarly treatment, perhaps the best example of this being the works of H.L. Gupta.[2] However, these tend to be mostly perfunctory. Fisher, interested in the relationship between the paramount power and the princely states, has explained that "[t]he greatest instability in a relationship between an Indian Ruler and a Resident thus came at the time of a succession on either side."[3] Fisher's work on the interplay between Residents and rulers, however, does not examine the relationship between rulers and their vassals, and any subsequent relationship between the vassal and the Resident. This was true both in the Western states that constitute McLeod's area of study, and certainly true for the Nizams of Hyderabad. While McLeod and Fisher both contribute to our understanding of succession, their focus (like many others) remains fixed on relationships at the highest level: those between the Indian Ruler and the Company or Raj. While this focus has served both to broaden and to deepen our understanding of the subcontinent's history, it does little to help us get inside of the many princely states and understand how internal successions and survival served as the building blocks on which many of the larger states, and their relationships with Raj, stood. Robbins Burling has taken an anthropological and comparative approach to the process. He has argued that successions are a particularly good time to examine political structures as, "ties of political strength and the fissures of political weakness that at other times may be more or less hidden from view then become obvious."[4] In Hyderabad, this becomes clear in the declining role of military power, and the increased importance of panoply and legal resolutions in succession disputes. Further, at the time of succession, Burling has suggested that participation in the process broadens.[5] The samasthans of Hyderabad faced succession issues not only from within their own families, but as members of a composite political milieu, they also faced pressure from above to find a suitable heir.

Wanaparthi: Son and Uncle

The Gadwal and Jatprole samasthans faced external succession issues, but this was not the case at Wanaparthi. The Wanaparthi succession dispute took place between an uncle and his nephew. In this sense, Wanaparthi's was a more typical succession, in which difficulties arose when an unexpected and sudden death raised questions about who had the legitimate claim to become raja. Here both uncle and nephew claimed they were the rightful heir, and more importantly, deserved control over part or all of the samasthan's revenue. These claims were based on differing ideas about the nature of the samasthan—was it a "simple" estate or a "noble" one? The former could be partitioned and the latter could not. To ascertain the truth, the history of the samasthan had to be examined in order to establish what, if any, custom of succession existed. This task was made somewhat easier by the work of Venkat Shastry, a Brahman scholar and poet who had compiled a family history. In the ensuing investigation, the very process by which the family history had been compiled came under scrutiny. In the end, after numerous appeals within the Court of Wards and Hyderabad's court system as well as cries of "communal" committee formulations, a decision was made not to partition the samasthan. Its integrity was preserved, and a sole heir was chosen.

At the core of the dispute was the question of not only *who* the rightful heir should be but also *whether* assets of the samasthan could be divided at all. In short, was the samasthan in any way partible? Raja Rameshwar Rao III, the grandson of the late Maharaja Rameshwar Rao II, argued that the samasthan was impartible because it was a "raj" or "state." His uncle, the son of the late maharaja, Raja Ram Dev Rao, argued that Wanaparthi was a "normal" estate (similar to a *jagir*) and, according to Hindu law, it could be partitioned among family members. The Wanaparthi samasthan case, a Hindu estate within Hyderabad—itself embedded within the British Raj—further raised questions as to which legal system applied: Hindu, Muslim, or European.

Evidence used in this succession dispute included a family history composed under the guidance of Maharaja Rameshwar Rao II, as well as his last will and testament. Early in the twentieth century, the maharaja brought to Wanaparthi Venkat Shastry. Shastry was called upon to set into verse the history of the samasthan that the maharaja dictated to him, which was based on family papers.[6] Shastry came from Pallavaram, a village in the Godavari district of the Madras Presidency. The maharaja paid him a salary and granted him a small *inam* with an annual income of about Rs. 300.[7] In October of 1922, the maharaja's ill health prompted him to prepare his will and settle his earthly affairs. He outlined the procedure to be followed upon his death. He had two sons: the elder, Krishna Dev Rao, and the younger, Ram Dev Rao. He also had two daughters who, following custom, would be left nothing.[8] In his will of 20 October, the maharaja wrote that "[m]y elder son Krishnadevarayulu is the heir to the Vanaparti Samsthanam."[9] In a separate form filed with the Hyderabad government, the maharaja again named the same heir: "Succession should be sanctioned in the name of the eldest son Krishna Dev Rao."[10] While Krishna Dev Rao was named heir to the Wanaparthi samasthan, Ram Dev Rao was bequeathed properties outside the samasthan in the Chitoor district and elsewhere in the Madras Presidency.[11]

Since Ram Dev Rao was still only a minor (sixteen years old in 1922), the maharaja in a subsequent document of 23 November spelled out the nature of the relationship between the two brothers. He instructed Ram Dev Rao to heed his older brother "for your good and get properly educated: and as soon as you become a major, take charge of your properties." The burden of guardianship was placed squarely on Krishna Dev Rao. He was nineteen years old and able to "look after all his affairs" and "manage them properly and work with interest in the matter of education and other affairs of Ramadevarayulu."[12] Thus the maharaja carefully explained in whose name the succession was to be granted. But, he could not have foreseen the sudden death of his elder son and the dispute that ensued.

The maharaja died on 27 November 1922. Since both sons were minors, the samasthan was taken into the Court of Wards. Krishna Dev Rao, already married (to Sarala Devi), had a young son, Rameshwar Rao III. But his health was fragile, and he died unexpectedly on 11 April 1924.[13] A few days following his death, Rameshwar Rao III, with his mother acting as guardian, filed a petition with the Hyderabad government asking to be named the legal representative of his father and thus heir to the samasthan. One week later, on 30 May 1924, Rameshwar Rao's uncle Ram Dev Rao filed a counterclaim asking that *he* be declared the rightful heir of his deceased brother. Thus, in death the dispute was born.

As long as the Court of Wards managed the samasthan, the question at hand was whether it could be divided between the son and uncle, or if it was to have a sole heir. The initial decision came from the Atiyat Court, which acknowledged that while Rameshwar Rao was the rightful heir to the estate, until he reached majority, his uncle Ram Dev Rao was to be given possession of the samasthan. As to Wanaparthi's status as a "state," which Rameshwar Rao had claimed, the opinion was clear: "The claim of being a state is only imaginary and baseless."[14] This decision was not amenable to either side, and the case was reheard by the appellate court. Aqeel Jung (minister to the *paigah* estates) agreed with the court that Rameshwar Rao, as son of the eldest son, was the rightful heir, but he did not agree that the samasthan should be placed in the temporary possession of Ram Dev Rao. Rather, he felt that it should remain under the supervision of the Court of Wards. He suggested that in the interim, Ram Dev Rao should be given a suitable allowance. These decisions were again appealed, each side angling for a better judgment.

A committee was formed that included Aqeel Jung, Richard Trench (Revenue and Executive Council member) and Mirza Yar Jung (Hyderabad's chief justice). Trench believed the samasthan should remain in the Court of Wards.

> His Exalted Highness's Farman undoubtedly permits the grant of temporary possession and management to any competent person, but, having regard to the relations that exist between him and his nephew, Ram Deo Rao is clearly the last man to whom they should be entrusted. The Court of Wards is the proper guardian of Rameshwar Rao's interests and should continue to hold charge of the Samasthan.[15]

The committee applied a model already in use outside Hyderabad to determine Wanaparthi's exact status. This was John Herbert Harington's analysis of estates in India.[16] Harington (1764–1828) had been Secretary of the Asiatic Society in the time of Sir William Jones and served (among other posts) as a member of the Supreme Council of Bengal. His ten-part list provided a useful paradigm against which the committee members could evaluate Wanaparthi. The first point concerned the period in which a family survived and possessed their estate. The Wanaparthi family could trace its history to five centuries, during which time the estate had covered roughly the same geographical area. Following that was the issue of succession to a single heir in comparison with other comparable families. When evaluated against Gadwal or Jatprole, both of which had maintained a line of sole heirs, the practice of impartibility at Wanaparthi was clearly in accordance with traditions of other samasthans. The relationship between the sovereign power and that of the subordinate power was important to ascertaining the latter's position within the polity. Wanaparthi had begun as a kind of "contractor" providing military service to earlier regimes, and had gradually attained its high position within the state. Next was the question of how the family had addressed the case of multiple heirs. When there previously had been multiple heirs at Wanaparthi, only one person had ever been made heir to the estate, and the other junior members abided by that practice. Titles and the accoutrements of power were vital to kings both large and small. At Wanaparthi, these had increased over time: from confirmation as raja and maharaja, to the position of samasthan member within the state, as well as recognition by the Company and the Raj. The size of the estate in question was further important to establishing its prestige.

Wanaparthi was among the largest samasthans within the Nizam's dominions and commanded a high degree of prestige. How junior members of the family were treated was also important to establishing the families' overall status. It appears that when several family members had previously vied for succession, those who had failed had been well-treated by the chosen heir, and their maintenance had been provided for. Harington then queried whether at any time part of the estate could have been claimed, and thus partitioned, but was not. For several generations Wanaparthi heirs had been adopted, so only one heir was able to claim heirship. As such, the samasthan had never been partitioned. This test, difficult to prove one way or another, clearly showed that Wanaparthi had not been radically partitioned during its long history.[17] Returning to more ceremonial matters, the moment or process of installation was seen as important in establishing the family's prestige. Heirs to the throne, appropriately installed with suitable pomp, had invariably conveyed notice to the rulers of Hyderabad. Finally, Harington's analysis questioned how smoothly the transition occurred between heirs of one generation and the next. At Wanaparthi, it appears that the samasthan had regularly enjoyed smooth passage from one heir to the next, either by the action of the raja or by savvy adoption practices of a wife. To what extent junior members of the family had always enjoyed maintenance is difficult to establish, but evidence of impartibility suggests that the estate had not previously been divided between senior and junior members.

Wanaparthi clearly met Harington's criteria and the committee members delivered their opinions. Aqeel Jung recognized that Wanaparthi was geographically impartible, but did not believe that it was a kind of "state" or "raj." He granted that a samasthan was impartible, "But it cannot be admitted that it is such a 'Raj' that can be owned by only one person or whose rights are higher than those of any Jagirdar."[18] He went on to opine that a samasthan was held by *peshkush*, and was thus like any other *jagir*. He also argued that while the samasthan could not be physically divided (since Rameshwar Rao was still a minor), its revenue could be divided between him and his uncle. What Aqeel Jung's analysis failed to note was the rajas of the samasthans had always held sole power and not divided it among family members. Thus, his opinion went against custom and was later challenged.

Trench agreed that the samasthan was not a "raj," and that it was impartible. He reiterated the policy of the Hyderabad government concerning the divisibility of landholdings: "The physical impartibility of State grants in the shape of land is an axiom of Atyat policy in Hyderabad."[19] Further, he argued that impartibility had to be established by some other means than the nature of the estate. Mirza Yar Jung stated that the samasthan's "importance grew in every generation in such a way that ultimately the title of Raja began to be conferred on its owner by H.E.H. Nizam's Government. And finally Raja Rameshwar Rao, the last holder, was honoured with the title of maharaja in the same manner as the holder of Gadwal Samasthan."[20] Mirza Yar Jung recognized the difference between the origin and the current status of the samasthan. "It is possible that it may have originated that way, but the origin is one thing and the end is a different thing altogether. The origin of big estates had been with small estates and weak powers but they ended in big kingdoms and strong powers."[21] He felt that the samasthan might have been divisible at an earlier time, but this was no longer the case.

While the samasthan was out of danger of being physically partitioned, its revenue was not. Ram Dev Rao and Rameshwar Rao appealed again. Arguing in favor of partibility, Ram Dev Rao suggested that Wanaparthi had begun in service to larger regimes as a sort of *theka* (military contractor). As such, its revenue would have been partible. The family had been granted a certain number of villages to maintain, which they had eventually come to own. Revenue had been collected and a portion of it was paid to the sovereign; the expense of maintaining troops had been deducted from the remainder. All this would have been the nature of a contract relationship, and would not have been an incorrect description of Wanaparthi. However, though the samasthan had begun as a contractor, it had changed over time. Ram Dev Rao's argument that the samasthan had never risen to any higher level than that of its origin could not be sustained.

Two central issues confronted the litigants from Wanaparthi. First, Hyderabad was governed by Muslim rulers, and much of its legal reference was Indo-Muslim. How were the claims of non-Muslim litigants to be handled?[22] What was to be done with regard to succession where Hindu and Muslim customs were different? The answer was neatly provided by the government's Revenue Department: "Succession relating to Mohammadan claimants will be decided according to Mohammadan law and that of Hindus according to Hindu law."[23] Since Wanaparthi had a Hindu ruler, Hindu law would be brought to bear upon matters relating to succession. Second, under Hindu law, eligible heirs to such estates were entitled to inherit a "fair portion" of revenue, land, or both.[24] However, in a clause that reflected the vast array of local practices, the law also made allowances for custom.[25] A "custom" was defined as "any rule, which having been continuously and uniformly observed for a long time, has obtained the force of law among Hindus in any local area, tribe, community, group or family."[26] For instance, if custom determined that an estate was awarded to a sole heritor, and was not divided between eligible heirs, then that custom had the force of law.[27] For Rameshwar Rao, establishing the custom of sole inheritance was critical. He needed to demonstrate that this custom had been exercised over an extended period of time. This was not easily done. "Custom is such a thing that its effect falls on every mind in various ways. Family accounts, family anecdotes, family usage; when all these things combine, only then the custom obtains the force of Law."[28] But thanks to the work already done by his grandfather, Maharaja Rameshwar Rao II, the task was made somewhat easier. In addition to questions of Hindu or Muslim law, the Hyderabad government sought to prevent repeated partitions that would result in smaller estates. The Atiyat Court reported, "Wherever more than one person claim[s] to succeed at the same time, instead of dividing it according to proportional shares, the whole mash is given into the possession of a single person." Further explaining why the Nizam's Government did not divide estates.

> This rule is entirely based on farsightedness and the policy of the Government because if a partition is permitted within a short time, in a few generations neither the dignity of the jagir remains nor the position of the jagirdar. Keeping in view the interest of the jagirdar as well of the ryots, partition and joint possession are prohibited.[29]

If partition was to be allowed, it would place the "dignity" as well as the territory itself in jeopardy. In this way, the government supported samasthans, *jagirs*, and *paigahs* that had been granted to only one family member. Thus, Rameshwar Rao and Ram Dev Rao could be assured that their case would follow Hindu law, and that partitioning the estate would remain a last choice, but Rameshwar Rao still faced the task of establishing a custom of undivided successions.

Rameshwar Rao III put forward the history of the samasthan composed at the time of his grandfather to demonstrate a custom of sole heirship. The history was carefully scrutinized by the committee members. The testimony of its author about the work and about his relationship with the maharaja sheds light on the relationship between kings, pundits, and history as it stood in the early twentieth century.

From Venkat Shastry's testimony, we learn something of the collective writing process between him and the maharaja. The maharaja, according to Shastry, "collected in one place all the sanads" that the family had issued and that it had received from its sovereigns. The maharaja had also rechecked details and correlated them with printed books. In Shastry's words, he "drew up a note of the same and handed it over to me. With the help of those notes of the said Maharaja, I used to verify the facts and read out the same to him, and he used to approve of the same. And whenever he desired me to amend or add anything to the same I used to do so accordingly."[30] After the maharaja had initially gathered the documents, Shastry composed and polished the final text in verse form.[31]

The maharaja was actively involved in the process of helping write his family history, yet Shastry's testimony shows that other forces were also at work. For the purposes of the case, everyone was most concerned with the custom of succession within the family, and the committee questioned Shastry about how successions had taken place in prior generations. He answered, "I have not mentioned anything about the other [wives?] having children. It is the rule with us always that we write about the line of those who are rulers."[32] It is nonetheless fascinating that the "rule" Shastry referred to, and the "us," was ambiguous. Was this a Brahmanical custom? Or, is this the case of a historian revealing an omission of fact in the writing process? Shastry's history depended on information first culled by the maharaja who approved its compilation before passing it back to Shastry. "Wherever I have not made any mention of the issue [child heir] it means that he had no issue. If he had issue the Raja Saheb would have written and given it to me."[33]

Shastry also took some liberties in shaping the material into verse form. For instance, in telling the story of Veer Krishna, the founder of the samasthan, Shastry had written that Krishna had acquired certain villages by "killing" either their owners or their inhabitants. To say that Krishna had killed villagers was a powerful assertion, and in his testimony Shastry revealed that this description was his own, and was not based on any fact. "[T]hese words may or may not have been said; they are mine, it is the beauty of the poem." At another time, when four sons had been born to one raja, questions were raised as to whether they had jointly administered the territory upon their father's death, or if only one son had succeeded to the throne. Shastry replied, "I have written that the four brothers were like four hands of Vishnu and four oceans together and united. <u>I have written that only one ruled and not four together</u>. He ruled together with them is only a poetic beauty."[34] This particular poetic liberty received, along with others, criticism from the committee members.

The first salvo against Shastry's work came from Aqeel Jung. He noted that during several generations, a custom of impartibility could be established, yet that at other times, there had been only one heir so partition had not been an option. Shastry's work had demonstrated *who* was heir, but not the process by which the heir was chosen. Aqeel Jung added, "The family history of the period before this [the most recent eight generations] is very vague and is filled with poetic exaggerations; and it is incomplete. Reliance cannot be placed on this."[35] A second attack on Shastry came from Trench who questioned the validity of the pundit's work. Translations of Shastry's work made for Trench prompted him to quip, "[i]t is no reflection on their historical value to say that they show the Pundit to be a man of considerable imagination and poetic fancy." Trench continued:

> Leaving aside the various conditions that a custom must thus fulfill, how is it possible to accept the Pundit's narrative where it deals with the pre-documentary history of the Samasthan as evidence that is clear and unambiguous? All we know is that the earlier portion of the Pundit's so-called history was compiled from the late Maharaja's notes and that those notes were prepared from Sanads.[36]

He further questioned Shastry's narrative concerning the four sons. Trench referred to the "flowery language of the poet," and then dismissed the section completely. He stated, "But what evidence is all this, if it deserves to be termed evidence, that a custom existed whereby the revenue of the family estate, whatever the estate may then have comprised, was indivisible? It does not even approach being the strict and positive evidence of exclusin [*sic*] necessary to establish custom." While it was ultimately dismissed for this lack of precision, it helped to confirm a tradition of sole heirship. Further, Shastry's history and testimony shed light on the process of history writing at the time.

Ram Dev Rao again appealed in late 1931, but in the summer of 1932 Trench firmly rejected the appeal. Clarifying his opinion on the establishment of a family custom, he restated his position: there was ample evidence to show that Wanaparthi had never (in recent generations) been partitioned. Nor could Trench concede that Rameshwar Rao had established the prior existence of a clear custom of impartibility. "What Rameshwar Rao seeks to establish is the existence of a family custom of complete impartibility and in doing so he sets himself an impracticable task."[37] Trench suggested that Rameshwar Rao, upon reaching majority, should be granted possession of the samasthan, but until that time the Court of Wards should administer the estate.[38] Trench was thus able to prevent the partition of the samasthan.

The final decision in the case came from Osman Ali Khan to whom all earlier opinions had been submitted. The Nizam, in a *firman* of 1 June 1933, agreed with the committee. Rameshwar Rao was the rightful heir to the estate; Ram Dev Rao was entitled to maintenance; and the samasthan should remain in the Court of Wards until Rameshwar Rao reached majority.[39] With that, the samasthan's immediate future was settled. It would not again come into the public eye until 1945, when Rameshwar Rao III assumed his responsibilities as raja of Wanaparthi. This succession case was more "typical" in that it arose between members within a family. Yet, perhaps less typical was the interview with Shastry and the use of history itself to establish a custom within the samasthan.

Gadwal: Interstate Disputes

At Gadwal, the issue of succession brought together the samasthan, the Nizam, the Court of Wards, and the Resident in sometimes contentious ways. Ultimately, this case demonstrated that while the Nizam's personal interests in the case were strong, the judicial machinery put in place—especially that of the Court of Wards—counterbalanced his authority. Unlike other successions, that at Gadwal suffered complications from unprecedented interference by Osman Ali Khan as well as the Resident. Much of the Nizam's meddling came by way of ceremonial avenues, and his behavior brought sharp criticism from the Residency. As Gadwal formed one piece of Hyderabad's composite political and social milieu, for the Resident, questions arose as to how much, if any, advice or interference he could offer. After the death of the maharaja, events transpired to bring the Gadwal samasthan and the Nizam to the brink of armed conflict, thus the Resident was pressed into taking action. Throughout the tensions, the press from the neighboring Madras Presidency carefully followed these unprecedented events and wove them into the larger narratives of the emerging nationalist movement.

The maharaja of Gadwal (photo 5.1), Sita Rambhupal II, died on 12 May 1924. His grandfather, Sita Rambhupal I, had adopted two sons, Sombhupal II and Rambhupal II.[40] Sita Rambhupal and his wife, Maharani Adi Lakshmi, had two daughters but no sons. The daughters, Varalakshmi and Lakshmi, aged ten and seven at the time of their father's death, held keys to the future of the samasthan. Their mother wanted to administer the samasthan until a son was born to one of the daughters. She would then adopt that child as heir. Ideally, adopting a grandchild would help lessen the chance of disputes or interference from within the family. However, given the youth of her daughters, she calculated that it

Photo 5.1 Maharaja Sita Rambhupal

would be some time before any children were born to them. Thus, it was her intent that either she or the Court of Wards would administer Gadwal. Adi Lakshmi had little time to think through her options because two days after her husband's death, Osman Ali Khan ordered Gadwal to be put under the Court of Wards. Gadwal's revenues were placed into the *khalsa*, that category of estates that paid revenue directly to the government. The Nizam justified his decision by claiming that the state needed Gadwal's revenue for security—a point to which we shall return later. He made provisions for the maintenance of Adi Lakshmi and her daughters; yet, for the family, placing Gadwal into the *khalsa* must have seemed tantamount to its dissolution. In addition to this action taken immediately after the maharaja's death, it was not clear why Gadwal should be placed in the Court of Wards in the first place. Legally, the Court of Wards covered any "*jagir*," and Hyderabad's Court of Wards considered a samasthan a category of *jagir*.[41] However, landholdings were to be administered by the Court of Wards only if no suitable person from the family were able to do this work. In the case of Gadwal, the Nizam ignored the fact that Adi Lakshmi was an able administrator.[42]

Why would the Nizam usurp the maharani's right as heir and put Gadwal into the Court? He justified his action with financial and military reasons. "It is up to my Government," the *firman* stated,

> to have regard to real and legitimate grounds and they should not pay any attention to feeble facts. Inasmuch as at present it is incumbent on us to better our financial situation, that is to say, we should adopt means for improving it so that by means of that we will be able to accomplish other important matters. For instance, we have got to maintain a large army so that in the present days of noise and unrest, it may be of use.[43]

But this assertion seems dubious at best. At this time, the Nizam's desire for *nazr* was at its height, and with Gadwal under the Court of Wards, he could more easily co-opt its revenue for his own private use.

An instance of this abuse of ceremony is found in an incident that took place shortly after the maharaja's death. Before he died the Nizam had sent the maharaja some mangoes as well as a reclining chair. This followed his habit of sending meaningless gifts to his nobles and demanding a generous *nazr* in return. With these items the Nizam wrote, 'Mangoes two sovereigns. . . . The easy chair cost me Rs. 800 exclusive of freight. So send Rs. 1,000 B.G. notes. You will find it very useful."[44] Operating in a culture of honor, gift giving, and loyalty, Sita

Rambhupal dutifully paid for the chair and the mangoes. However, only days after his death, the Nizam ordered the Court of Ward's chief officer to reclaim the chair. Such behavior, coupled with the loss of the samasthan's autonomy, prompted swift action from Adi Lakshmi.

On 21 June 1924, she took her grievances to the Hyderabad Executive Council. She argued before the Council that she was the rightful heir to the samasthan, and that in lieu of being placed under the Court of Wards, she should have been left free to manage the samasthan herself. Within Hindu family successions, a son of the deceased would have been the first rightful heir. Next in order would be the widow, the daughter, and the daughter's son. Thus, Adi Lakshmi had both legal authority and precedent to administer the samasthan. Moreover, her grandson, when born, would be legally next-in-line to succeed.[45] The case moved forward after continued pressure on the Executive Council and the Residency brought by Adi Lakshmi and her counsel, Diwan Bahadur Aravamudu Ayyangar.[46] At this point, with Adi Lakshmi pressing her case to the Executive Council, and the Nizam behaving erratically, the Resident felt called to step in. First, in a letter to Delhi, then Resident William Barton sought authority as to whether he "would be justified in offering advice to the Nizam regarding the settlement of the succession to the Gadwal Samasthan."[47] It is interesting that Barton sought to advise the Nizam, and not to directly advise members of Gadwal's family. He was told that such advice should be proffered by letter, by personal meeting, or indirectly through one of the Nizam's council members. To do otherwise would be a violation of protocol. At the same time, Barton offered his own opinion of the situation: "I would suggest that the Rani should be permitted to adopt and that during the minority of the heir she should administer the Samasthan. This is a settlement which would give general satisfaction and reassure many people who live in dread of high-handed interference with their estates on their death."[48]

The Residency was interested in the Gadwal succession because Gadwal was important for its income, size of some 800 square miles, location in the rich Raichur *doab*, and prestige as the premier samasthan. With an annual revenue of nearly three lakhs, a smooth succession that maintained regular payment of revenues to the Nizam was important. Yet, income, size, and location were not the primary reasons for British involvement. Gadwal was largely autonomous, and paid only its annual *peshkush*. Moreover, by the 1920s the *doab* was peaceful and Gadwal was no longer at the center of military operations.[49] Further, by that time, the "high noon" of the Raj was long past, and there was little value or loyalty to be gained from interfering in the dispute.[50] If the Resident could gain little from direct involvement, then his indirect influence must have turned on other considerations.

Within Hyderabad, Gadwal's considerable size made it a critical region within the state, so a smooth succession would have helped to maintain a broader peace. Since the Gadwal family was considered a pillar among the landed Hindu nobility, its absorption by the "Muslim" Hyderabad government would only stoke communal tensions. Additionally, any conflict over Gadwal's annexation had the potential of drawing in other participants along caste lines as the samasthan family belonged to the powerful Reddy community of south India. Thus, whatever interest the Resident took, it was likely to be indirect, with the hope of heading off communal or caste conflicts and the potential of broader political disruptions. With growing interest in the case, Osman Ali Khan must have sensed the potential for trouble and proceeded to back-peddle from his earlier attempt at outright annexation.

On New Year's Eve 1924, the Nizam issued a *firman* indicating that the succession would go to Adi Lakshmi's grandson.[51]

> After mature deliberation I have come to the following conclusion in respect of the Gadwal Samasthan, where no male issue or an adopted son was left by the deceased Raja. The Raja, however, had once spoken to me that he would apply to my Government for permission to adopt one of the sons of his daughters. My decision therefore is that arrangements may be made according to the wishes of the deceased Raja, whose faithful and loyal conduct towards his master had all along been exemplary. I therefore order, with a view to perpetuate the name of the deceased Raja, and for the permanency of the Samasthan, that the reinstatement of this Estate be kept in abeyance till one of the two daughters of the Raja gives birth to a male issue, who after receiving due education reaches the age of 21. In other words the Samasthan should, till then, remain under control of a Revenue Manager, like the Vanaparthi Samasthan. An adequate allowance determined by the President in Council and finally sanctioned by me should, however, be paid to the Maharani and other members of the deceased Raja's family. This case may now be filed.[52]

While this was partly amenable to the maharani, it did not remove Gadwal from jurisdiction under the Court of Wards. With Adi Lakshmi's daughters so young, the order meant that Gadwal would remain in the Court of Wards for many years. On her behalf, Ayyangar argued that Adi Lakshmi should be allowed to succeed her husband based on grounds of law and precedent.[53] A custom had been established within the samasthan itself, whereby, when a raja died and left no male heir, a wife succeeded to the throne. When necessary, a wife had been allowed to adopt an heir of her choice. This pattern had been followed at Gadwal throughout the eighteenth and nineteenth centuries. Women rulers there included: Ammakka and Lingamma (1724–1740); Mangamma and Chokkamma (1742–1746); Venkatlakshmiama (1840–1845); Lakshmi Devamma (1845–1901), and Adi Lakshmi Devi (1928–1940). All these women had ruled in their own right, and then adopted heirs to continue the family line. Ayyangar argued that women of the samasthan had "been recognised as rulers without there being any male ruler on whose behalf they could be said to have managed."[54]

The women rulers of Gadwal, Wanaparthi, and Jatprole, whether ruling as Regents with the Nizam's blessing (Jatprole), with the help of the Court of Wards (Wanaparthi), or independently prior to the Court's establishment (Gadwal) were part of a greater number of women rulers in the Deccan, and beyond. Of course, female power (*shakti*) has ancient origins, and there is no shortage of examples of women who command power and demand worship. For instance, Sita, the heroine of the great epic *Ramayana* is often regarded as the "ideal" (Hindu) woman. More recent from the Islamicate Delhi sultanate is Raziya Sultana who ably led that sultanate for four years (1236–1240). Still closer physically and chronologically to the eighteenth century samasthan women is Tarabai (1675–1761). At only twenty-five, Tarabai commanded Maratha forces for the seven-year period from 1700 to 1707 against then Mughal Emperor Aurangzeb. A large portion of her midlife was spent under arrest, only for her to emerge in the twilight of her life as a powerful dowager. Tarabai and the eighteenth-century women at Gadwal share several characteristics: both had control over armed forces, both carried out external political correspondences and relations, while at the same time managing internal domestic affairs, and both served at one time or another as Regents to future heirs.[55] While there is no definitive proof of contact between Tarabai and the Gadwal samasthan, it is entirely possible that the women of Gadwal were aware of Tarabai's impressive exploits. Tarabai's successors, the Maratha *peshwas* would have more direct contact with Gadwal, for a time bringing that samasthan under their policy of *chauth*, or one-quarter tax remission to the Maratha treasury.

Returning to the increasingly tense situation between the Nizam and Adi Lakshmi, Gadwal's plight began to ripple outward from its epicenter at Hyderabad to the Madras Presidency. Among the first responses was a memorial addressed to the Nizam, signed by forty-three "ladies" on behalf of Adi Lakshmi. Signatories included Britons and Indians, wives of members of the Madras Bar, and "other leading members of Indian society in Madras."[56] Sympathy for Adi Lakshmi, and outrage at the Nizam's actions, were likely centered along caste lines. The Gadwal family, and the late raja in particular, were considered leaders of the Reddy community of south India. The raja "was noted for his benevolence and charity and was held in great esteem and veneration by many Hindus in Southern India, and more especially by the Reddi community throughout the Madras Presidency, who looked upon him as the head of their caste and community and frequently referred important caste disputes to him for decision."[57] Frustration also mounted along communal lines. Then Resident, Charles Russell, commented that the Nizam's action could be, "calculated to arouse considerable feeling amongst the Hindu population."[58] Two weeks later and under a deluge of protests, Russell again wrote, "the Hindu community has been much stirred by the orders issued by His Exalted Highness regarding the Gadwal Samasthan, and telegrams have been received by me from the Hindu residents of various places outside the State."[59] Russell seems to have been aware that the dispute was quickly taking on a communal tone. The press also began to take note of events in Gadwal. The *Congress* of Rajahmundry in the Madras Presidency wrote, "Should H.E.H. the Nizam from the selfish motive that the finances of his Government will improve if Gadwal remains under him, flout the opinion of the Andhras, they should cross the Tungabhadra at Kurnool and start a righteous and non-violent *satyagraha*."[60] In an effort to resolve the dispute, the Nizam pressured Adi Lakshmi to sign a declaration accepting his New Year's *firman*. The Revenue secretary, Nawab Fasih Jung on 8 March 1925, conducted this diplomatic effort. She refused. What happened next was neither righteous nor in the spirit of nonviolence.

On 9 March 1925, the Nizam ordered 100 troops and a machine gun to Gadwal where they took up positions outside the palace. Since armed conflict had long ceased in the Hyderabad countryside, the Nizam's action was likely designed to intimidate rather than suppress.[61] He claimed that "outsiders" were unfavorably influencing the maharani and intruding in Hyderabad affairs. On 12 March 1925, the head of the Court of Wards sent Adi Lakshmi a note stating that if she failed to agree with the Nizam's proposal, the samasthan would be completely confiscated and her allowance ended. Adi Lakshmi, sensing a need to defuse the situation, responded a week later and reaffirmed her loyalty to the Nizam. No shots were fired and on 22 March, the troops were recalled.

This standoff had immediate consequences. As part of an effort to ameliorate the situation, the Nizam appointed a committee to investigate Adi Lakshmi's claims. The committee, created by *firman* on

22 March, consisted of Nawab Zulkander Jung, High Court Judge; Nawab Fasih Jung, Revenue secretary; and Nawab Akbar Yar Jung, Judicial and Police secretary. The committee met and heard testimony from both sides. Work proceeded slowly, being "intentionally delayed" so that it was not done until October. This delay enabled the Nizam to hold Gadwal revenues that much longer within the *khalsa* account. In this, his efforts were aided by two of the committee members who were "utterly unprincipled and ready in all things to conform to the caprice of their Ruler."[62] The committee did little to help, and William Barton explained that their inaction was probably due to fear.

> Various efforts have recently been made to intimidate the Rani's counsel and although over two months have elapsed since the latter's written arguments were placed before the Committee, its members seem loath, apparently for fear of incurring the Nizam's displeasure, to come to a decision, and it is probable that they will defer their report indefinitely.[63]

As the committee continued to deliberate and delay, the affairs of Gadwal continued to attract the attention of the press.

Press reports and commentary reflected regional and national trends. This was the time of the Indian nationalist movement as well as a period when linguistic and caste identities (here, Telugu and Reddy) were coming to the fore. The Gadwal case became a rallying point to "awaken" communities in south India and urge them to come to the aid of the samasthan. The newspaper the *Congress* of 19 March 1925 reported:

> The Nizam has acted like Lord Dalhousie who had annexed the Native States on the grounds that there were no heirs to the rulers. Gadwal is a thoroughly independent Zamindari except that it pays a subsidy to H.E.H. the Nizam. The Nizam wanted to swallow all its rights in one gulp . . . Now, another opportunity presents itself to the Andhras to show their manliness, courage and self-respect. Will the Andhra leaders at least now come forward and show the work that the Andhras should do, so that Gadwal may be returned to the Rani?[64]

Unjust action, comparisons with the Raj, and a plea to the Telugu speaking Andhras of the Madras Presidency were themes repeatedly invoked by the press. Two weeks later the *Congress* reported: "The Western Andhras are not even in a position to discuss these questions [the incorporation of Gadwal and other samasthans in Hyderabad State]. What then is their duty? . . . The only political question that presents itself to the Andhras at present is that of Gadwal. So the whole Andhra country should set up an agitation in respect of this matter."[65] Evident from these accounts is a growing "Hindu" and "Andhra" identity in opposition to the "Muslim" committee created to remedy the situation.

The press also pursued an attack on the composition of the committee, which as noted, consisted of three Muslim members. Rallying against this "Muslim" committee, the press decried its inadequacy to handle the matter at hand, deciding the fate of a "Hindu" kingdom. With the increasingly communal nature of the tensions, it was only natural that Gadwal was now very much "Hindu," while the committee and Hyderabad were clearly "Muslim." The *Swadeshabhimani* sarcastically carried this theme further.

> Our readers know quite well how his Hindu subjects are being loved by the Nizam . . . Now, by doing one more wonderful act, he has furnished yet another vivid illustration of "Mussalman justice." When the Hindu Raja of Gadwal died recently, the Nizam appointed a Commission consisting of three Mussalmans to adjudicate the claim of the Raja's widow for her husband's throne and has now issued a firman that the Maharani has no right to the throne.[66]

Further, the *Andhra Patrika* invoked "tradition" and antiquity to justify the maharani's claims. "According to Hindu traditions, the practice of the wife managing all the estates of her husband after his death has been obtaining from time immemorial."[67] Finally, the *Tamil Nadu* portrayed the events at Gadwal in a stridently communal light. The paper argued that a committee composed only of Muslims could not possibly understand a "Hindu" kingdom. "It is not at all proper to appoint Muhammadans to decide the question as to whether a Hindu State should continue to exist or not. It will be just and equitable on the part of the Nizam to appoint some Hindus also on this committee, as Hindus alone can understand the tenets, customs and injunctions of their religion."[68] This approach to Hindu-Muslim relations was a portent of things to come.[69] The success of Hyderabad's composite culture began to give way to communalist and nationalist sentiments.

Under the mounting pressure and criticism, Osman Ali Khan issued two new *firmans*. These seemed designed to humiliate the samasthan family, and in some way justify his action. The first came on 10 May 1925. In it, he stated that Gadwal held a debt of 8.5 lakhs. This debt was used post facto as justification for placing Gadwal into the Court of Wards—gross debt was one condition under which an estate could be put into the Court.[70] Ironically, if the samasthan carried such debt, the reasons lay not with mismanagement of the samasthan, but in the avarice of the Nizam himself. During the last years of his life, Maharaja Sita Rambhupal, in the grip of the Nizam had been so squeezed for large amounts of money that he had not only accumulated great debt, but had come to avoid trips to Hyderabad. Barton noted, "If the finances of the Samasthan are in a bad way as is stated by the Nizam—and in my view of the foregoing it is quite credible that they are—the cause is not far to seek."[71] A calculation later done by the Residency showed that Gadwal was in fact owed a *refund* of H.S. 238,227.[72] This refund was due because Gadwal had paid *nazr* in its own coinage, which had traded higher against the Nizam's coin and the Indian imperial rupee. Thus, the Nizam's first *firman* concerning Gadwal's debt was dubious at best. The second *firman* issued on 13 August 1925 reduced the allowance given to the maharani. This was done presumably to reduce the samasthan's expenditure, but coming in the heat of the conflict between Osman Ali Khan and Adi Lakshmi it seems to have been calculated to embarrass and cause inconvenience more than economize.

By early the next year, having witnessed the firestorm over the Nizam's actions, British officials were increasingly concerned that the Gadwal situation could erupt into a much larger conflict. The succession dispute, when mapped onto growing communal and nationalist movements throughout the subcontinent, provided ample tinder for an errant spark to ignite. In lengthy consultations with the Resident, officials outlined a suggested strategy to approach the Nizam, offer advice, and bring the matter to a close.

> It therefore seems desirable that such advice as is offered to the Nizam should be based mainly on the danger of giving legitimate offence to Hindu sentiment. The Resident might emphasise the delicate nature of H.E.H.'s position as the feudal lord of this very ancient Hindu Estate, the preservation of which as a semi-independent entity is evidently a matter of great concern to Hindu sentiment throughout Southern India. Any affront, real or fancied, to such sentiment would be a matter of embarrassment to the British Government as well as to H.E.H. [73]

The concern from New Delhi was with protecting "Hindu sentiment." The Nizam's position, as "feudal lord" of Gadwal was—though not directly mentioned—especially difficult as he himself was Muslim. Hyderabad State's composite identity was, along with the rest of India, beginning to breakdown into its constituent parts; here, "Hindu" and "Muslim."

Finally, Gadwal's fortunes were beginning to change. First, the Court of Wards supervised the marriage of Varalakshmi, the older daughter, see photo 5.2. This marriage, costing a lavish 1.5 lakhs, was performed on 6 June 1927. Varalakshmi was married to the prince of Domakonda, Someshwar Rao.[74] A son born from that marriage was eligible to become

Photo 5.2 Princesses Varalakshmi and Lakshmi

the Gadwal heir. Second, continued efforts by Adi Lakshmi helped build momentum toward releasing the samasthan from the Court of Wards. Ayyangar noted:

> She [Adi Lakshmi] is very well educated in her vernacular, which is the vernacular of the State, namely, Telegu. She can read and write Telegu very well. I am prepared to submit my personal testimony as regards her capacity of understanding matters of State and of her ardent desire to be a just ruler. I have no doubt that she will discharge satisfactorily the responsibilities devolving on her in regard to the administration of the State. The only thing that she wants is that she should be given a capable, faithful and upright officer as her Dewan or Minister to assist her in the administration.[75]

Another positive report about Gadwal came from Theodore Tasker. Tasker first visited Gadwal in 1926 in conjunction with the Court of Wards. His positive impression of Adi Lakshmi and of Gadwal would aid in its release. At Gadwal, as in Wanaparthi and Jatprole, Hindu rulers worked in accord with Muslim dewans and other ranking officials. At that time, Nawab Malik Yar Jung Bahadur was the *talukdar* for Gadwal under the Court of Wards, and from Tasker's notes, we can discern the positive relationship between Malik Yar Jung (as well as Yavar Ali and Aziz Hassan, both of whom later served as *talukdars* for Gadwal) and the maharani. Tasker stated that these men "enjoyed the confidence both of Government and the Maharani Saheba."[76]

Finally, in 1928 Gadwal was one of the thirteen estates recommended and approved for release from the Court of Wards. This was due partly to an effort by the Court, under the direction of Tasker and Trench, to reduce the number of estates under its supervision. The Resident commented: "Almost the first positive outward fruits of the reforms introduced in the administration of Hyderabad are seen in the recent release of some 13 estates from the Court of Wards, including the well-known Gadwal Samasthan, an event which cannot but have a favourable repercussion on Hindu sentiment."[77]

But the release was not without conditions. The first was "[t]hat the Maharani manages the *Samasthan* by obtaining the services of a Government officer (whose position will be equal to that of a 1st Taluqdar). The selection of this officer will lie with the Government."[78] This allowed Adi Lakshmi to manage the affairs of Gadwal, but at the same time, inserted a government official in a high position within the samasthan administration. In fact the maharani had previously asked for a "faithful and upright" officer to assist her, so this condition does not seem unwarranted. It was also to the Court's advantage to have an officer at Gadwal to mediate between itself and Adi Lakshmi. If anything were to happen to the maharani, and the samasthan returned to the Court of Wards, having a knowledgeable officer in place would be invaluable.

The second condition was perhaps more invasive and damaging to Gadwal's autonomy. It is worth citing in full because its language reveals the somewhat paternal attitude of the Court of Wards.

> That the supervision of the Revenue Department over the administration of the *Samasthan* should continue to the extent that the annual budget sanctioned by the Revenue Department and the *Samasthan* should be bound to obtain sanction of the Revenue Department to transfer any amount from one major head to another of the sanctioned budget. Besides this, the Revenue Department will be at liberty, until all debts are liquidated, to check the accounts of the *Samasthan* at its own will, whenever it deems necessary. After a practical experience of five years, however, the question of curtailing the supervision of the Revenue Department may be considered.[79]

The Revenue Department allowed itself the "liberty" to check accounts at any time, under any pretext, clearly binding Gadwal's administrative authority to the Court and government. The Court of Wards stipulated that whatever conditions it imposed could (and would) be repealed after a period of time. The third and fourth conditions were less invasive: the third required that the samasthan undertake the survey and settlement of its hitherto unused lands. This work was to be done by the Hyderabad government, following standard procedure for estates under the Court of Wards. Finally, the fourth condition allowed Adi Lakshmi to adopt a child from one of her daughters and continue to administer Gadwal until that child came of age.[80]

From 1927 to 1934 further events took place in Gadwal. The first came in 1928 when Varalakshmi gave birth to a son, Krishna Rambhupal.[81] He would eventually lead the samasthan out of the Court of Wards, and see it through to its end in 1949. Second, in 1930, the Nizam visited Gadwal while on tour. These types of visits were largely ceremonial, and this one did not involve any *nazr* bidding as in previous trips. Gifts were offered, *pan* shared, a photo taken, and the Nizam departed. Tensions between the Nizam and the rani seem to have dissipated. Finally, in 1932, a second son was born to Varalakshmi.

The following year Tasker returned to visit Gadwal a second time. Tasker's tour notes provide a glimpse of the projects taking place in the samasthan. They also, if only briefly, catch Tasker (an otherwise quiet and business-like official) in a sentimental mood. He met with Adi Lakshmi and discussed events pertinent to Gadwal, "in all of which the Maharani showed herself well informed." He continued:

> On the personal side I may note that, whereas five years ago there was no adopted son in sight, on this occasion we were greeted inside the Fort by the four-year-old son of the elder daughter, in full uniform with sword and mounted on a pony, commanding a personal body-guard of small boys in khaki. In addition to "Pedda Buchi Raja" (as he is known to all) there is now Chinna (i.e., younger) Buchi Raja, a very vigorous brother of five months. The second daughter's marriage has not yet been arranged.
>
> I noticed outside the Fort a lofty new erection for housing temple raths, and work was proceeding night and day on a new temple car. The Maharani Saheba has also recently purchased three elephants.[82]

Upholding the duties of a ruler, the maharani continued to patronize nearby temples with new temple chariots as well as maintaining her and her family's honor with the purchase of three new elephants. With Gadwal under the maharani's supervision, it was only a matter of time before Krishna Rambhupal was adopted as heir. This took place in late December 1940. Of the maharani's administration the *Deccan Chronicle* wrote: "On the somewhat premature demise of her husband, the Maharani of Gadwal assumed the administration of the Samasthan, and conducted its affairs with tact and skill, reminiscent of the Hindu queens of yore. She has been a generous patron of education and the Fine Arts, and has continued the traditions of the Samasthan for liberality and hospitality."[83]

In accordance with custom, Adi Lakshmi offered *nazr* to the Nizam for the adoption and recognition of her grandson as heir. The amount given was 125 *ashrafis*, or about Rs. 6,000. This sum caught the attention of the Resident, Claude Gidney, who inquired within Hyderabad circles whether "the amount of this presentation [was] in accordance with custom or in excess of it."[84] It should be remembered that this inquiry came at a time when Osman Ali Khan was again seeking large *nazr*. This time, however, there was no problem. Krishna Rambhupal was duly adopted by his grandmother and became Gadwal's last official raja; the Nizam accepted the *nazr* and authorized the adoption; and Gidney was satisfied that the amount given was within the bounds of custom. Ultimately the samasthan was returned to its ruling family and continued to function until 1949. The legal machinery of Hyderabad had operated slowly, and with frequent interference from the Nizam, but in the end it fulfilled its purpose. Lessons from Gadwal's succession were not lost on the other samasthan nobles. It is to the east of Gadwal to Jatprole that we now turn for an entirely different strategy for a successful succession

Jatprole: The Exception

One name is conspicuously absent from the Court of Wards roster, from the Residency records, and from the Nizam's files: Jatprole. Unlike Wanaparthi and Gadwal, and many of the other smaller samasthans, Jatprole avoided both time in the Court of Wards and a difficult succession path as its ruling family successfully strategized to maintain their autonomy and power. Where heirs were chosen from the immediate families at Wanaparthi and Gadwal (a son and grandson), the raja of Jatprole in the first decades of the twentieth century, Lakshma Rao, and his heir were part of a larger, vibrant network of families. These families, related by blood, history, and caste, prepared Lakshma Rao for his successful tenure as raja and made it possible for him to adopt a viable heir as he entered the twilight of his life. Lakshma Rao was a product of what I have called the "great generation," and this background accounts in part for his talent in handling the samasthan and the eventual succession. However, it was also in the order of events, which allowed the family to make adequate arrangements. When Lakshma Rao died in 1928, he had witnessed events at Wanaparthi and Gadwal.[85] His own efforts to adopt an heir began as early as 1915, but took some time to reach fruition. His chosen heir was a child at the time of his death, so his wife, Rani Ratnammba, served as Regent (with the Nizam's blessing) and led the samasthan for nearly two decades. Her talent accounts for the samasthan's vibrancy and its success in avoiding interference from the Court of Wards, the Nizam, and the Residency.

Lakshma Rao's background and the broader network of interrelated families to which he belonged also contributed to his deft handling of the samasthan's affairs. The heads of the Jatprole family belonged to the Velama caste. Their ancestors had come to the Mahbubnagar district area centuries earlier, while other members of the family settled in Venkatagiri in the Nellore district. As events unfolded in south India, Jatprole found itself embedded within the Muslim regimes north of the Krishna river, while Venkatagiri and the other related samasthans of Pithapuram in the Godavari district, and Bobbili in the Vizianagaram district found themselves within British India. These families continued to participate in each other's social events (weddings, installations, adoptions, etc.), and took an active part in the politics of the Madras Presidency and Hyderabad State. In the late nineteenth century, a turn of events would once again bring the families even closer together, despite geographical differences, and produce a remarkable period in their kingship and rule.

In the second half of the nineteenth century, Jagannath Rao II, then raja of Jatprole, had no son.[86] He was a frequent visitor in the Madras Presidency and a respected noble of south India. Fond of sport, he established the "Jatprole Cup" at Madras, competed in races in Bangalore, and hunted and participated in other popular sports of the day.[87] Jagannath Rao also attended family functions held at the homes of his relatives. For instance, he attended a wedding at Venkatagiri in 1875, where he was "one among the chief guests."[88] Three years later, he attended the coronation of the eldest Venkatagiri son as raja of that samasthan. At that time, he made plans to adopt the youngest son of that family to succeed him.[89] While final approval rested with the Nizam, Jatprole and some of the other samasthans repeatedly looked outward to the Madras Presidency rather than to Hyderabad for adoptions, new administrative ideas, and social events. Geographically, Kollapur was closer to Kurnool and to the Madras Presidency than to Hyderabad city. Second, a visit to Hyderabad usually meant giving *nazr* to the Nizam, which could be a costly affair. Third, Lakshma Rao's own birthplace was Venkatagiri. His brothers resided in the Madras Presidency samasthans, and so he had personal reasons for looking to Madras rather than to Hyderabad. Fourth, his upbringing in Venkatagiri exposed him to the culture of the Raj. When he assumed his own *gaddi* (literally cushion, used here to mean throne) he implemented reforms (social, educational, legal, etc.) borrowed from the Madras Presidency. Finally, among Velama samasthans, Jatprole was the only Velama domain in Hyderabad State. Thus, when looking for a member of the same caste to adopt, the family had every reason to look beyond Hyderabad's borders.

The beginning of the twentieth century was a unique moment: the Jatprole, Bobbili, and Pithapuram samasthans were all without heirs. Fortuitously, the elder raja of Venkatagiri, Yachama Naidu, had several sons who formed a coherent generational block. These sons were adopted by the families of the other samasthans. The sons were: Rajagopala Krishna Yachendra who remained at Venkatagiri; Rungamannar Krishna Yachendra, given to Bobbili; Ramakrishna Yachendra, given to Pithapuram (he would later marry into the Nuzvid samasthan); and finally, Lakshma Rao (né Navanitha Krishna Yachendra), given to Jatprole. This cohort formed what might be called a "great generation."

A generation can be defined biologically: descendants of a common ancestor who usually take about thirty years to marry and produce offspring of their own. It can also be defined according to the nineteenth-century scholar Wilhelm Dilthey as comprising those people who in adolescence shared a common set of "formative impressions."[90] As youth, at Venkatagiri, Lakshma Rao and his brothers likely circulated in the political and social milieu of the Madras Presidency. This included circles that intersected high-ranking British officials as well as fellow Indian nobles, and joined with a variety of emerging social options; from "pegs" at the club, to big-game hunting, to portrait sittings, to owning the latest American-made automobiles.

Lakshma Rao, born on 2 September 1865, was adopted by Jagannath Rao when he was fourteen. This ceremony took place at Tirupathi on 7 March 1879.[91] Two weeks later, with appropriate pomp, he entered Jatprole for the first time. He seems to have remained in the samasthan for several years, learning the intricacies of its administration. When he reached his nineteenth year, he took the name Lakshma Rao, and in March of 1884 was given full administrative powers by his adopted father. This happy event was followed two years later by his marriage to Rani Ratnammba in 1886 at Venkatagiri. Here, he and his brothers were once again reunited.[92] His formal accession took place on 6 March 1887, and was recognized by the Nizam, Mahbub Ali Khan. Lakshma Rao became a favorite of the Hyderabad court; he and the Nizam were almost exactly the same age and shared a love of big-game hunting.[93] Both Lakshma Rao and his daughters were excellent hunters.

Once established at Kollapur, the new raja began an impressive program of building, reform, and socializing. Kollapur had been the capital of the samasthan for several generations, and Lakshma Rao wished to modernize and beautify the town. His adopted father had begun to construct a new palace atop the older fort. This new palace, the Chandra Mahal, completed in 1871, was constructed in part by craftsmen brought from Venkatagiri. Strong architectural similarities exist between buildings in Kollapur and those at Venkatagiri. The masonry work is identical, the pillars and porticoes are similar, and the overall façade of the Kollapur palace clearly resembles that of the main Venkatagiri palace. Further construction included the Vijiah Mahal and the Shadi Mahal in 1916, the Jammi Mosque, the Jagannath Bagh, a hospital, school, and a printing press.[94] These structures, in addition to the new samasthan administrative offices, all bore identical finials, marking them as official buildings of the samasthan.

The situation at Kollapur was a product of Lakshma Rao's contact with his family members in the Madras Presidency. While ruling in different samasthans, he and his brothers seem to have had ample reasons for visiting each other. This great generation was first reunited in 1878 when the eldest brother was installed at Venkatagiri. In attendance were the brothers from Bobbili, Pithapur, and Jatprole. From the Bobbili family history we learn that "[i]t is a very happy event to note here that the three brothers . . . came together there for the first time after their adoption."[95] The brothers would continue to meet as weddings and family crises afforded them with opportunities to see one another. For instance, in 1883, the third brother, Krishna Yachendra, who had been adopted at Bobbili, returned home to Venkatagiri to attend his eldest brother's wedding. Three years later, he made the same journey to attend the wedding of brother number four, Lakshma Rao of Jatprole. Also present was the eldest brother who had remained at Venkatagiri. In 1898, the Venkatagiri and Pithapur brothers attended the wedding of their younger brother at Bobbili. Despite the distances, the brothers regularly visited back and forth to attend celebrations and look after intrafamily matters.

As we might expect, disputes occasionally broke out within this generation, and certain members of the family were consistently called upon to broker the peace. The raja at Bobbili, Krishna Yachendra, seems to have been the key family peacemaker. When in 1889 his father and younger brother Muddu Krishna had a dispute over money, it was Krishna Yachendra who made the journey from Bobbili to Venkatagiri to help restore the peace. Again, in 1897, when a dispute erupted over the maintenance of Muddu Krishna, his brother from Bobbili was called to work out a settlement. Krishna Yachendra appears to have taken a great interest in the nobility of India. For instance, he authored a book entitled *Advice to the Indian Aristocracy*. One of the chapter titles is "Some Bad Habits" where he pleas to his fellow nobles to have only one wife. He laments, "I need hardly say that no man should have more than one wife at the same time. But some of our present-day Zamindars, I regret to say, marry more than one, generally two wives."[96]

From 1920 to 1928, Lakshma Rao corresponded with his nephew and brother at Pithapur. The letters that survive are only those sent *from* Lakshma Rao, but they hint at the qualities of the contact maintained by the brothers and their families. In a letter of 1921, Lakshma Rao asks his Pithapur kin what kind of automobile he should purchase. He asks, "Recently I came to know that Bobbili raja bought a car for 16,000. What make is it? What body is it?"[97] Later he learned that in Pithapur they were driving a Chevrolet, but had recently purchased a Studebaker, and he inquires into this. This sort of communication among brothers would be no more out-of-place today than it was nearly a century ago. Lakshma Rao also writes about more administrative matters, displaying his concern for the samasthan. In a letter of 29 November 1926, he says, "I have so many problems here. Especially without rain it is a great difficulty. Because of these reasons, for the first time, I am forced to take a loan. I have never done like this, that is why my heart is not at peace."[98]

In addition to his program of construction, Lakshma Rao also employed savvy political strategies to neutralize communal tension within Kollapur. In one instance from early 1925, a dispute arose between Muslims attending the Jammi Mosque and Hindus attending the temple adjacent to the mosque. The matter was quickly submitted to the Department of Religious Affairs at Hyderabad, which, after making its suggestions, passed the matter to the Nizam. A response came in April, and besides pointing to the kinds of communal tension experienced across the subcontinent, it praised Lakshma Rao for his neutral stance and prompt handling of the situation. The Nizam agreed with the Religious Affairs department, which had issued several orders regarding the matter. First, the common boundary wall between the temple and mosque was to be raised "as high as possible" so that neither group might easily see each other. Second, prayers at the temple that used a bell were to be reduced in number so that they would not offend those offering prayer at the mosque. Third, both sides were to strictly follow government orders whenever processions were taken out or bands played in the street. In addition, music coming from a nearby girl's school, a *dasi* (slave, prostitute) home, and a liquor store were to be shifted elsewhere. Finally, "[t]he garbage dumping and pig breeding nearby the mosque should be prohibited."[99] The problems faced by the Hindu and Muslim residents of Kollapur regarding noise, processions, and unclean areas are no less familiar to Hindus and Muslims of contemporary India. However, what is notable in this situation is the praise given to Lakshma Rao by the Nizam himself. The Nizam writes, "Further, it gave me great pleasure that the ruler of the Samasthan remained neutral and has not supported either of the parties." The Nizam went on to contrast Lakshma Rao's conduct of affairs with that of Shah Abdur Raheem of Bidar. The latter "caused enmity among both the communities, Hindus and Muslims, should be warned, that such acts in the future would lead to severe punishment and he should be monitored for a period of time . . ."[100]

Lakshma Rao's actions, and the setting of Kollapur, fit well with scholarly interpretations of communal relations in the princely states.

For instance, Ian Copland's five-point paradigm for better communal relations in the princely state is well suited to explain the events at Kollapur.[101] First, the town had a relatively small Muslim population that was well integrated, physically and occupationally with the larger Hindu community. The samasthan itself for many years had a Muslim *dewan*. Second, Kollapur was far from Hyderabad, and removed from British India by its embedded location with in a larger princely state. Thus communal troubles across the Krishna river, or in Hyderabad city, were distant affairs. Third, while much of Hyderabad State was somewhat "backward" or "behind" the rest of India, Kollapur seems to have been an exception. Ample housing, electricity, town-planning, and benevolent rule all made the town somewhat of a model. Fourth, Kollapur's relatively small size allowed that its residents met face-to-face on a regular basis. As Copland notes, "it is potentially easier to strike a stranger one will never see again than to trade blows with a person one is likely to run into next day in the street or at the bazaar."[102] Finally, with the palace in Kollapur's center, and the rajas of Jatprole at the heart of the palace and the samasthan, the town and its head ran along traditional monarchical policies: the raja observing his ritual obligations and fulfilling his *rajadharma*, while at the same time, participating in Hyderabad State and the Nizam's composite cultural and political milieu.

By 1920, Lakshma Rao and his wife, Rani Ratnammba had two daughters of their own, Rajeswari and Saraswati, but no sons.[103] Lacking a male heir, adoption of a son from another branch of the family was the most suitable option. Murali Krishna Rao of the Pithapuram samasthan was of the proper age for adoption, and so the two families made the necessary arrangements. What remains of this agreement is the written contract from Murali Krishna Rao to Lakshma Rao that provides a glimpse into the inner-workings of two families' and their union.[104] Murali Krishna Rao was the son of Raja Suriyamahipathi Ram Krishna Rao, raja of the Pithapuram samasthan. At the time of the adoption agreement, Murali Krishna Rao was nineteen years old. Notable in the agreement was the fact that two-thirds of its contents pertained to Murali Krishna Rao's treatment of Rani Ratnammba and her daughters. The document outlined in detail the financial compensation he would provide the women of the Jatprole family. There are ten clauses within the document; surprisingly few given the fact that Murali Krishna Rao would be responsible for the samasthan's administration. *How* he was to govern the samasthan was knowledge he presumably already possessed; but how he would treat the women of the family was not yet known (and had to be established), so it was spelled out in some detail. The adoption agreement began, "Having no male issue you are intent on taking [me for] adoption, for the perpetuation of your family and to reign over your Samasthanam and as required by you fo[r] the purpose I execute willingly this agreement with the conditions as mentioned hereunder."[105]

The first three clauses spell out the intended relationship between Lakshma Rao and Murali Krishna Rao. The first clause of the agreement allowed for the possibility that Lakshma Rao might have yet fathered a son "by God's grace."[106] In that event, the samasthan would pay Murali Krishna Rao Rs. 1,000 per month, or a lump sum of Rs. 250,000 as maintenance. The second clause addresses the possibility that Murali Krishna Rao and Lakshma Rao might in the future have a "disagreement . . . for living together." In such a circumstance, the samasthan would pay Murali Krishna Rao an allowance of Rs. 500 per month, and he would not be entitled to enter the samasthan until after Lakshma Rao's death. The third clause dealt with the possibility of disagreements between Murali Krishna Rao and Rani Ratnammba. In such a case, half of the zenana buildings (under construction in 1915 and finished by 1916) would remain with Rani Ratnammba, along with her servants "without reducing the establishment of her servants . . . the list in the pay bill [of] all her establishment [would] be born by the Samasthanam. Her prestige will be maintained without any defect."[107] She would also receive Rs. 1,000 per month allowance for life. Of these possible conditions it was a kind of disagreement that proved insurmountable for Murali Krishna Rao and his adopted family.

The fourth to eighth clauses pertain to the treatment of Lakshma Rao's younger daughter, Saraswati. In addition to the maintenance provided for her in her father's will, Murali Krishna Rao agreed to pay an additional Rs. 500 per month to her for life, so that she would be able to live in an "honourable fashion." If Murali Krishna Rao and Saraswati did not get along, he further agreed to construct a new home for her. Regardless of this, he agreed to provide her with a, "first-class ration of food."[108] Finally, Murali Krishna Rao agreed that Saraswati's husband—not yet decided on at that time—would be paid Rs. 200 per month and added, 'I will be treating him well with [all] Samasthanam respects." The ninth clause allowed that Murali Krishna Rao would pay any outstanding debts of his adopted father at the time of the latter's death. The final clause stated that the adoption was subject to the Nizam's approval. This was a formal recognition of the ties and relationships that had long existed between the samasthan and the Nizam. If not approved by the Nizam, Murali Krishna Rao would have no further claim to the samasthan. While the agreement was between the two samasthans, it was actually executed under the authority of Hyderabad State, thus ultimately the Nizam's approval was necessary for the adoption to take place. On 8 May 1916, the Nizam's government formally granted permission for Lakshma Rao to adopt Murali Krishna Rao. At the same time, Lakshma Rao stated that he himself had no sons; a legal requirement for the adoption. Sometime after 1915, Murali Krishna Rao came to Kollapur and began living in the palace. For reasons that remain unclear, he did not stay and went back to his family at Pithapuram, thus nullifying the adoption agreement.

Lakshma Rao tried a second time to adopt an heir. He did not look to Pithapuram since earlier events had strained relations between the two families. Instead, he looked to Bobbili. The Bobbili family offered for adoption the young Jagannath Rao, the grandson of the maharaja of Bobbili, Venkata Swetachalapati Ranga Rao. On 22 January 1922, Lakshma Rao filed a petition with the Nizam's government asking for its approval of the adoption of Jagannath Rao as heir. The adoption procedure included public notices of the adoption, supported by the statements of officials and the testimony of witnesses. All this was meant to reaffirm that Lakshma Rao himself had no sons, and that Jagannath Rao would be his sole heir. On 10 February 1922, notice of the intended adoption was given. This notice allowed any objectors to file a claim against the adoption. On 21 March 1922, the government confirmed that Lakshma Rao had no other adopted or natural sons, and gave support to the adoption. On 2 June 1922, in a show of broader support between the samasthans, Maharaja Sita Rambhupal of Gadwal, and Raja Venkatama Reddy, Hyderabad's police chief, both testified that Lakshma Rao had no other sons. On 21 July, Osman Ali Khan gave orders for the adoption. Three months and two days later, the formal adoption took place, and Jagannath Rao's position as heir to the Jatprole *gaddi* was secure. On 3 November, in accordance with the law, Lakshma Rao notified the Revenue Office of the adoption. It appears that he left nothing to chance, since two years later, on 15 April 1925, he filed an affidavit with the Nizam's government stating (again) that his adopted son was the sole legal heir to the samasthan and swore to this.

At the same time, Lakshma Rao managed to keep Jatprole out of the Court of Wards, even though the samasthan had faced difficulties. This was unusual and was largely due to his leadership. Sometime prior to 1928, Theodore Tasker, at the request of Lakshma Rao, had visited Kollapur and toured the samasthan. The purpose of this visit was to impress upon him the quality of the local administration, and to clear the way for Rani Ratnammba to become the samasthan's Regent. This planning would keep the samasthan free of the Court of Wards and allow its administration remain in family hands.[109] Tasker was impressed with what he saw, prompting him apparently to write that the samasthan was an "oasis in the desert."[110] Placing the samasthan under the Court would have inserted an undesirable layer of bureaucracy between the samasthan and its residents. As a result, Jatprole remained under the administration of its ruling family. Lakshma Rao, most likely having seen the difficulties faced by other samasthans in the region, prepared in advance for his death. This forethought aimed to ensure a smooth transition of power from himself to his wife, and then to their adopted son. When Lakshma Rao died on 15 April 1928, he was 62 years old.

The Jatprole family and its relations in the Madras Presidency, however, continued to command the attention of both the Resident and the Nizam. Three years after Lakshma Rao's death, the Resident, Terence Keyes, in a letter to the Government of India, mentions his own suggestions that a samasthan member be placed on the Nizam's Executive Council. The individual Keyes had in mind was none other than young Jagannath Rao's uncle, Krishna Rao. Keyes writes:

> His Exalted Highness agreed that it was advisable to appoint a Hindu to Council when Maharaja Sir Kishen Pershad goes . . . His Exalted Highness is rather bitten with my suggestion that he should think over some of the members of the Samasthan families, as they, while being genuine Hindus (unlike Kishen Pershad who is half a Muhammadan and has had three Muhammadan wives and several children who are brought up as Muhammadans), represented the landed classes, stability and the "State" patriotism. The one I know who should make a good Member is the uncle of the young Raja of Jatprole. He is broad-minded, intelligent and enterprising. He at one time kept his own pack of hounds, and now hunts in Madras. He is closely connected with the Rajas of Bobbili and Venkatagiri in the Madras presidency; and is probably known to the Viceroy.[111]

Krishna Rao, like Lakshma Rao before him, came from the political milieu of the Madras Presidency. He likely knew the right people, practiced the right hobbies, and was related to the right families. Further, young and dashing Krishna Rao represented the samasthan, and more broadly the "landed classes" and "stability," important components of Hyderabad's composite political fabric. Keyes considered the idea before leaving office. However, he was "warned off" further action on the matter.

> I advised him to give, first to some minor office to, and then bring into Council, Krishna Rao, uncle of the Raja of Jatprole, who is a sporting

> young fellow who had his own pack of hounds, and has taken his pilot's certificate. I had to drop this idea when I was warned off reforms by Watson; but the increase in Members and the addition of a Hindu must come to the fore any day now.[112]

Tragically, even if the Nizam had wanted to appoint Krishna Rao to the Executive Council, the dashing Uncle died in a plane crash in August 1935.

By the 1930s, Hyderabad State's three largest samasthans had all negotiated successions to the next generation of rulers. At Wanaparthi, young Rameshwar Rao III remained firmly under the Court of Wards umbrella while issues regarding the nature of his samasthan, the applicability of Hindu or Muslim law, and the uses of "history" had all been resolved. At Gadwal, Rani Adi Lakshmi administered the samasthan with help from the Nizam's government and Court of Wards after defusing a potentially violent clash, and seeing her plight become entangled in the larger fray of south India's political and communal tensions. At Jatprole, for reasons of intrafamily linkages and Lakshma Rao's position among a great generation of rulers, he helped keep his samasthan out the Court of Wards and continuing along a path of sound administration and management. Each samasthan, embedded within Hyderabad's composite geographical and political realm, was able to preserve its integrity at the critical moment of succession. All three samasthans' rajas would emerge from the Court of Wards, or a period of Regency, to rule again, if only for the last fading years of Hyderabad State.

Conclusion

In February 1937, one year late, Mir Osman Ali Khan celebrated his silver jubilee. While his reign was marked with various innovations and reforms, it is from this point that the sun began to set on Hyderabad and the samasthans. In the decade prior to India's independence, the Nizam undertook a series of evaluative steps and reforms. Osman Ali Khan faced growing pressure from the Residency as well as the swelling nationalist and independence movement to make changes in his government. During the first year of India's independence, Hyderabad State remained outside of the new Indian union as the Nizam fostered hopes of creating an independent state of his own. However, those dreams were short lived. As Hyderabad was forcefully integrated with the rest of India, the Nizam's reign as well as that of the samasthan rajas came to an abrupt end.

Once India attained independence, the samasthan rajas twice entered into negotiations, first with the military governor of Hyderabad and then with the Indian government. On both the occasions, the core issue was how the samasthans were to be defined, and what financial compensation was to be given based on this definition. Their identity as valuable members of Hyderabad's composite political and social milieu was never in doubt, yet when a rupee amount was to be attached to their estates, and their rank vis-à-vis each other and Hyderabad's other landholders was to be determined, the families contested the way in which they were defined by the interim Hyderabad government. They used their history (as descendents of pre-Muslim Deccan empires, and as valuable buttresses to the Golconda and Asaf Jah regimes) to distinguish their status from that of the *paigah* and *jagirdar* estates. Between these periods of negotiation and dispute, in the fall of 1949, the samasthan rajas handed over their domains to the interim Hyderabad government. In these last events, continuity with older ceremonial practices commingled with ideas central to the new Indian nation.

"Tower of Strength"

At his silver jubilee celebration in 1937, the Nizam delivered a speech in which he clearly articulated the position of the state's nobility. "My principle has always been," he said,

> that, as far as possible, Jagirs should continue to be preserved and that they should be saved from extinction. But this, to some extent, rests with the Jagirdars themselves. If they keep themselves free from the burden of debt and avoid litigation in matters of succession and look after the management of their Jagirs well, specially if they make efforts for the well-being of their tenants, I have every hope that this class will prove a tower of strength and a source of pride to the State.[1]

In this context, the *jagirdars* the Nizam spoke of included the samasthan rajas and *paigah* nobles. Permeating his speech was the confidence and paternalism that only the head of India's premier princely state could summon. That the *jagirs* should be "saved from extinction" alluded to the Nizam's own power to absorb them via the Court of Wards, and references to litigation and succession were aimed, in part, at the samasthan families who were regularly engaged in these costly affairs. Yet, temporarily, other events overtook any further discussion or reform within the state's landholding tenures.

World War II erupted in Europe, and the Nizam gave generously to Britain, donating some 25 million pounds sterling. At the war's end, Hyderabad pressed for the return of lands ceded to the Company and Crown dating from the late eighteenth century. These negotiations were carried out by the state's prime minister, the Nawab of Chattari, who also served as president of the Executive Council. Particularly important were the rich agricultural fields of Berar as well as the ceded coastal districts that would give Hyderabad access to the sea. Any bid for independence by Hyderabad would depend largely on sea access both for economic and military reasons. In addition to the Berar issue, the granting of dominion status to Hyderabad and the accession of the state to the Indian Union were the major talking points between the Hyderabad delegation and members of the Political Department.[2] While no progress was made on those fronts, the Government of India did cede to the Nizam a small section of the Secunderabad cantonment area.

Returning to domestic reforms, in early 1947 the Nizam ordered a commission to investigate the circumstances and problems within the samasthans, *paigahs*, and *jagirs*. The commission began its work in January and completed it by May. Perhaps as the idea of granting independence to India grew certain, the Nizam sought to shore up his domestic political house. A report that evaluated and made recommendations toward some reforms of the samasthans, *paigahs*, and *jagirs* would go some way toward this end. The chairman was Sir Albion Rajkumar Banerji, former *dewan* of Mysore; six other members of the state's elite rounded out the panel, including Raja Someshwar Rao of the Domakonda samasthan.

The commission's findings included suggestions for reform in most areas of administration, but its members were not in full agreement. Someshwar Rao gave his signature to the final report, subject to a minute of dissent. His objections are illustrative of the unique position he and the samasthan rajas saw themselves in. Far from being defined as a kind of *jagir*, Someshwar Rao argued that the samasthans were unique within Hyderabad and thus deserved special consideration. His main point of dissent surrounded the samasthans' payment of *peshkush*. He began his comments by reminding the commission that the samasthans were fundamentally different in their origins from the *jagirs* and *paigahs*. "These Samasthans were not free grants but were the creation of the Rajas themselves. They are in a more compact form, as these Rajas consolidated their villages to facilitate better administration and protect their ryots from outside interference, intrusion and aggression."[3] He then explained the nature of the payment made by the samasthan families to the different rulers of the Deccan.

> Having done so much, these Rajas at the ascendancy of every ruling dynasty over the Deccan considered it safe to pay some annual amount as tribute, which is called Peshkash, to the successive rulers of the Deccan, in recognition of the latter's suzerainty over them. The rulers in return protected them from foreign invasion and never interfered with the internal administration by the Rajas.[4]

Payment by the samasthans was not in return for land grants, as was the case with the *paigahs* or *jagirs*, but represented the continuation of a preexisting practice that stretched back to the Kakatiya and Vijayanagar empires.

What Someshwar Rao sought was the abolishment of *peshkush*, and a uniform tax applied to the samasthans and *jagirs* alike, to cover expenses incurred by the government on their behalf. By way of comparison, he referred to the land reforms in Mysore where such payments were abolished.

> It would be sheer justice and a gracious gesture on the part of the Government if the Peshkash, an old-time remnant, is abolished, as has

> been done in the case of Mysore by the Paramount Power. If a just and uniform policy in regard to all the Jagirs is to be adopted, it can only be done if the Peshkash is abolished and the Samasthans, like the other Jagirs are taxed in a uniform manner.[5]

His suggestion would entail the end of a practice that had bound the samasthan families to the powers at Golconda and Hyderabad, and assured them of their survival. By the mid-twentieth century, such ceremonial payments as *peshkush*—even to the samasthan rajas—seemed outdated, and a type of "uniform tax" seemed more equitable.

However, events much larger than the issue of *peshkush* overtook Someshwar Rao's minute of dissent and the commission's report. In August 1947, India was free, and all but three of its princely states had joined either India or Pakistan. Hyderabad, Kashmir, and Junagadh held out. While the latter was soon invaded by India, and while Kashmir has remained a tragically embattled state to the present day, Hyderabad "stood still." The issue of *peshkush* or a uniform tax gave way to whether Hyderabad State itself was to survive. Three months after India had made its "tryst with destiny," the Nizam signed a standstill agreement with Prime Minister Nehru, thus buying each side time to negotiate an end to the impasse. Since India had been partitioned along largely religious and communal lines, Osman Ali Khan could not easily join either India or Pakistan. As a Muslim, he identified with the goals of Mohammad Ali Jinnah, Pakistan's founder, in seeking a homeland for South Asia's Muslim community and wanting to avoid becoming a permanent minority in a dominantly Hindu India. Yet, the population of Hyderabad was predominantly Hindu, and following the same communal logic, Hyderabad belonged with India. By early fall of 1948, Sardar Vallabhbhai Patel, Nehru's deputy prime minister, lost his patience with the Nizam and ordered a police action dubbed "Operation Polo." In fact, this was a military operation, and India's army quickly subdued Hyderabad's forces.[6] The Nizam, tired of negotiation and bloodshed, settled with Nehru and allowed the integration of Hyderabad State into the Indian union. He retired to his palace and was rarely seen in public.

Reform and Refusal

In early 1949, two years after independence and a year after Hyderabad's annexation by the Indian Union, the samasthan rajas—facing dissolution—proposed changes to the way their territories were being defined for the purpose of compensation by the government. Landholders from the Nizam down to the smallest *jagir* were to be compensated as their lands became the property of the state. They would be allowed to keep properties clearly belonging directly to the family: palaces, gardens, and some agricultural land, but the rest was to be turned over.[7] As such, the samasthan rajas sought the best possible compensation. To do this required defining themselves differently from their *paigah* and *jagir* counterparts, a tactic different from Someshwar Rao's minute of dissent from a decade earlier. Even as their epitaphs were being carved, their definition continued to be debated within the nascent Indian state.

The initial foray by the group came in a letter to the military governor of Hyderabad, J.N. Chaudhuri. Twelve heads of samasthans signed the letter requesting the military governor to extend the discussion on *jagir* administration in the state to avoid a rushed and unfair judgment.[8] At stake was the compensation to be allotted to the samasthan families. If they were defined as *jagirs*, their compensation would be less than if they were defined in their own right as samasthans. A week later a second petition was again addressed to Chaudhuri by the samasthan heads. This time the authors made five major claims regarding their identity, followed by a point-by-point rebuttal to the proposed *jagir* reform. First, "That the memorialists beg to submit that their status is different and distinct from that of the Jagirdars so called."[9] The second point claimed that the samasthans' legal status was different from that of the *jagirs*. Third, "[t]hat while they are desirous and anxious to co-operate with Government in regard to their general policy with regard to this question, they beg that in reaching final conclusions on this matter, their special status and position ought not to be disregarded."[10] The grounds for their "special status" are illuminated in later correspondence, but in short, the samasthan heads rightly claimed that their origin predated the Asaf Jah dynasty, and thus their relationship to their land was fundamentally different from the relationship bestowed by the Asaf Jah rulers on the *paigahs* and *jagirdars*. The fourth claimed suggested that each samasthan engage in individual and direct bilateral negotiations with the government concerning their financial settlements. From the rani of Gadwal and of Amarchinta to the rajas of Wanaparthi and Jatprole, the samasthan leaders saw themselves as states within a state, commanding the right to negotiate on their own terms.

But the memorialists' letter to Chaudhuri seems to have fallen on deaf ears, and by late May they again addressed their claims to the secretary of the Ministry of States in New Delhi *through* Chaudhuri. The letter, in continuation of their 26 February 1949 correspondence, was entitled "Draft Jagir Administration Regulation Memorial Submitting Points of

Difference Between Samasthans and Jagirs." Their first point of disagreement with the draft *jagir* regulation came from the nature of the ruler's tenure in a samasthan as opposed to a *jagir*. The regulation stated that the grant of both *jagirdars* and samasthan holders was for the lifetime of the holder only. While this was true for the *jagirdars*, the samasthans in fact enjoyed de facto perpetual hereditary rights. The second point extends the definition of the samasthans further noting that:

> while Jagirs were specific grants made by the Asaf Jahi Kings or their predecessors in consideration of past services or as marks of favour, the same kind of characterization cannot be made in the case of Samasthans which were in existence long before the Asaf Jahi dynasty came to power in Hyderabad and whose origin was generally independent of any grant.[11]

The preexistence of the samasthans made them different from *jagirs*, and as the memorialists continued, even if the Asaf Jahi dynasty confirmed their successions, that should not have fundamentally changed their unique nature. "These memorialists submit that it would be contrary to all principles of justice, equity and good conscience to say that although the nature of an estate at its origin was a perpetual one, still because of confirmation by the Asaf Jahi Kings, or by their sanctioning recognition of the succession to these estates, they have lost their original character."[12] Again, the samasthan rajas sought a distinct definition for their estates. Origin, succession, geography, and service are elements that they repeatedly included in their arguments for a distinct identification.

Handover

Despite ongoing contestations and definitional wrangling, in September of 1949, the samasthan rajas were about to take center stage for the last time. In a five-day period, six of the samasthans, as well as the *paigahs* and many *jagirs*, would sign instruments of accession, thus ending their existence. Working under Chaudhuri was L.N. Gupta, *Jagir* Administrator. On 7 September he sent notification to the rajas and other landholders of their accession order and dates. Wanaparthi would be first on 15 September followed by Gadwal and Gopalpet two days later, Amarchinta on 18, Paloncha on 19, and Jatprole on 20.[13] These final acts were out of any ceremonial order. Gadwal might have been first, followed by Wanaparthi and Jatprole, yet the heyday of ceremonialism and ranking of the samasthans was over. Only ceremonial courtesies could now be paid on a local and individual level. What then was this final accession ceremony to look like? Like the durbars of earlier times, the handover would be meticulously organized and would recognize, one last time, the medieval origins of the samasthans. Wanaparthi's was the first such ceremony, and an examination of its course is indicative of what transpired that week.

In 1949, Rameshwar Rao III had been guiding Wanaparthi as raja since he assumed control four years earlier. From the Ramsagar Palace in Wanaparthi town, he carefully managed the arrangements for the ceremony. In a letter to Chaudhuri, Rameshwar Rao outlined the plan for the day. "After I speak on the occasion, the keys of the Treasury and the seals of office would be presented to you. Then we expect you would say a few words taking over charge of the administration. All this would take place in a sort of formal Durbar."[14] In addition, Rameshwar Rao asked that Chaudhuri lay the cornerstone for the Sarala Sagar Dam project, and that Gupta might also address the gathering. Chaudhuri responded, making a few changes to the proposed schedule. He added, "As regards the Darbar, as this will be an extremely historic occasion, it would be a good thing in my opinion if all concerned were suitably dressed for the occasion. We are perhaps a little apt to get slack over dress, particularly on such ceremonial occasions and I am sure, you will agree with me here."[15] Chaudhuri's concern over dress and ceremony echoes sentiments that had been expressed by Hyderabad's nobles for centuries—from Rameshwar Rao's great-grandfather requesting the Nizam to update his uniforms, to Mahbub Ali Khan's own orders governing dress for his durbars, this concern and practice had long antecedents. These comments also reveal that the time when appropriately formal dress for a durbar was automatically assumed had now passed. In addition to being an important event, the durbar would be attended by the press and by residents of Wanaparthi town. In the spirit of Lord Lytton, a "bit of bunting" was necessary.[16] Chaudhuri's comments were nuanced by his later suggestion that Rameshwar Rao does not "make any special arrangements for catering, etc. In the long run we are both, I think, basically simple people and appreciate simplicity rather than anything else."[17] The durbar would be a public event with an audience looking on while a later dinner between the two men was a private affair and thus more relaxed.

The durbar itself was to be divided into five main events. These were carefully ordered in advance so the affair would proceed without incident. First, Rameshwar Rao would address the crowd. Then, immediately following his speech, trays would be brought forward bearing the seals of office, a garland, and the key to the treasury. The raja would present these to Chaudhuri, and this would be followed by a short speech by Gupta. An address on behalf of the residents of Wanaparthi was then to be made, followed by a brief address by Chaudhuri. The whole affair would close with a prayer.

As the crowd and guests settled into their seats, Rameshwar Rao rose to address them. His speech (delivered in English) recounted the samasthan's history, his own achievements as raja, and finally, a glimpse of the future. He began by recalling Wanaparthi's origins "as a feudatory chief of the ancient forgotten empire of Vijayanagara." He reminded the guests that the family and samasthan had served the sultans of Golconda, the Mughals, and then the Asaf Jahs. "It is with pride and gratification that we can look back and say that throughout this period we have never bowed our heads before insolent might."[18] While the samasthan served these larger regimes, Rameshwar Rao reminded the audience that Wanaparthi had maintained its authority (and implied dignity) in relations to higher powers. Looking to the present and future, he highlighted the projects still to be completed, including the Sarala Sagara Irrigation Project. At that time only half complete, it would eventually irrigate over 4,500 acres in the area around Wanaparthi town. Rameshwar Rao thanked his uncle, Ram Dev Rao, not present that day, for his guidance and cooperation. Although years earlier the two had been party to a succession struggle, they had long since mended differences between them. As he handed over the keys to the major general, closing the curtain on the history of his samasthan, Rameshwar Rao said, "This would probably be the last official act I perform as the ruler of this Samasthan and as a parting request I ask my people to cooperate with the new administration to their utmost as they have done with me in the past and help in making the change smooth and dignified."[19]

L.N. Gupta, the *Jagir* Administrator spoke next, and was followed by an address to Chaudhuri given on behalf of the "Public of Mahbubnagar." The address marked a new sense of public and democratic participation in government that had taken hold, and this, in the eyes of the authors, extended not just to the residents of Wanaparthi, but included the entire district. This brief "Welcome Address" praised the work that Chaudhuri had been doing as military governor, complemented the work of Lady Chaudhuri for her work, and reflected positively on the short administration of Rameshwar Rao as raja. In praise of the *jagir* regulations being implemented, the address stated, "This regulation is a great step forward in the amelioration of the lot of Common man [*sic*] which was so dear to the heart of our great Leader, and Father of the Nation, Mahatma Gandhi."[20] Thus a link was forged between the change at Wanaparthi, the plight of the common man, and the creation of a new nation. Commenting on the transition from feudal to more democratic landholding schemes, the *Deccan Chronicle* noted, "It is but proper that in a country like India, where Agriculture is the bedrock of national economy that there should be no intermediary between the landholder and the Government."[21]

By 1950, the government was in the process of settling the commutation of the samasthans. Yet, even at this late date, the definition of a samasthan and the nuances between Hyderabad State's landholders was still contested terrain. In January of that year, the government published the "Hyderabad *Jagirs* (Commutation) Regulation." This regulation allowed that each landholder would be paid for his lands based on a standard calculation. Payment was fixed in relation to annual revenue. An important caveat in this calculation was that those estates listed as *jamiat jagirs* would reduce their calculation of annual income by 20 percent.[22] Among the estates listed as *jamiat jagirs* were Gadwal and Wanaparthi. With a reduction in the samasthan's calculated income, and commutation at hand, Rameshwar Rao challenged the classification of Wanaparthi as a *jamiat jagir*. In a petition addressed to the chief minister of Hyderabad State, Rameshwar Rao contended that "The classification of Wanaparthi Samasthan as a 'Jamiat *Jagir*' is unwarranted and is the result of the improper appreciation of the nature of the tenure of the Samasthan."[23] To bolster this claim, a body of experts' testimony was included. The jurist Alladi Krishna Swami stated that the samasthan was held on *bilmakta*, or a fixed payment, with no clause for service Moulvi Ahammed Shareef also stated that the samasthan paid an annual *peshkush*, and that this was not related to maintenance of troops. Further, the petition amply quoted the earlier *Report of the Royal Commission on Jagir Administration and Reforms* to establish specifically which territories were the *jamiat jagirs*, and to clearly show that Wanaparthi did not belong to that group. Wanaparthi, which, along with Gadwal was listed in 1950 as a *jamiat jagir* (a *jagir* who provided troops). This was done during the time of the interim Government of Hyderabad while all of the estates were being dismantled. The government considered Wanaparthi a *jamiat jagir* because over the years, Rs. 16,000 was withheld from the *peshkush* for *jamiat hamrahi* (personal escort) of the Wanaparthi rajas. However, had the funds been for the maintenance of troops, it would have been labeled *nigahdasht jamiat* (government troops). This distinction was critical in fixing the true income of the samasthan, and the compensation that was eventually given to Rameshwar Rao III and his family.[24]

Conclusion

The samasthans are now gone. One by one, their rulers signed accession documents. The interim Hyderabad government gave the families that had ruled the samasthans compensation for the loss of their territories. Many of the employees of the samasthan administrations were incorporated into the new Hyderabad government. Residents of the samasthans watched as "their rajas" either faded from public view or assumed new positions within a new state and nation. Further, they watched as new forms of democratic governance made their way to the samasthan capitals and their villages.

The last Nizam and the nobles who served under him faced sharp criticism for their seeming "backwardness." For instance, freedom fighter and later diplomat K.M. Munshi's claim that the *jagirdars* (a title that he lumped the samasthans under) held power "at the sweet will of the Nizam" is clearly an overstatement.[25] In fact, as we have seen, much of the Nizam's power rested on the support (financially and militarily) of these polities, and his "sweet will" was tempered by legal institutions such as the Court of Wards. Up to and through the nineteenth century, the samasthan kingdoms provided both military service and tribute to their overlords. In return, first the Qutb Shahs of Golconda and then the Asaf Jahs of Hyderabad granted them a considerable degree of autonomy. By the late nineteenth century, under the reforms of Salar Jung and the increasing influence of the British Raj, peace had broken out within the Deccan, and the samasthans were no longer called upon to provide military service. Where the ability to command troops once signified rank within Hyderabad's durbar, the ensuing vacuum was filled with court ceremonialism. The samasthan rulers vied with each other and other court nobles for ceremonial honors that reaffirmed and cemented their position within the state's composite hierarchy. They competed for accoutrements such as titles, elephants, and visits by the Nizam. The sixth and seventh Nizams, Mahbub Ali Khan and Osman Ali Khan, used court ceremony to bind together the myriad of Hyderabad's nobles. This ensured their loyalty, revenue, and some degree of peace.

But ceremonialism could not mediate every situation or resolve every dispute. At the end of the nineteenth century, the Hyderabad government implemented a legal venue for resolution of disputes. The Court of Wards juggled lingering ceremonialism and "interference" by the Nizams, but largely was able to provide for the samasthan heirs and its other wards. The samasthan rulers were brought into the Court when no heir was available. The majority of the samasthan families found themselves within the Court at one time or another. At times, the families and the Court had an adversarial relationship (as seen with Gadwal), while at other times they were able to avoid the Court entirely (as seen with Jatprole). For the Hyderabad government, the Court was a means to direct the fate of these estates and prevent them from repeated partitions. The Court's work also helped assure that the samasthans paid revenue, and at times, served to modernize the estates within its charge.

In conclusion, two further points can be made concerning the samasthans of Hyderabad. While Hindu rulers governed the samasthans, their overlords were Muslim. This might have been an invitation for communal tension, yet evidence suggests that when tension arose it was mediated. Further, power was negotiated between the samasthan rajas, the Nizams, and the British. This ability to mediate and negotiate becomes more important in the twentieth century as much of the subcontinent became plagued by communal conflict. This suggests that the strategies of accommodation and compositeness (economic, ceremonial, and legal) within Hyderabad State helped keep communalism at bay. Further, this offers modern India another local model of positive relations between Hindu and Muslim communities. Second, work on Hyderabad and the princely states of India has largely focused on relationships between elites; studies on the Nizams and their British counterparts are abundant. Here I have sought to redirect attention to the vertical structure of Hyderabad, shifting our gaze from the metropolis to the countryside, and to local history. By examining local records, such as those proffered by the Court of Wards and the families themselves, we can recover the voices of those who have not yet been heard; many of the samasthan and zamindar histories remain to be told. Perhaps, like those within Hyderabad examined here, their family records still exist and await the inquisitive historian's discovery. Their histories can add valuable accounts of power-holders at the local level. Finally, as Mukerhjee reminds us, "Many today feel that if only there had been no zamindars, everything would have been perfect. But there *were* zamindars and whether we like it or not, we, as students of history, have to take notice of what they said or did."[26]

There are many competent histories on different aspects of Hyderabad State; yet the state's history continues to be viewed as the city's history, thus leaving the people and affairs of the countryside largely untouched. Further, the institution of the Court of Wards connected Hyderabad with much of the subcontinent. These Courts played an important role in the internal administration of Hyderabad State as well as in the presidencies. While some tightly focused work has been done on particular local Courts, a broad history of their function across the subcontinent remains to be done. The samasthans within Hyderabad's dominions participated in a network of adoptions and marriages that not only crisscrossed Hyderabad, but extended beyond into the Madras Presidency. Histories of southern India have tended to focus on political divisions, for instance, on the Madras Presidency *or* on Hyderabad State. But, as we have seen, the samasthan families (and certainly other nobles) participated in a network of connections that crossed these political boundaries. As seen in the generation of Velama kings in the Madras Presidency and Hyderabad State, a new and different image of politics in south India emerges as connections between the two states are examined. Within Hyderabad and perhaps many other princely states, we still do not know enough about their internal workings. Work that focuses on princely states is abundant, but these works restrict themselves to discussion on the relations with the Raj; thus we could further profit by examining princely states' internal composition and administration. This work has brought to light elements of Hyderabad's internal, multiethnic structure, taking the samasthans as examples; yet one could easily take up the *paigahs* or *jagirs* as well. In the same way, in-depth histories of any one samasthan would be a valuable contribution to local history as well as to that of Hyderabad State. Reflecting on Hyderabad, Theodore Tasker suggested that it was "an important political fact" that they (the samasthans) continued "being."[27] To some degree, it is hoped that this work has explained this "being," and how these samasthans survived and made vital contributions to India's premier princely state.

Appendices

Appendix 1

Nizam's of Hyderabad

Mir Qamaruddin Chin Qilij Khan	Asaf Jah I	1724–1748
Mir Ahmad Khan	Nasir Jung	1748–1750
Hidayat Mohiuddin Khan	Muzaffar Jung	1750–1751
Syed Muhammed Khan	Salabat Jung	1751–1762
Mir Nizam Ali Khan	Asaf Jah II	1762–1802
Mir Akbar Ali Khan	Sikandar Jah, Asaf Jah III	1802–1829
Mir Farqunda Ali Khan	Nasir ud daula, Asaf Jah IV	1829–1857
Mir Tahniat Ali Khan	Afzal ud daula, Asaf Jah V	1857–1869
Mir Mahbub Ali Khan	Asaf Jah VI	1869–1911
Mir Osman Ali Khan	Asaf Jah VII	1911–1948

Appendix 2

Residents of Hyderabad

Date of Assumption of Office	
John Holland	16 April 1779
James Grant	2 July 1781
Richard Johnson	20 January 1784
John Kennaway	28 April 1788
William Kirkpatrick	15 November 1797
James Achilles Kirkpatrick	18 September 1798
Henry Russell	1 September 1805
Thomas Sydenham	3 January 1806
*Charles Russell	20 May 1810
Henry Russell	17 April 1811

Charles Theophilus Metcalfe	1 December 1820
*Hugh Laird Barnett	4 August 1825
William Byam Martin	29 September 1825
*Edward Cockburn Ravenshaw	7 August 1830
Josiah Steward	6 November 1830
*James Cameron	12 January 1838
*James Wahab	16 June 1838
*George Tomkyns	8 July 1838
James Stuart Fraser	1 September 1838
*Cuthbert Davidson	11 December 1852
*John Low	7 March 1853
Cuthbert Davidson	5 September 1853
George Alexander Bushby	1 December 1853
*Anthony Robert Thornhill	31 December 1856
Cuthbert Davidson	16 April 1857
Anthony Robert Thornhill	31 December 1862
George Udny Yule	31 January 1863
Richard Temple	14 April 1867
*John Graham Cordery	5 January 1868
Charles Burslem Saunders	10 June 1868
*Peter Stark Lumsden	16 July 1872
Charles Burslem Saunders	11 October 1872
Richard John Meade	5 December 1875
Steuart Colvin Bayley	24 March 1881
*George Herbert Trevor	1 June 1882
John Graham Cordery	21 April 1883
Oliver B. Coventry St. John	10 April 1884
John Graham Cordery	10 July 1884
*Edward Charles Ross	12 April 1886
John Graham Cordery	15 October 1886
*Donald Robertson	1 November 1887
John Graham Cordery	1 December 1887
*Arthur Pearse Howell	14 March 1888
Dennis Fitzpatrick	6 August 1889
Trevor John Chichele-Plowden	12 November 1891
*Kenneth James Lock Mackenzie	23 March 1895
Trevor John Chichele-Plowden	14 October 1895
*James Adair Crawford	30 July 1898
Trevor John Chichele-Plowden	31 October 1898
David William Keith Barr	24 February 1900
Charles Stuart Bayley	1 March 1905
*Michael Francis O'Dwyer	14 May 1908
Charles Stuart Bayley	29 November 1908
*Evelyn Berkeley Howell	14 August 1909
*Michael Francis O'Dwyer	24 April 1909

Charles Stuart Bayley	4 December 1909
Alexander Fleetwood Pinhey	24 February 1911
Stuart Mitford Fraser	8 March 1914
Alexander Fleetwood Pinhey	29 October 1914
*Alfred Beckett Minchin	8 April 1916
Stuart Mitford Fraser	25 July 1916
Charles Lennox Somerville Russell	1 January 1921
*Stuart George Knox	1 November 1921
Charles Lennox Somerville Russell	1 November 1922
William Paton Barton	1 July 1925
*Leslie Maurice Crump	20 May 1927
William Paton Barton	27 November 1927
Terence Humphrey Keyes	9 February 1930
Duncan George Mackenzie	1 July 1933
*John Creery Tate	3 May 1934
Duncan George Mackenzie	9 November 1934
*Claude Henry Gidney	23 April 1937
Duncan George Mackenzie	23 October 1937
Claude Henry Gidney	30 October 1938
Arthur Cunningham Lothian	15 October 1942
Charles Gordon Herbert	25 November 1946

* Officiating or acting Residents.

Appendix 3

Heads of Gadwal Samasthan

Pedda Veera Reddy aka Venkatabhuapaladu
Peddanna Bhupaladu
Sarga Reddy
Veera Reddy
Kumara Veera Reddy
Lingamma
Somanna
Ammakka and Lingamma
Thirumal Rao
Mangamma and Chokamma
Pedda Ram Rao
Somanna aka Sombhupal I
Rambhupal I
Sita Rambhupal I
Venkatlakshmamma
Sombhupal II
Venkatlakshmamma
Rambhupal II

Raja Sita Rambhupal II
Raja Krishna Rambhupal

Appendix 4

Heads of Jatprole Samasthan

Pillalamari Bethala Naidu aka Chevi Reddy
Damara Naidu
Vennama Naidu
Dacha Naidu aka Erradacha
Singama Naidu
Annapotha Naidu
Dharma Naidu
Thimma Naidu
Chitti Daccha Naidu
Annapotha Naidu
Chinnamada Naidu
Errasoora Naidu
Madha Naidu
Mulla Naidu
Peda Naidu
Mulla Bhupati
Pedamalla Naidu
Mulla Bhupati
Madhava Raidu
Narasingha Raidu
Chinna Madhava Rao
Bari Gadupala Rao
Pedda Rama Raidu
Pedda Jagannath Rao I
Venkat Lakshma Rao I
Venkat Jagannath Rao II
Venkat Lakshma Rao II
Jagannath Rao III

Appendix 5

Heads of Wanaparthi Samasthan

Veer Krishna Reddy
Venkat Kumar Rao I
Ram Krishna Reddy
Pedda Venkat Reddy I
Immidid Venkat Reddy II

Ashta Basha Bahairi Gopal Rao II
Gopal Rao III
Janamma
Suvai Venkat Reddy
Bahiri Gopal Rao IV
Suvai Venkat Reddy IV
Bahiri Gopal Rao V
Raja Ram Krishna Rao II
Raja Rameshwar Rao I
Raja Ram Krishna Rao III
Maharaja Rameshwar Rao II
Raja Rameshwar Rao III

Glossary

Ashrafi	Gold coin
Bahiri	Eagle
Bajra	A type of millet
Beriz	Total amount of revenue assessment
Bil-maqta	Land given to an influential person in return for an annual fixed cash rent
Dasi	Slave. Also prostitute
Deshmukh	Officer exercising limited police and/or revenue authority over a district
Dewan	Revenue minister
Dewani	The office, jurisdiction, emoluments of the *Dewan*
Doab	Land between two rivers
Durbar	A ruler's court, the administration of his or her state and the ceremonies therein
Fauj	Army
Firman	Imperial order or edict
Gaddi	Cushion. Used here as the royal throne ensemble of a Hindu ruler including cushion and chair
Habshi, Habashi	Ethiopian
Har	Jeweled neckware
Ilaqa	A property, an estate. *Ilaqadar:* one who has or possesses property. In Hyderabad State, the premier type of *jagirdar*
Inam	Gifted hereditary rent-free land grant
Izzat	Personal honor, prestige, reputation
Jagir	A land tenure in which public revenues were made over to a servant of the state. *Jagirdar:* one who has or possess. *Al-tamgha:* as special favors, revenue-free, permanent, perpetual, and hereditary. *Jamiat:* for maintenance and provision of troops. *Madad mash:* for the

	maintenance of the recipient. *Mashrooti:* for the maintenance of some service. *Mokassa:* for a special purpose or individual who remitted one-fourth or one-third of the revenue. *Tankha*: for the salary of those rendering some service. *Zat:* for the maintenance of the grantee
Jamadar	Local military commander
Jambia	Dagger, sword, knife
Jaridah	A register, account book, an official notice or publication in such
Jatra	Fair, market; annual festival of a Hindu temple
Jawan	Soldier or police officer. Literally "a young man"
Jawar	A type of millet
Jinn	Ghost, spirit
Khalsa	Lands from which a ruler directly collects revenue
Khilat	Robe of honor, presented with title or appointment to nobility
Khutba	Friday prayer
Kotwal	Police chief
Lakh	100,000
Mahal	District, palace
Majlis	Board or court; an assembly
Makhta	Fixed rate or rent; land of that nature. *Makhtadar*, one who has or possess
Mala	The Telugu equivalent of an outcaste
Muniwar	Traditional police official
Masnad	Throne
Mohur	Gold coin; a seal or seal ring
Maulvi	Muslim legal scholar, learned man
Mufassal	Countryside, provinces
Mulki	Son of the soil, indigenous. Used in distinction to non-*mulki* or outsider
Nagagoud	Authority to administer and rule land
Nayaka, naik	A leader or chief; head of a small body of soldiers
Nazim	Chief administrator; supervisor
Nazr	Gift, usually gold; a present or offering
Nizam	Title of Hyderabad ruler
Paigah	Lands held on military tenure by certain noblemen
Pan-maqta	Land given in return for an annual fixed cash rent
Pargana	A district, a province, a tract of land
Peshkar	Generally an agent, deputy or manager; in Hyderabad a specific office below that of the minister

Peshkush	Payment, tribute
Poligar	Lesser king, territorial chieftain
Putti	Basket boat
Qiladar	Fort commander
Rajadharma	Duties of a king
Ryot	A subject, cultivator, peasant
Sahookar	Banker, merchant
Samasthan	Hindu noble or chief; area ruled by such a family
Sanad	Royal letter, decree or contract
Sawar	A rider, a horseman
Sherwani	Men's knee-length coat, buttoned at the neck
Shikar	Hunt, hunting
Serishtadar	Record keeper, accountant
Sibbandi	A force, a small army, troops
Sicca	A stamped coin; silver coin used by the Company and princes
Siddi	Muslim African descendant; also *sayyad*
Subah	A province, a large subdivision. *Subahdar:* one who has or possesses
Taluk	District, division of a province, an estate (usually smaller than a zamin) *Talukdar:* one who has or possesses
Toshakhana	Special treasury
Vakil	Agent or intermediary between rulers. Also at times a lawyer
Zamin	Earth, ground, land, soil. *Zamindar:* one who has or possess
Zat	Personal rank held by a Mughal officer

Notes

Introduction

1. "Hyderabad Silver Jubilee Durbar," *Time*, 22 February 1937, p. 20.
2. Mirza Mehdy Khan, *Imperial Gazetteer of India Provincial Series Hyderabad State* (Calcutta: Superintendent of Government Printing, 1909; repr., New Delhi; Atlantic Publishers, 1991), p. 24.
3. Barbara Ramusack has argued that the princes of India provided continuity between India's precolonial and colonial periods, and even into the postcolonial period. Barbara Ramusack, *The Indian Princes and Their States* (Cambridge: Cambridge University Press, 2004), p. 2.
4. Karen Leonard, "The Deccani Synthesis in Old Hyderabad: An Historiographic Essay," *Journal of the Pakistan Historical Society* 30, no. 4 (1973). pp. 205–18.
5. In describing the Gadwal samasthan, then Resident William Barton referred to it as a "little State." Barton to GOI, 7 December 1925, R/1/1/1469, OIOC.
6. Complete information was not available for: Domakonda, Rajapet, Dubbak, Papanapet, and Sirnapalli. Population data was collected from the Gadwal, Wanaparthi, Jatprole, and Amarchinta samasthans. The Gadwal samasthan was in the Raichur district. The population of the Gadwal samasthan grew steadily at about a rate of 4.6% from 1911 to 1931. The population in 1911 was 113,818, in 1921 it dropped to 109,427, but by 1931 was 119,146. In that year, the samasthan had about 125 villages and towns. Nearly 75% of these were villages with a population of 1,000 or less. The largest town was Gadwal with a population of 12,982. In 1931, populations within the Wanaparthi, Jatprole, and Amarchinta samasthans were 90,318, 50,442, and 48,297 respectively. In this same order, these three samasthans had higher population growth rates than those at Gadwal. In the two decades from 1911 to 1931, Wanaparthi grew 20%, Jatprole 30%, and Amarchinta 12%. As in the Gadwal samasthan, the largest town in the Wanaparthi samasthan was Wanaparthi itself with a population of 5,076. Also like the Gadwal samasthan, Wanaparthi, Jatprole, and Amarchinta's majority of inhabitants lived in villages with populations under 1,000. Mazhar Husain, *Hyderabad District Gazetteers: Raichur* (Hyderabad- Deccan: Government Central Press, 1941), pp. 4, 6–7, *Hyderabad*

District Gazetteers: Mahbubnagar (Hyderabad-Deccan: Government Central Press, 1940), pp. 2–3, 6–7.

7. Khan, *Imperial Gazetteer of India Provincial Series Hyderabad State*, pp. 296–99.
8. Government Order 633, 25 June 1914, Political Department, TNA. Wanaparthi, or "Wanparti" is cited in: *The Imperial Gazetteer of India*, vol. XXIV (Oxford: Clarendon Press, 1908), p. 355.
9. The samasthans had already been left out of important official documents such as the 1891 census of Hyderabad State. In that document, when describing the different types "territorial divisions" within the state, no mention is made of the samasthans, and only "*jagirs*" were listed. Mirza Mehdy Khan, *Census of India, 1891. Volume XXIII. His Highness the Nizam's Dominions* (London: Eyre and Spottiswoode, 1894), pp. 28–29.
10. For a full-length treatment of maps and empire to the mid-nineteenth century, see: Matthew H. Edney, *Mapping an Empire* (New Delhi: Oxford University Press, 1999).
11. The relationship between state/nation, imagination, and maps has been addressed by Benedict Anderson in *Imagined Communities* (London: Verso, 1991), pp. 170–78.
12. Political Secretary's Office, file A6, 5 June 1923, APSA.
13. Some exceptions do exist. Chinna Somanna, "The Economic History of the Samsthanas in Mahaboobnagar District (1900–1948)" (MA thesis, Osmania University, 1994).
14. Gadwal samasthan's population was 91% Hindu, with 7% Muslim, and the rest identified as tribal, Christian, Sikh, and one Zoroastrian. Nearly 90% of the Wanaparthi samasthan was Hindu, with 5,624 Muslims (about 6%) and 681 Christians (the most of any samasthan). The ruling family of Wanaparthi was supportive of Christian missionary efforts within the samasthan; thus the overall number of Christians in that samasthan is higher than elsewhere. Jatprole samasthan had 8,831 Muslims, or about 17%. Amarchinta samasthan had 3,332 Muslims, about 6%. Husain, *Hyderabad District Gazetteers: Raichur*, pp. 10–11; *Hyderabad District Gazetteers: Mahbubnagar*, pp. 10–11. Paul D. Wiebe, *Christians in Andhra Pradesh* (Madras: The Christian Literature Society, 1988), p. 75.
15. Gadwal samasthan had 507 Hindu temples, and 59 mosques. In Wanaparthi, Jatprole, and Amarchinta there were 217, 111, and 97 Hindu temples, with 30, 18, and 11 mosques respectively. Husain, *Hyderabad District Gazetteers: Raichur*, pp. 14–15; *Hyderabad District Gazetteers: Mahbubnagar*, pp. 14–15. Some of the larger temples include: the Agasthyesvara Swamy temple near Jatprole, the Madhava Gopala Swamy temple at Kollapur, the Chenna Kesava Swamy temple at Gadwal as well as the nearby Venkateswara Swamy temple, and the Sri Ranganayaka Swamy temple at Srirangapur near Wanaparthi.
16. V. Sadasiva Sastrulu, *Sri Surabhivari Vamsa Charitramu* (Madras: Saradamba Vilasa Press, 1913), pp. 124–25.

17. The samasthan rajas were occasionally visited by guests or requests for information. For instance, from his position within the Madras Presidency, C.P. Brown procured (likely by way of an assistant) a rare Telugu poem ("Sri Kalahasti Mahatmyam") from Gadwal. Peter L. Schmitthenner, *Telugu Resurgence C.P. Brown and Cultural Consolidation in Nineteenth-Century South India* (New Delhi: Manohar, 2001), p. 97, note 72. Another visitor to the Gadwal court in the early nineteenth century was Colin Mackenzie's assistant, Narrain Row. Row was searching for genealogical data about the Gadwal family. Row, Mackenzie, and the raja of Gadwal are all explored in chapter 3.
18. Omar Khalidi, ed., *Memoirs of Cyril Jones* (New Delhi: Manohar, 1991), p. 41.
19. Mazhar Husain, *List of Uruses, Melas, Jatras, Etc. in H.E.H. the Nizam's Dominions 1349f (1940 A.D.)* (Hyderabad: Government Central Press, 1940), p. v.
20. Ibid., pp. 22, 82, 83.
21. Phillip Wagoner, " 'Sultan among Hindu Kings': Dress, Titles and the Islamicization of Hindu Culture at Vijayanagara," *The Journal of Asian Studies* 55, no. 4 (1996): 851–80.
22. S. Nurul Hasan, "Zamindars under the Mughals," in *Land Control and Social Structure in Indian History*, ed. Robert Frykenberg (Madison: University of Wisconsin Press, 1969), pp. 17–32. See also Richard Barnett, *North India between Empires: Awadh, the Mughals, and the British, 1720–1801* (Berkeley: University of California Press, 1980). Thomas Metcalf, *Land, Landlords, and the British Raj* (Berkeley: University of California Press, 1979).
23. *The Imperial Gazetteer of India*, p. 277.
24. Michael H. Fisher, *A Clash of Cultures: Awadh, the British, and the Mughals* (New Delhi: Manohar, 1987), pp. 141–42.
25. Ibid., p. 223.
26. A further comparison could be made with the zamindars of Bengal. For example, they shared with the samasthans an extensive practice of gift giving. John McLane, *Land and Local Kingship in Eighteenth-Century Bengal* (Cambridge: Cambridge University Press, 1993), p. 2. One work that takes up a single Bengal zamindar's life as its focus is that of Nilmani Mukherjee. He has produced an exhaustive work on the life and times of Jaykrishna Mukherjee (1808–1888), zamindar of Uttarpara. Nilmani Mukherjee, *A Bengal Zamindar* (Calcutta: Firma K.L. Mukhopadhyay, 1975). See also Partha Chatterjee who has explored the strange events in the Bhawal estate. Partha Chatterjee, *A Princely Imposter?* (Princeton: Princeton University Press, 2002).
27. Thornton describes this as "[h]aving had for generations to govern and conciliate a large and not unwarlike Hindu population, the ruling classes of Hyderabad are singularly free from religious bigotry." Thomas Henry Thornton, *General Sir Richard Meade and the Feudatory States of Central and South India* (London: Longmans, Green, and Co., 1898), p. 251.

28. Thomas R. Metcalf, "From Raja to Landlord: The Oudh Talukdars, 1850–1870," in *Land Control and Social Structures in Indian History*, ed. Robert E. Frykenberg, (Madison: University of Wisconsin Press, 1969), p. 127.
29. Hyderabad has been the subject of several as of yet unpublished Ph.D. theses. These include: John Roosa, "The Quandary of the Qaum: Indian Nationalism in a Muslim State: Hyderabad 1850–1948" (Ph.D. thesis, University of Wisconsin, 1998), Peter Wood, "Vassal State in the Shadow of Empire: Palmer's Hyderabad, 1799–1867" (Ph.D. thesis, University of Wisconsin, 1981).
30. William Dalrymple, *White Mughals: Love and Betrayal in Eighteenth-Century India* (London: HarperCollins, 2002), especially the note, p. xxxviii. A welcome corrective to this lacuna is Richard Eaton's social history of the precolonial Deccan as told through biographies of eight Indian lives. Through biography, Eaton is able to both bring the detail and color of the early modern Deccan to light, while at the same time stitching together a larger narrative of the region. Richard Eaton, *A Social History of the Deccan, 1300–1761: Eight Indian Lives* (Cambridge: Cambridge University Press, 2005).
31. Karen Leonard, "The Hyderabad Political System and Its Participants," *Journal of Asian Studies* 30, no. 3 (1971). p. 573.
32. K. Krishnaswamy Mudiraj, *Pictorial Hyderabad*, vol. 2 (Hyderabad: Chandrakanth Press, 1934), pp. 618–40.
33. Sastrulu, *Sri Surabhivari Vamsa Charitramu.*
34. Vajapeya Yajula Ramasubbaravu, *Sri Surabhi Venkatalaksmaraya Nijam Navajyant Bahaddarvari Jivitamu* (Hyderabad: Kovvuru, 1929).
35. Rachayata Krishna, *Wanaparthi Samasthana Charitra* (Kurnool: Hyderabad Printers, 1948).
36. *Sri Raja Prathama Rameshwara Rayalu* (Hyderabad: Orient Longman, 1990).
37. A. Mohan Reddy, *Wanaparthi Samasthan Telugu Sahityaseva* (Hyderabad: Orient Longman, 1998), Namatari Venkat Shastri, *Wanaparthi Samasthan Charitra* (Hyderabad: Orient Longman, 1992).
38. Acharya Tumati Donappa, *Andhra Samasthamulu Sahitya Poshammu* (Hyderabad: Pravardana Publications, 1969), Raman Raj Saksenah, *Qadim Dakani Saltanaten Aur Samastan* (Hyderabad: Husami Book Depot, 1996).
39. Harriet Ronken Lynton and Mohini Rajan, *Days of the Beloved* (Berkeley: University of California, 1974), pp. 173–89.
40. Two brief but notable exceptions exist, both by M. Ramulu: "Gadwal Samasthanam: A Study" (MA thesis, Telugu University, 1989), "Gadwala Samsthanam—A Historical Perspective," *Itihas* vol. 16, no.1 (January-June 1990): 117–24.
41. See for instance, the revised edition of an earlier work: Narendra Luther, *Hyderabad a Biography* (New Delhi: Oxford University Press, 2006).
42. Sarojini Regani, *Nizam-British Relations: 1724–1857* (Hyderabad: Booklovers Private Limited, 1963), Vasant Kumar Bawa, *The Nizam*

between the Mughals and British: Hyderabad under Salar Jung I (New Delhi: S.Chand and Co., 1986), Bharati Ray, *Hyderabad and British Paramountcy 1858–1883* (Delhi: Oxford University Press, 1988).

43. See for example: Nani Gopal Chaudhuri, *British Relations with Hyderabad* (Calcutta: University of Calcutta, 1964). Five of seven chapter headings bear the word "interference."
44. Karen Leonard, *Social History of an Indian Caste* (Hyderabad: Orient Longman, 1994).
45. Margrit Pernau, *The Passing of Patrimonialism* (New Delhi: Manohar, 2000).
46. Lucien D. Benichou, *From Autocracy to Integration* (Hyderabad: Orient Longman, 2000), Omar Khalidi, ed., *Hyderabad: After the Fall* (Wichita: Hyderabad Historical Society, 1988).
47. Henry George Briggs, *The Nizam*, vol. 1 (1861; repr., Delhi: Manas Publications, 1985), J.D.B. Gribble, *A History of the Deccan*, vol. 1 (1896; repr., New Delhi: Rupa & Co., 2002).
48. Bernard Cohn, "Political Systems in Eighteenth Century India: The Banaras Region," *Journal of the American Oriental Society* 82, no. 3 (1962): 312–19.
49. Rajayyan further elaborates the role of these territorial chieftains ("little kings") in Tamil Nadu. He writes that the "chiefs" were "a second line of defense against external aggression and as guardians of public order and peace against internal commotion . . . As an intermediary authority, they performed what the rulers normally neglected to do in the field of public welfare. While the common people found it beyond their reach to gain positions in the central administration, they experienced no such difficulty in the poligari establishments. This created and nurtured a bond of affinity between the poligars and the masses." K. Rajayyan, *South Indian Rebellion: The First War of Independence 1800–1801* (Mysore: Wesley Press 1971), pp. 23–24. A *polligar* is a petty chieftain, associated with south India, and existing predominantly through plunder while occasionally being held in-check by an overlord. The term was applied to Gadwal by Mughal Emperor Aurangzeb. "Enclosure No. 1. Memorandum," R/1/1/1469, OIOC.
50. Nicholas B. Dirks, *The Hollow Crown* (Cambridge: Cambridge University Press, 1987).
51. Pamela Price, *Kingship and Political Practice in Colonial India* (New York: Cambridge University Press, 1996).
52. For some summary of the debates surrounding "little kings," see: Rahul Peter Das, "Little Kingdoms and Big Theories of History," *Journal of the American Oriental Society* 117, no. 1 (January-March 1997): 127–34.
53. Ramusack, *The Indian Princes and Their States.*
54. Ian Copland, *State, Community and Neighbourhood in Princely North India, C. 1900–1950* (New York: Palgrave Macmillan, 2005), pp. 23 and 45.
55. For an examination of recent communal problems in Hyderabad city, see Ashutosh Varshney, *Ethnic Conflict and Civic Life* (New Haven: Yale University Press, 2002), pp. 171–200. More historical approaches can be

found in Dick Kooiman, *Communalism and Indian Princely States* (New Delhi: Manohar, 2002), pp. 165–215.

56. P. Sundarayya, *Telangana People's Struggle and Its Lessons* (Calcutta: Desraj Chadha, 1972), pp. 9–10.
57. Leonard, *Social History of an Indian Caste*, p. 571. See also reference to paintings done at the Gadwal and Wanaparthi courts in: George Michell and Mark Zebrowski, *Architecture and Art of the Deccan Sultanates* (Cambridge: Cambridge University Press, 1999), p. 221.
58. Regani, *Nizam-British Relations*. For a broader analysis of the Residency system and indirect rule, see: Michael H. Fisher, *Indirect Rule in India* (Delhi: Oxford University Press, 1991), pp. 386–401.
59. P. Seetapathi, "Introduction," in *Enugula Veeraswamy's Journal*, ed. P. Sitapati and V. Purushottam (Hyderabad: Andhra Pradesh Government Oriental Manuscripts Library & Research Institute, 1973), p. x.
60. Enugula Veeraswamy, *Enugula Veeraswamy's Journal (Kasiyatra Charitra)*, trans. P. Sitapati (Hyderabad: Andhra Pradesh Government Oriental Manuscripts Library & Research Institute, 1973), p. 17.
61. Ibid., p. 18.
62. Syed Siraj ul Hassan, *Castes and Tribes of the Nizam's Dominions*, vol. 2 (New Delhi: Vintage, 1990), p. 340.
63. The English translation employs limited diacritical marks; however, they are not consistently applied nor helpful in understanding commonly used terms (Nizam, zamindar, etc.), thus I have left them off. Veeraswamy, *Enugula Veeraswamy's Journal*, p. 19.
64. Ibid., p. 20.
65. Villages visited by Veeraswamy between the Krishna river and Hyderabad city include Pentapalle, Pangal, Tummagunta, Chinnamandi, Wanaparthi, Cholapuram, Manojipet, Ganapuram, Mulakarra, Koturu, Aluru, Jadcherla, Balanagar, Faruknagar (aka Janampet), Palamakula, Shahpuram, and Hyderabad.
66. Skirmishes occurred not only between one samasthan and another, or against other nobility, but were often types of "civil wars" between family members within one samasthan. Such was the case at Paloncha in the spring of 1798 when the raja and his brother engaged in a protracted battle for power. This battle not only led to the "ruin" of the family, but also to trade within the region. "This civil war lends to the ruin of both parties, as the merchants passing through are liable to many exactions and vexations and the chief resource depending upon the customs levied upon the merchants they must of course suffer a diminution of revenue when no trade is carried on." April 1798, Mss Eur F48, OIOC.
67. Robert E. Frykenberg, "Introduction," in *Land Control and Social Structure in Indian History*, ed. Robert E. Frykenberg (Madison: University of Wisconsin Press, 1969), p. xv.
68. Gribble, *A History of the Deccan*, vol. 2, pp. 5–6.

69. While the samasthans form a specific group within Hyderabad's polity, these rajas were not alone as similar types of rulers and territories can be found elsewhere within the subcontinent. However, the nomenclature becomes increasingly complicated as we move outside of Hyderabad. For instance, in the Madras Presidency there were several notable samasthans: the great Velama estates at Venkatagiri, Bobbili, Pithapuram, and Nuzvid. These families played key roles in the history of the Coromandel Coast. Bobbili was the sight of the infamous "battle of Bobbili," while the rajas of Pithapuram and the other families were generous patrons of the arts during the late nineteenth and early twentieth centuries. Yet, in the literature generated *by* these samasthans, they refer to themselves both as zamindars *and* samasthans without explanation as to the difference. A brief history of Pithapuram can be found in: K. Satayanarayan Varma and C. Papayashastri, *Andhra Bhoja Shri Suryaraya Maharaja Prashti* (Pithapuram: 1966). On Bobbili, see: Velcheru Narayana Rao, David Shulman, and Sanjay Subrahmanyam, *Textures of Time Writing History in South India 1600–1800* (New Delhi: Permanent Black, 2001), pp. 24–92. Velamas are a caste group in southern India, generally holding landlord or royal positions and highly regarded as leaders within their communities. See for example: Alladi Jagannatha Sastri, *A Family History of Venkatagiri Rajas* (Madras: Addison Press, 1922). T. Rama Row, *Biographical Sketches of the Rajahs of Venkatagiri* (Madras: Asiatic Press, 1875). Venkata Swetachalapati Ranga Row, *A Revised and Enlarged Account of the Bobbili Zamandari* (Madras: Addison and Co., 1900). Also, on Velamas, see: Edgar Thurston, *Castes and Tribes of Southern India*, vol. 7 (Madras: Government Press, 1909), pp. 336–42.
70. A late-eighteenth-century account of powers in the Deccan recounts, "Still however some descendants of the ancient Hindoo Princes retained their authority in the Deckan as the Rails [*sic* Royals] of Aneconda [Anagundi] . . ." Mss Eur Mack. General, XLIII, OIOC.
71. In the Madras Presidency, two types of zamindars (really samasthans) existed: those of ancient origin who could not be sold or dismantled, and secondary "ordinary" estates that were the "creation" of the Raj. Of the former, the following were all samasthans, some closely related to those in Hyderabad State: Vijayanagaram, Venkatagiri, Ramnad, Shivaganga, Pithapur, Carvetnagar, Kalahasty, Nidadvole, Nuzvid, Bobbily, Parlakinmedy, and Jeypore. Maclean, C.D. *Manual of the Administration of the Madras Presidency*, vol. 1 (Madras: Government Press, 1885), pp. 54–61 and 119–20.
72. *Nazr* is different from *peshkush* or *beriz*. The former was given upon receiving an appointment or at the renewal of a grant. *Beriz* was the amount of revenue assessed for a landholding. *Nazr* was the symbolic gift, a rendering of fealty, given from a subordinate to a superior. See Wilson, H.H., *A Glossary of Judicial and Revenue Terms*, 2nd ed. (Delhi: Munshiram Manoharlal, 1968), pp. 72 and 415. Robert Frykenberg has called the administration of some zamindaris one of "myopic self-interest" suggesting

an isolationist type of administration. See Robert E. Frykenberg, *Guntur District, 1788–1848. A History of Local Influence and Central Authority in South India* (Oxford: Clarendon Press, 1965), p. 146.

73. Barton to GOI, 7 December 1925, R/1/1/1469, OIOC.
74. Khan, *Imperial Gazetteer of India Provincial Series Hyderabad State*, pp. 296–99.
75. Dirks, *The Hollow Crown*. Paloncha was also home to the majority of the "hill Reddis" of Hyderabad State. Christoph von Furer-Haimendorf, *The Aboriginal Tribes of Hyderabad*, vol. 2: *The Reddis of the Bison Hills* (London: Macmillan & Co., LTD, 1945), pp. 29–30.
76. Cheragh Ali, *Hyderabad (Deccan) under Sir Salar Jung*, vol. 1 (Bombay: Education Society's Press, 1885), p. 11.
77. Reilly, H.D.C. *Report of the Paigah Commission* (Hyderabad, 1345 H. [1926–1927]. p. 86.
78. Khusro, A.M., *Economic and Social Effects of Jagirdari Abolition and Land Reforms in Hyderabad* (Hyderabad: Osmania University, 1958), p. 6.
79. Khan, *Imperial Gazetteer of India Provincial Series Hyderabad State*, pp. 294–96.
80. Khusro, *Economic and Social Effects of Jagirdari Abolition*, p. 4.
81. Ibid., p. 12.
82. Anwar Iqbal Quershi, *The Economic Development of Hyderabad* (Bombay: Orient Longmans Ltd., 1947), pp. 114–18.
83. Dirks, *The Hollow Crown*. Price, *Kingship and Political Practice in Colonial India*. Joanne Punzo Waghorne, *The Raja's Magic Clothes: Revisioning Kingship and Divinity in England's India* (University Park, Pennsylvania: Pennsylvania State University Press, 1994).
84. John Richards, *Mughal Administration in Golconda* (Oxford: Clarendon Press, 1975), pp. 116–22.
85. Stewart N. Gordon, "Scarf and Sword: Thugs, Marauders, and State-Formation in 18th Century Malwa," *The Indian Economic and Social History Review* 6, no. 4 (1969): 403–30.
86. Hyderabad's durbar, because of its multiple polities, was somewhere between a pure "Oriental despot" and what Geertz has described for Bali as "an expanding cloud of localized, fragile, loosely interrelated petty principalities." Clifford Geertz, *Negara: The Theatre State in Nineteenth-Century Bali* (Princeton, NJ: Princeton University Press, 1980), p. 4.
87. Anand Yang, "An Institutional Shelter: The Court of Wards in Late Nineteenth-Century Bihar," *Modern Asian Studies* 13, no. 2 (1979): 247–64.

Chapter 1: At the Edge of Empire

1. Rameshwar Rao to GOI, 12 September 1857, Foreign Department, NAI.
2. For a biography of Rameshwar Rao, see: *Sri Raja Prathama Rameshwara Rayalu* (Hyderabad: Orient Longman, 1990).

3. Mudiraj, *Pictorial Hyderabad*, vol. 2, p. 628.
4. Cynthia Talbot, *Precolonial India in Practice: Society, Religion, and Identity in Medieval Andhra* (Oxford: Oxford University Press, 2001), pp. 67, 150.
5. Wagoner, "Sultan among Hindu Kings." p. 853.
6. Rameshwar Rao to GOI, 12 September 1857, Foreign Department, NAI.
7. Cuthbert Davidson to Fort William, 14 September 1857, Foreign Department, NAI.
8. Susan Bayly, *Saints, Goddesses and Kings Muslims and Christians in South Indian Society 1700–1900* (Cambridge: Cambridge University Press, 1989), p. 50.
9. One link between the Kaktiyas and Wanaparthi is the use of the eagle (*garuda*) in their family crest. Racharla Ganapathi, *Subordinate Rulers in Medieval Deccan* (Delhi: Bharatiya Kala Prakashan, 2000), pp. 1–2.
10. For some description of Velamas in the Nizam's territories, see: Hassan, *Castes and Tribes of the Nizam's Dominions*, pp. 635–40. For the Reddy community of greater Andhra, see: K.S. Singh, ed., *People of India: Andhra Pradesh*, vol. 13, Part 3 (New Delhi: Affiliated East-West Press, 2003), pp. 1476–637.
11. Sastrulu, *Sri Surabhivari Vamsa Charitramu*, p. 85.
12. He is also intricately related to the Padmanayakas, now associated with modern Velamas. Talbot, *Precolonial India in Practice*, pp. 189–94.
13. The practice of tracing family histories back into mythology was common in the post–Vijayanagara period. Nobuhiro Ota, "Beda Nayakas and Their Historical Narratives in Karnataka during the Post-Vijayanagara Period," in *Kingship in Indian History*, ed. Noboru Karashima (New Delhi: Manohar, 1999), p. 163.
14. Some sources trace the family back ten generations to Hemadri Naidu and Bhimaraju, but it is with Chevi Reddy that the stories of the family's origin begin to coalesce. A different version of this story suggests that "Rechan" was the village where the family resided, and that there was no Mala. Sastrulu, *Sri Surabhivari Vamsa Charitramu*, pp. 4, 10.
15. *The History of Surabhi Family and the Rajah Saheb of Jatprole* (Madras: The Indian Encyclopedias Compiling & Publishing Coy), p. 2. Reddy had two political capitals, one at Amanagallu in Nalgonda and the other at Pillallamari in Mahbubnagar district. His name was taken from the later.
16. N.G. Chetty, *A Manual of the Kurnool District in the Presidency of Madras* (Madras: R. Hill, 1886), p. 23.
17. Ramulu, "Gadwal Samasthanam: A Study," p. 17. Gona-Vitthala was a general under Pratapa Rudra and conquered territory in the Raichur *doab*. P.V.P. Sastry, *The Kakatiyas of Warangal* (Hyderabad: Government of Andhra Pradesh, 1978), p. 170.
18. 1925, R/1/1/1469, OIOC.
19. *Imperial Gazetteer of India*, vol. 5 (Oxford: Clarendon Press, 1908). A story exists concerning the Anagundi family headdress. When the Vijayanagar forces were defeated, the head of the Anagundi family took flight. His crown

accidentally fell from his head and was captured by the Qutb Shah forces. In memory of this shameful event, the raja no longer wore a crown on his head, but instead tied a scarf. Mss Eur Mack. General, Vol. X, OIOC.

20. Stein states that "during the Vijayanagara period there came into existence, or at least into sharp focus, a level of supralocal chieftainship which appears to be different from anything which existed before." "But, in the degree of power of these chieftainships, in the magnitude of local resources commanded and redistributed, in their independence from local social and cultural constrains, their ability to intrude into local society, and in their persistent independence from and occasional opposition to superordinate authority, this political category is unprecedented." Burton Stein, *Peasant State and Society in Medieval South India* (Delhi: Oxford University Press, 1980), pp. 369–70.
21. Burton Stein, *Vijayanagara* (Cambridge: Cambridge University Press, 1993), p. 91.
22. Bayly, *Saints, Goddesses and Kings Muslims and Christians in South Indian Society 1700–1900*, p. 23.
23. Ibid., pp. 48–49.
24. This distinction between north and south, and between *nayaka* and samasthan is evident in the bibliographic essay of Stein's, *Vijayanagara*. Works on states to the south of Vijayanagar are those concerned with *nayakas*, works on those states that fell under the Qutb Shahs of Golconda remain nameless, but in fact were the samasthans. Stein, *Vijayanagara*, p. 151.
25. The samasthan letterhead for sometime bore the name of Sugur (Soogoor). It seems that in 1686 the capital of the samasthan was again shifted, from Sugur to Kotha Kota (new fort). Kotha Kota appears on early maps of this region, and from that town, the road bent southeast to Kurnool. The capital then moved to Sri Rangapur in the mid-eighteenth century under Venkat Reddy (possibly in 1727), and finally shifted to Wanaparthi in 1807. Mudiraj, *Pictorial Hyderabad*, p. 622. The Bedars were a tribe of warriors who settled in the Raichur *doab* area and eventually consolidated their power to the north in and around Shorapur. Syed Siraj ul Hassan, *Castes and Tribes of the Nizam's Dominions*, vol. 1 (New Delhi: Vintage Books, 1990), pp. 34–43.
26. Sastri, in his history of the family, notes that the samasthan location was good because of forests and proximity to Hyderabad and the Madras Presidency. Sastrulu, *Sri Surabhivari Vamsa Charitramu*, p. 123.
27. Phillip Wagoner, *Tidings of the King* (Honolulu: University of Hawaii Press, 1993), p. 87.
28. Jos Gommans, "The Silent Frontier of South Asia C. 1100–1800," *Journal of World History* 9, no. 1 (1998): 2.
29. For the intricate "criss-cross" alliances of the eighteenth- and nineteenth-century polities in Hyderabad State, see: Sunil Chander, "From a Pre-Colonial Order to a Princely State: Hyderabad in Transition, C. 1748–1865" (Ph.D. thesis, Cambridge University, 1987), p. 5.

30. For a complete history of the Qutb Shah rulers, see: H.K. Sherwani, *History of the Qutb Shahi Dynasty* (New Delhi: Manoharlal Publishers, 1974).
31. Wagoner, *Tidings of the King*, p. 121.
32. Mahomed Kasim Ferishta, *History of the Rise of the Mahomedan Power in India till the Year A.D. 1612*, trans. John Briggs, vol. 3 (Calcutta: R. Cambray & Co., 1910), p. 348. The list of forts taken by Sultan Quli Qutb Shah is impressive. As given by Ferishta, "Rajconda, Kovilconda, Dewurconda, Pangul, Gunpoora, Jirconda, Yelgundel, Mulungoor, Etgeer, Meduk, Bhowungeer, Belumconda, Wurungole, Cumamett, Indraconda, Ramgeer, Condapilly, Ellore, Chitcole," p. 353.
33. Adam Watson, *The War of the Goldsmith's Daughter* (London: Chatto & Windus, 1964).
34. Rameshwar Rao, WFP, p. 3. Several histories of different lengths and quality exist for Wanaparthi. Produced by the samasthan, see: *Wanaparthi Samasthana Paripalana Vidhanamu* (Wanaparthi: Wanaparthi State, 1948). Krishna, *Wanaparthi Samasthana Charitra*.
35. Gijs Kruijtzer to author, personal communication. This information comes from a letter in Dutch VOC records. Letter from Masulipatnam to Pulicat, 24 April 1684.
36. Sastrulu, *Sri Surabhivari Vamsa Charitramu*, p. 110.
37. Briggs, *The Nizam*, vol. 1, p. 121.
38. Richards, *Mughal Administration in Golconda*, p. 116.
39. Ibid., p. 116.
40. Ibid., pp. 116–17.
41. Richards identifies a fourth son, Gopalin Rao. However, no record of this son exists in the Jatprole family history. Given that Gopalin Rao was granted *muniwar* (police) powers, it may be that he was the same person as Gopal Rao, or perhaps one of his sons.
42. Richards, *Mughal Administration in Golconda*, p. 121.
43. Farruksiyar to Lingamma, 26 August 1715, R/1/1/1469, OIOC, p. 26.
44. Richards, *Mughal Administration in Golconda*, p. 269. Richards suggests that Venkat belonged to Jatprole because of its proximity to Pangal, but Wanaparthi shared a similar proximity and had a ruler of the same name at this time.
45. Asaf Jah I to Gopal Rao, 10 April 1734, WFP.
46. The Raja of Gadwal met Salabat Jung (1751–1762) on 24 February 1755 while the latter marched south, crossing the Krishna and Tungabhadra rivers.
47. Intelligence reports make frequent mention of Jagannath Rao's activities. In June 1799, then Resident James Kirkpatrick received information that Rao had amassed nearly 2,000 soldiers as well as elephants and camels. Board Collection, F/4/76/1665, OIOC.
48. Jagannath Rao had in 1796 run afoul of Muhammad Ameen Khan who was an Arab revenue farmer for the region. Rao had fortified his stronghold at Bolavaram, which Khan considered an act of rebellion. Six years later, a

British force was sent against Rao to pursue the rebellious raja. Chander, "From a Pre-Colonial Order to a Princely State: Hyderabad in Transition, C. 1748–1865," p. 63 note 42, p. 98. The East India Company was also very much interested in the military strength of the samasthans, let alone their skirmishes. Assessments of Paloncha, Narayanpet, Jatprole, Gadwal, Wanaparthi were made, as well as other unidentifiable powerful landholders. Mss Eur Mack. General Vol. XLVI, OIOC.

49. Barton to GOI, 7 December 1925, R/1/1/1469, OIOC.
50. "Copy of a confidential note by Diwan Bahadur Aravamudu Ayyangar, Counsel for the Rani of Gadwal, on the Gadwal Case," in Barton to GOI, 6 November 1926. Foreign Dept., R/1/1/1469, OIOC, p. 24.
51. Philip Meadows Taylor, ed., *The Story of My Life* (1882; repr., New Delhi: Asian Educational Services, 1986), p. 164.
52. Fraser to Elliot, 4 February 1851, in Briggs, *The Nizam*, vol. 2, p. 327.
53. Bushby to GOI, 11 September 1856, R/1/1/1469, OIOC, p. 4.
54. Mudiraj, *Pictorial Hyderabad*, p. 620 W. See also: Davidson to GOI, 12 October 1860, Mss Eur D728, OIOC.
55. Rameshwar Rao to GOI, 12 September 1857, Foreign Department, NAI.
56. Secretary to Rameshwar Rao, 21 October 1857, Foreign Department, NAI.
57. Davidson to Rameshwar Rao, 28 February 1862, WFP.
58. Hastings Fraser, *Our Faithful Ally the Nizam* (London: Smith, Elder and Co., 1865), p. 311.
59. See: Omar Khalidi, *The British Residents at the Court of the Nizams of Haydarabad* (Wichita, Kansas: Haydarabad Historical Society, 1981); Regani, *Nizam-British Relations: 1724–1857.*
60. This romantic tale of "east meets west" has been carefully retold. See: Dalrymple, *White Mughals: Love and Betrayal in Eighteenth-Century India.*
61. Fisher, *Indirect Rule in India*, pp. 293–94 and p. 397.
62. 16 January 1972, Mss Eur, D7985, OIOC.
63. On the importance and "re-introduction" of geography in India's history, see: André Wink, "From the Mediterranean to the Indian Ocean: Medieval History in Geographic Perspective," *Comparative Studies in Society and History* 44, no. 3 (2002). pp. 416–45.
64. P.M. Joshi, "The Raichur Doab in Deccan History—Re-Interpretation of a Struggle," *Journal of Indian History* 36, no. 3 (1958): 393.
65. Ibid., 394.
66. Ibid., 184. Ferishta, *History of the Rise of the Mahomedan Power in India till the Year A.D. 1612*, vol. 2, pp. 389–90.
67. Ibid., p. 355.
68. Richards, *Mughal Administration in Golconda*, map 1. Also table 4.2, p. 88.
69. There is both inscriptional evidence of this as well as first-hand accounts. M. Somasekhara Sarma, *History of the Reddi Kingdoms* (Waltair: Andhra University, 1948), p. 391.
70. Ferishta, *History of the Rise of the Mahomedan Power in India till the Year A.D. 1612*, p. 371.

71. Robert Sewell, *A Forgotten Empire*, 2nd ed. (New Delhi: National Book Trust, 1970), p. 250. The basket boats were also used in 1812 by the British to transport their heavy arms over the Tungabhadra river.
72. Chetty, *A Manual of the Kurnool District in the Presidency of Madras*, p. 27.
73. Stein suggests that "others believe" Tirumala took refuge at Tirupati. Stein, *Vijayanagara*, pp. 119–20.
74. Ferishta, *History of the Rise of the Mahomedan Power in India till the Year A.D. 1612*, p. 454.
75. Richards, *Mughal Administration in Golconda*, p. 209.
76. For a description of the various kinds of ornaments worn by rulers, especially from the pre-Muslim era in the Deccan, see Sarma, *History of the Reddi Kingdoms*, pp. 295–303.
77. Omar Khalidi, *The Romance of the Golconda Diamonds* Middletown, New Jersey: Grantha Corporation, 1999.
78. Ferishta, *History of the Rise of the Mahomedan Power in India till the Year A.D. 1612*, p. 407.
79. Ibid., p. 453.
80. Abdul Majeed Siddiqui, *History of Golconda* (Hyderabad: The Literary Publications, 1956), p. 350. Richards, *Mughal Administration in Golconda*, p. 15.
81. R.H. Major, ed., *India in the Fifteenth Century* (New York: Burt Franklin), p. 30.
82. Sewell, *A Forgotten Empire*, p. 369.
83. "A Description of the Diamond-Mines as It Was Presented by the Right Honourable, the Earl of Marlbal of England to the R. Society," *Philosophical Transactions* XII (1677), p. 899.
84. Ibid., p. 915.
85. Siddiqui, *History of Golconda*, pp. 348–49. My emphasis.
86. Sarma, *History of the Reddi Kingdoms*, p. 382.
87. For a description of the different types of jewels and clothes popular in nineteenth century Hyderabad, see: Sheela Raj, *Medievalism to Modernism* (London: Sangam Books, 1987), pp. 68–74.
88. This was true, for instance, in Arcot dating from 1801. Bayly, *Saints, Goddesses and Kings Muslims and Christians in South Indian Society 1700–1900*, p. 158.

Chapter 2: Soldiers, Mercenaries, and Moneylenders

1. William Barton, *The Princes of India* (London: Nisbet & Co. Ltd., 1934), p. 193.
2. These small armies were frequently called *sibbandi* (a force, troops). They were employed for a few weeks during the spring and fall seasons for revenue collection. Generally these forces were ragged and prone to plunder and rapine.

3. Chander, "From a Pre-Colonial Order to a Princely State: Hyderabad in Transition, C. 1748–1865," p. 47.
4. Salar Jung was a favorite of the Residents, and worked with them to modernize the administration so that it mirrored much of that in British India. He had a private estate of considerable size, 1486 square miles, and a prestigious lineage. The family claimed descent from Shaikh Owais of Karan dating from the time of the Prophet. Ten descendants later, members of the family settled in the Deccan at the time of Ali Adil Shah (1656–1672) of Bijapur. Further descendants served the late Mughal emperors Aurangzeb, Bahadur Shah, and Farrukhsiyar. When Asaf Jah came to the Deccan, he brought with him Shaikh Muhammad Taki. The latter was made commander of garrisons and all forts. From him derive a line of noblemen who served with distinction in the Deccan and in Hyderabad. Among them was Salar Jung's maternal great-grandfather, Mir Alam. Mir Alam negotiated with Lord Cornwallis, and commanded troops in Hyderabad's battle against Tipu Sultan in 1799. When Salar Jung became minister in 1853, he brought the state out of a political and fiscal nose-dive. He reduced taxes; sharpened the powers of the *talukdars*; banned the sub-letting of land by them; made subordinates in the countryside directly responsible to the government, and improved the functions and precedents of the legal courts. Vasant Kumar Bawa, *Hyderabad under Salar Jung I* (New Delhi: S.Chand & Company Ltd., 1996). Khan, *Imperial Gazetteer of India Provincial Series Hyderabad State*, pp. 294–96. Ali, *Hyderabad (Deccan) under Sir Salar Jung*, vol. 1, p. 76.
5. Nizam ul Mulk to Ammakka and Lingamma, 3 September 1727, R/1/1/1469, OIOC, p. 30. All that remains from these early communications are the English translations of Persian documents.
6. Nizam ul Mulk to Ammakka and Lingamma, 13 November 1729, R/1/1/1469, OIOC, p. 31.
7. Chetty, *A Manual of the Kurnool District in the Presidency of Madras*, p. 34.
8. Mss Eur Mack. General Vol. XLVI, OIOC.
9. Briggs, *The Nizam*. See letter from Lord Mornington to Henry Dundas, 23 February 1798, p. 304.
10. André Wink, *Land and Sovereignty in India* (London: Cambridge University Press, 1986), pp. 44–47.
11. Briggs, *The Nizam*, p. 332.
12. Ray, *Hyderabad and British Paramountcy 1858–1883*, p. 5.
13. An account of Shorapur from 1799 states that the raja maintained 9,000 troops and 3,000 horses, "and he will not mind any one; and no one can hurt him." 29 August 1799, Mss Eur F48, OIOC.
14. The Company was deeply concerned about the affairs of Hyderabad State and the Marathas. Thus, Gadwal's payment of *peshkush* to the Maratha treasury in 1818 caused a certain amount of concern. "Note on Kittoor," 1818, Eur Mss F/151/26, OIOC.
15. C.U. Aitchison, *A Collection of Treaties, Engagements and Sanads*, vol. 9 (Calcutta: Superintendent Government Printing, 1909), p. 72. Ray, *Hyderabad and British Paramountcy 1858–1883*, p. 24.

16. Harriet Ronken Lynton, *My Dear Nawab Saheb* (Hyderabad: Disha Books, 1991), p. 20.
17. In Hyderabad today the African presence is still felt in the names of some locations such as Habshiguda and Siddi-Ambar bazaar.
18. For the meeting of the Islamic world with the subcontinent, see André Wink, *Al-Hind*, vol. 2 (New Delhi: Oxford University Press, 1999).
19. Sarma, *History of the Reddi Kingdoms*, pp. 239–41.
20. R.R.S. Chauhan, *Africans in India: From Slavery to Royalty* (New Delhi: Asian Publication Services, 1995), p. 217. The Nizams of Hyderabad also had Africans in their forces. For instance, there was an Amazon Guard comprising African women posted at the Nizam's palace. For a reference to these "unusual" forces, see: Maud Diver, *Royal India* (New York: D. Appleton-Century Company, 1942), p. 174.
21. Chandu Lal to Ram Krishna Rao, 25 December 1817, in: *Translations of some sanads and documents*. Hyderabad: [Privately published], 1950, p. 6.
22. Barton, *The Princes of India*, p. 197.
23. Reginal Burton, *A History of the Hyderabad Contingent* (Calcutta: Central Printing Office, 1905), p. 4.
24. Ibid., pp. 49–50.
25. Qadir Khan Munshi, *Tarikh-E-Asaf Jahi*, ed. N.R.V. Prasad, trans. Zaib Hyder (Hyderabad: Andhra Pradesh Government Oriental Manuscript Library and Research Institute, 1994), pp. 138 and 141.
26. Burton, *A History of the Hyderabad Contingent*, p. 117.
27. See, for example, skirmishes in October 1829 and again in May 1831. *The Chronology of Modern Hyderabad 1720–1890* (Hyderabad: Central Records Office Hyderabad Government, 1954), pp. 192 and 199.
28. Zubaida Yazdani, *Hyderabad during the Residency of Henry Russell, 1811–1820* (Oxford: University Press, 1976), p. 39.
29. Taylor, ed., *The Story of My Life*, p. 332.
30. Fraser to Dalhousie, 16 May 1849, in Hastings Fraser, *Memoir and Correspondence of General James Stuart Fraser* (London: Whiting & Co., 1885), p. 293.
31. Dalhousie to Fraser, 30 May 1849, in Ibid., pp. 294–95.
32. Ibid.
33. Ibid., p. 239.
34. Wanaparthi was not alone in its difficulties with creditors, Arab or otherwise. In 1890, the raja of Anagundi lost several villages to Bansi Raja, his creditor, when he was unable to repay a debt. *Hyderabad in 1890 and 1891* (Bangalore: Caxton Press, 1892), p. 34.
35. In 1829, Nasir ud Daula succeeded Sikander Jah (1803–1829) as the fourth Nizam, and he asked that the supervision of the Nizam's government by the Residency be stopped. It was, and the "evil effects of the change became manifest, in the turbulent conduct of several of the influential Zemindars." Fraser, *Our Faithful Ally the Nizam*, p. 236.
36. Khan Bahadur Ahmed Khan to Rameshwar Rao, 2 April 1846, WFP.

37. Rameshwar Rao to Raja Ram Baksh, 7 May 1846, WFP.
38. Ibid.
39. *Madras Spectator*, 9 June 1846. Narayanpet was northwest of Wanaparthi, and Makhtal ("Goormukhtal?") south of Narayanpet.
40. Fraser, *Our Faithful Ally the Nizam*, p. 207.
41. Gribble, *A History of the Deccan*, p. 198.
42. Fraser, *Memoir and Correspondence of General James Stuart Fraser*, p. 209.
43. James Stewart Fraser, 21 September 1846, WFP. At the same time, Fraser interviewed some Rohillas who were owed money, paid them, and had them escorted to the state's border to facilitate their permanent departure. Fraser, *Our Faithful Ally the Nizam*, p. 248.
44. A. Claude Campbell, *Glimpses of the Nizam's Dominions* (Philidelphia: Historical Publishing Co., 1898), p. 359. *Englishman*, 11 July 1850. The Arabs of Hyderabad had their own system of jails, which they operated without government regulation. This continued until their incorporation under the reforms of Salar Jung in the following decades.
45. Two accounts of this event exist: one states that Rameshwar Rao came to Hyderabad to escape capture by the Arabs, but was then turned over by the minister. The second states that the Nizam himself summoned the raja from Wanaparthi to Hyderabad under the guise of a dinner invitation and then had him arrested. The former seems less credible as Rameshwar Rao's great grandson, in his own telling of events, states that the Nizam and the raja had in fact had dinner before the latter was arrested. Unpublished notes by Rameshwar Rao, p. 19. WFP, Hyderabad. See also: Lynton and Rajan, *Days of the Beloved*, p. 179.
46. Talib ud Daula served intermittently as police chief of Hyderabad under Nasir ud Daula. *The Chronology of Modern Hyderabad 1720–1890*, p. 264. However, he is reported as the *talukdar* of Wanaparthi elsewhere. *Englishman*, 11 April 1851.
47. *Englishman*, 17 April 1851.
48. *Englishman*, 26 April 1851.
49. *Englishman*, 4 February 1852. Arabs fired on British troops in September 1853, and in August of 1855 an Arab moneylender/mercenary turned his Hyderabad home into a fort in preparation for reclaiming a debt. Fraser, *Our Faithful Ally the Nizam*, pp. 278–79.
50. Penderel Moon, *The British Conquest and Dominion of India*, vol. 1 (New Delhi: India Research Press, 1999), p. 656.
51. Edmonstone to Rameshwar Rao, 21 April 1855, Foreign Department, NAI.
52. *Englishman*, 19 April 1855.
53. *Englishman*, 19 May 1855.
54. Rameshwar Rao was so well known for both his assistance to the British and his occasional banditry that he (and Ram Bhupal of Gadwal) were included in the massive Bowring Collection. "This Chief holds a fief in the Hyderābād territory said to yield 1 1/2 lac yearly, and situated in the Pāngal District. The present is Raja named Sawai Rājā Rāmesar Balwant Bahādoor

and commands a Regiment of Horse in the Nizam's service. During the Crimean campaign, as also at the time of the mutiny in 1857 he offered his powerful aid to the British Govt to extinguish their foes. His career is said to have been wild and eccentric, and at one time he was imprisoned for dacoity." Mss Eur G/38/3/26, OIOC.

55. Military Dispatches Book for 1863, 22 January 1862, WFP.
56. Ibid.
57. Rameshwar Rao. WFP, p. 18.
58. *Englishman*, 6 December 1859.
59. Ibid.
60. Ibid.
61. Gordon, "Scarf and Sword: Thugs, Marauders, and State-Formation in 18th Century Malwa," p. 415.
62. Care for the roads had fallen to the Nizam's government by 1867.
63. Sherwani, *History of the Qutb Shahi Dynasty*, p. 499.
64. See also Robert E. Frykenberg, "On Roads and Riots in Tinnevelly: Radical Change and Ideology in Madras Presidency During the 19th Century," *South Asia* 4, no. 2 (1981): pp. 42–45.
65. Military Board to Rameshwar Rao, 30 April 1862, WFP.
66. Government to Rani of Wanaparthi, 9 October 1868, WFP.
67. Receipt Book of Letters of Rameshwar Rao, 16 June 1865, WFP. Government to Rameshwar Rao, 22 October 1868, WFP.
68. Government to Rameshwar Rao, 2 February 1850, WFP.
69. Government to Rameshwar Rao, 23 September, 4 October, 29 October 1861, WFP.
70. The role of Gadwal's women rulers is examined in chapter 5.
71. Raja Ram Baksh to Venkatlakshmi, 7 August 1845, R/1/1/1469, OIOC.
72. Yazdani, *Hyderabad during the Residency of Henry Russell, 1811–1820*, p. 26.
73. David Shulman has suggested that the south Indian bandit was a necessary counterforce to the king. Whether this remained true in the nineteenth century is unclear. Certainly Nagappa attracted attention, but perhaps by his time, the king's authority was no longer so closely bound to the suppression of bandits. David Shulman, "On South Indian Bandit Kings," *The Indian Economic and Social History Review* 17, no. 3 (1980): p. 305.
74. See J.F. Richards and V. Narayana Rao, "Banditry in Mughal India: Historical and Folk Perceptions," in *The Mughal State 1526–1750*, ed. Muzaffar Alam and Sanjay Subrahmanyam (New Delhi: Oxford University Press, 1998), pp. 491–519.
75. Boardman to Rameshwar Rao, 13 April 1859, Receipt Book of Letters from Major J.H. Boardman, WFP.
76. Boardman to Rameshwar Rao, 25 October 1859, Receipt Book of Letters from Major J.H. Boardman, WFP.
77. Boardman to Rameshwar Rao, 10 November 1859, Receipt Book of Letters from Major J.H. Boardman, WFP.

78. Mukhtar ul Mulk to Rameshwar Rao, approx. February 1862, WFP. This correspondence is not dated, but makes reference to a previous letter of 27 February 1862, thus the approximate date.
79. In one account, the raja's "brother" is said to have been responsible for Nagappa's capture. However, the raja was adopted, so this relationship—if true—would have been that of a fictive brother. The account comes from: *Englishman*, 16 December 1859.
80. Ibid.
81. Taylor's time in the Deccan can be divided into two eras: from about 1824 to 1839 when he worked for the Nizam's army, and from about 1840 to 1860 when he was the officer in charge in the Shorapur samasthan. See Taylor, ed., *The Story of My Life*. For a fictional account of banditry in the Deccan, see: Philip Meadows Taylor, *Confessions of a Thug* (1839; repr., Oxford: Oxford University Press, 1986).
82. Meadows Taylor to Rameshwar Rao, 12 March 1860, Receipt Book of Letters from Major J.H. Boardman, WFP.
83. The samasthan did not give up its entire armed forces. For example, we find Gadwal and Wanaparthi exempted from the Indian Arms Act of 1903, thus allowing them and their armed guards to travel through British India. (GOI to Barr, 17 October 1903, R/2/8/1192, OIOC.) The personal guards of the state's nobles became a point of contention when the Government of India tightened restrictions on carrying arms through its territories and under protest from the nobles, several were exempted from the Act including the rajas of Gadwal and Wanaparthi.
84. Richard Temple, *Journals Kept in Hyderabad, Kashmir, Sikkim, and Nepal*, vol. 1 (London: W.H. Allen & Co., 1887), pp. 21–22 and 137. See also 30 May 1867, Mss Eur F86/81, OIOC.
85. Richard Temple to Rani Shankaramma, 3 January 1867, WFP. Temple visited Wanaparthi in 1877.
86. 4 August 1867, Mss Eur F86/81, OIOC.
87. 10 August 1867, Mss Eur F86/81, OIOC.
88. Seshgir Rao to Nizam Mahbub Ali Khan, 3 November 1884, WFP. (At this time the Nizam was not yet invested with full powers, but the letter is addressed to him anyway as "The Honourable Ruler.")
89. Briggs, *The Nizam*, p. 121. The Arab guard did not entirely disappear with the end of the nineteenth century. The principal of Mahbubia Girls School, Miss. F.M. Wyld, provides the following account of the Arab guard from the decade between 1909 and 1919. "In the City there existed a Company known as The Arab Guard . . . From time to time, only about once in six months or so, one could hear in the distance, coming up from the City direction, a rhythmic chant which gradually grew louder, accompanied by the tramping of feet apparently with a sort of running movement. The chant grew louder and louder as it approached our gate, and died away in the distance as it went on its way. It was a picturesque procession, as the Arab Guard went past in strange motley uniforms of seemingly ancient date. This

somewhat ruffianly [*sic*] looking little procession, which looked neither right nor left, was actually in charge of large sums of money. This money was being transferred from the Treasury in the City to some destination . . . The protection of this treasure, was however, entrusted to the care of this strangely assorted band." Mss Eur B320, OIOC.

90. Barton, *The Princes of India*, p. 199. El Dorado in the sixteenth century was a fabulously wealthy city that explorers believed to be in South America.
91. H.D.C. Reilly, *Report of the Paigah Commission*, p. 86. Also: Nizam's Political Secretary to Resident, 2 January 1934, L/P&S/1/3/1/199, OIOC.

Chapter 3: Turbans, Titles, and Tigers: Symbols of Rulership

1. This is a point made by Eliot Weinberger in his introduction: J.R. Ackerley, *Hindoo Holiday*, ed. Eliot Weinberger (New York: New York Review Books, 2000).
2. David Cannadine, *Ornamentalism: How the British Saw Their Empire* (London: Penguin Group, 2001), p. 122.
3. Pamela Price, "Warrior Caste 'Raja' and Gentlemen 'Zamindar': One Person's Experience in the Late Nineteenth Century," *Modern Asian Studies* 17, no. 4 (1983): p. 564.
4. For an overview of Mahbub Ali Khan's reign, see: Lynton and Rajan, *Days of the Beloved*.
5. Fraser, *Memoir and Correspondence of General James Stuart Fraser*, Appendix, p. xlviii.
6. Ram Krishna Rao to Hyderabad Government, 10 February 1884, WFP.
7. Salar Jung to Ram Krishna Rao, 19 February 1884, WFP.
8. Hyderabad city, as it took shape in the eighteenth century, was a planned city with quarters set aside for different branches of government, society, and trade. For an overview of the city at this time, and its architectural underpinnings, see: Alison Mackenzie Shah, "Constructing a Capital on the Edge of Empire: Urban Patronage and Politics in the Nizams' Hyderabad, 1750–1950" (Ph.D. thesis, University of Pennsylvania, 2005.), pp. 51–76.
9. Dewan of Anagundi to Nizam's Private Secretary, 19 March 1895, Ceremonials File, APSA.
10. Vikar ul Umra to Tucker, 29 January 1895, APSA, Ceremonials File.
11. The raja and his men stayed in the safety of the Residency bazaar.
12. Malcolm likely traveled by way of Kurnool, and it is possible that the young raja that visited was one of the three samasthan rajas under consideration. The road from Kurnool to Hyderabad passed through both Wanaparthi and Jatprole, and close to Gadwal. The rajas of the time were Rambhupal I (Gadwal), Ram Krishna Rao II (Wanaparthi), and Jagannath Rao I (Jatprole).
13. John Kaye, *The Life and Correspondence of Major-General Sir John Malcolm*, vol. 2 (London: Smith, Elder, and Co., 1856), pp. 98–99.

14. This description is modified from Elphinstone and fits not only the Hyderabad durbar, but is general enough that it might describe others as well. Mountstuart Elphinstone, *The History of India* (Allahabad: Kitab Mahal, [Reprint 1966]1849), p. 174. See also Adrian C. Mayer, "The King's Two Thrones," *Man (N.S.)* 20 (1985). pp. 205–21.
15. Rajendra Prasad, *The Asif Jahs of Hyderabad* (New Delhi: Vikas Publishing House, 1984), p. 173.
16. Mudiraj, *Pictorial Hyderabad*, pp. 632 and 637.
17. The demands of protocol can be seen in accounts of the coronation durbar held in Delhi in 1911. In order to avoid offending India's princely nobility, Lord Lynton and his staff designed the seating for the coronation in a semicircle so that all of the suitably high-ranking nobility were equidistant to the king. See John Fortescue, *Narrative of the Visit to India of Their Majesties King George V. and Queen Mary and of the Coronation Durbar Held at Delhi 12th December 1911* (London: Macmillan and Co., 1912). Foldout following Appendix D. See also Robert Frykenberg, "The Coronation Durbar of 1911: Some Implications," in *Delhi through the Ages*, ed. Robert Frykenberg (Delhi: Oxford University Press, 1986), pp. 376–80.
18. Afsur Doula, 19 March 1902, Ceremonials File, APSA.
19. This is similar to the court of Awadh where the ruler bound himself more closely to landholders throughout his domain by symbolic incorporation done at durbars. Fisher, *A Clash of Cultures*, p. 12.
20. David Cannadine, "The Context, Performance and Meaning of Ritual: The British Monarchy and the 'Invention of Tradition,' C. 1820–1977," in *The Invention of Tradition*, ed. Eric Hobsbawm and Terence Ranger (Cambridge: Cambridge University Press, 1983), p. 102.
21. One success of the samasthan rajas was in 1903 when the raja of Wanaparthi attended the Delhi durbar with the Nizam. *The Coronation Durbar Delhi 1903. Official Directory (with Maps)* (Delhi: Foreign Office Press, 1903), p. 59.
22. A.J. Dunlop to Political Secretary, 4 November 1911, CW.
23. Kishen Pershad to First Assistant Resident, 17 February 1904, Foreign Department, NAI.
24. Afsur ud Daula was also a member of Lord Robert's coronation staff in London.
25. Lynton and Rajan, *Days of the Beloved*, p. 63.
26. After his father's death in 1911, Osman Ali Khan held a durbar to commemorate his ascension to the throne. A photograph of this event shows the new Nizam surrounded by the state's nobles, including Lakshma Rao of Jatprole, standing three people away from the Nizam on his left. Also from that year a photo taken after lunch at Maharaja Kishen Pershad's home shows Sita Rambhupal of Gadwal in attendance. Zahid Ali Khan, ed., *Images of Hyderabad* (Hyderabad: Siasat, 1994), pp. 97, 104.
27. Ibid., p. 97.
28. Ibid., p. 104.

29. Nicholas B. Dirks, "Colonial Histories and Native Informants: Biography of an Archive," in *Orientalism and the Postcolonial Predicament,* ed. Carol A. Breckenridge Peter van der Veer (Philadelphia: University of Pennsylvania Press, 1993), p. 296.
30. The following section is from: Narrain Row to Mackenzie, 1809. Trans. XII/14(5)[sheets 8–13v], Mackenzie Collection, Madras. I am grateful to Phil Wagoner for sharing this document with me. The original has many typographical errors, thus I have sparsely quoted from it. A subsequent use of this work is found in: Phillip B. Wagoner, "Precolonial Intellectuals and the Production of Colonial Knowledge," *Comparative Studies in Society and History* 45, no. 4 (2003). pp. 783–814.
31. For an analysis of Mackenzie's "native assistants," see: Dirks, "Colonial Histories and Native Informants: Biography of an Archive." pp. 275–313.
32. Bernard Cohn, "Representing Authority in Victorian India," in *The Invention of Tradition,* ed. Eric Hobsbawm and Terence Ranger (Cambridge: Canto, 1983), pp. 176–77.
33. This is somewhat in contradiction to Fisher's assertion that the pre-1857 period was one of increased intervention in the princely courts. Perhaps the preeminence of Hyderabad can help explain why the shoe issue was not more forcefully addressed. In the post-1857 period, the Residency did use the succession of the Nizam to implement change, and this is in accordance with Fisher's assertion that "[t]he Company often found the interregnum a particularly efficient time to alter the relationship between the throne and the Resident." Fisher, *Indirect Rule in India,* p. 186.
34. Fraser, *Our Faithful Ally the Nizam,* p. 321.
35. Hastings, *Our Faithful Ally the Nizam,* pp. 342–43.
36. Richard Temple, 9 April 1867, Mss Eur F/86/81, OIOC.
37. The shoe issue was not the only change made at the death and successions within the Nizamate. When the third Nizam, Secundar Jah, died, the terms of address used between the Company and the Nizam's government were changed at the request of the governor general. Prior to Secundar Jah's death, he had been addressed as "*mabu dowlat*" (royal self) and the governor general was "*niyazmund*" (petitioner). After the Nizam's death, these forms of address were dropped in order to attain equality between the governor and the Nizam. Hastings, *Our Faithful Ally the Nizam,* p. 235.
38. C.B. Saunders, "Administration Report of Hyderabad for 1869–1870, by C.B. Saunders, Esq., C.B., Resident at Hyderabad," in *Hyderabad Affairs,* ed. Syed Mahdi Ali (Bombay: Times of India Steam Press, 1869–1870), pp. 266–86.
39. Ibid.
40. Salar Jung to Yule, 3 April 1867, Mss Eur E357/28, OIOC.
41. F.W. Buckler, "The Oriental Despot," in *Legitimacy and Symbols: The South Asian Writings of F.W. Buckler,* ed. M.N. Pearson (Ann Arbor: The University of Michigan, 1985), pp. 176–87. Bernard S. Cohn, *Colonialism*

and Its Forms of Knowledge (Princeton: Princeton University Press, 1996), pp. 114–15.

42. Stewart Gordon, "Introduction: Ibn Battuta and a Region of Robing," in *Robes of Honour Khil'at in Pre-Colonial and Colonial India*, ed. Stewart Gordon (New Delhi: Oxford University Press, 2003), p. 21.
43. Ibid.
44. Ibid., pp. 22–23.
45. C. Defremery, B.R. Sanguinetti, and H.A.R. Gibb, eds., *The Travels of Ibn Batutta, A.D. 1325–1354*, vol. 3 (Cambridge: The University Press, 1971), pp. 662–63.
46. Niccolao Manucci, *Storia Do Mogar or Mogul India*, trans. William Irvine (repr., Calcutta: Indian Editions, 1966), p. 321. Other accounts of *nazr* giving can be found in: Percival Spear, *Twilight of the Mughuls* (Karachi: Oxford University Press, 1973), pp. 45–46, 76, 225.
47. Abd-er-Razzak, "Narrative of the Journey of Abd-Er-Razzak," in *India in the Fifteenth Century Being a Collection of Narratives of Voyages to India*, ed. R.H. Major (Repr. Delhi: Deep Publications, 1974), p. 31.
48. He gave a *nazr* of Rs. 2,100,000. Wink, *Land and Sovereignty in India*, p. 111.
49. Naidu was a noble in the Madras Presidency, so the title did little if anything for him either in Hyderabad or Madras. Frykenberg, *Guntur District, 1788–1848*, p. 43.
50. Cohn, "Representing Authority in Victorian India," p. 170.
51. Phillip Lawson, *The East India Company: A History* (London: Longman, 1993), p. 123.
52. Ibid., p. 129.
53. Fisher, *Indirect Rule in India*, pp. 269–82.
54. Cohn, "Representing Authority in Victorian India," p. 172.
55. Fisher, *Indirect Rule in India*, p. 183.
56. "Translation of H.E.'s order to the Private Secretary No. 49 dated 2nd Zeehaj 1319H," [12 March 1902], Ceremonials File, APSA.
57. Raja of Anagundi to secretary of Nizam, 26 September 1912, Ceremonials File, APSA.
58. Ray, *Hyderabad and British Paramountcy 1858–1883*, the map between pp. 142–43. The railway from Hyderabad south through Wanaparthi and Gadwal to Kurnool was built between 1909 and 1931.
59. Russell to Wood, 24–29 July 1921, R/1/1/676, OIOC.
60. Nizam to Sita Rambhupal, 24 July 1922, R/1/1/1469(1), OIOC.
61. Nizam to Russell, 9 January 1921, R/1/1/673, OIOC.
62. Charles Russell to Wood, 10 January 1921, R/1/1673, OIOC. This was not the last time that Osman Ali Khan's name was linked with being a miser. His obituary, carried in the United States, refers to "The Richest Miser." "Hyderabad Nizam Dies in India at 80," *New York Times*, 25 February 1967. p. 1.

63. Keyes to Watson, 13 July 1931, L/P&S/1/3/1199, OIOC.
64. Waghorne, *The Raja's Magic Clothes: Revisioning Kingship and Divinity in England's India*, p. 26.
65. R.I.R. Glancy to Rameshwar Rao II, 28 January 1914, WFP.
66. Colin Bruce, John Deyell, Nicholas Rhodes, and William Spengler, *The Standard Guide to South Asian Coins and Paper Money* (Iola, Wisconsin: Krause Publications, 1981), p. 181. Production of Gadwal's coin seems to have ended in 1899. Judicial Secretary to Nizam's Private Secretary, 7 February 1899, Private Secretary's Office Records, APSA. As early as 1800, the coins of Gadwal and Narayanpet were in circulation within the Anagundi samasthan. Mss Eur Mack. General XI.
67. Ram Prasad Tripathi, "The Turko-Mongol Theory of Kingship," in *The Mughal State 1526–1750*, ed. Muzaffar Alam and Sanjay Subrahmanyam (New Delhi: Oxford University Press, 1998), p. 121.
68. Richards, *Mughal Administration in Golconda*, pp. 35–36.
69. See the coins of Gadwal, Wanaparthi, Narayanpet, and Shorapur. Colin, Deyell, Rhodes, and Spengler, *The Standard Guide to South Asian Coins and Paper Money*, p. 181.
70. Saidul Haq Imadi, *Nawab Imad-Ul-Mulk* (Hyderabad: The State Archives Government of Andhra Pradesh, 1978), p. 38.
71. *Englishman*, 19 April 1855.
72. Mudiraj, *Pictorial Hyderabad*, pp. 620I, 636, 639.
73. For a full-length treatment on masculinity and empire, see: John M. MacKenzie, *The Empire of Nature* (Manchester: Manchester University Press, 1988).
74. Khan, ed., *Images of Hyderabad*, p. 89.
75. *Note Regarding the Visit of Their Excellencies Lord & Lady Willingdon to Hyderabad in November 1933 (Hyderabad-Deccan: Government Central Press, 1937)*, p. 35.
76. Dunlop to Faridoon, 22 February 1902, Private Secretary's Office File, APSA.
77. Faridoon to Raja, 26 February 1902, Private Secretary's Office File, APSA.
78. Hanklin to Faridoon, 3 March 1902, Private Secretary's Office File, APSA.
79. Faridoon to Raja, 27 July 1904, Private Secretary's Office File, APSA.
80. Dunlop to Faridoon, 14 February 1905, Private Secretary's Office File, APSA.
81. Faridoon to Raja, 11 April 1905, Private Secretary's Office File, APSA.
82. Wakefield to Faridoon, 13 June 1918, Political and Private Secretary's Office, APSA.
83. Wakefield to Faridoon, 13 June 1918, Political and Private Secretary's Office, APSA.
84. Wakefield to Faridoon, 27 June 1918, Political and Private Secretary's Office, APSA.
85. *Game Regulations, His Highness the Nizam's Dominions*, 1914, Hyderabad. Section 5.

86. For some insight into Mir Osman's social habits during the first two decades of his reign, see Vasant Kumar Bawa, *The Last Nizam* (New Delhi: Viking, 1992). Benjamin B. Cohen, "Gifts or Greed? Nazr in the Reign of Hyderabad's Osman Ali Khan," in *Paradigms in Indian History*, ed. V. Sadanandam (Hyderabad: Itihasa Prabhasa Publishers, 2004), pp. 105–16. D.F. Karaka, *Fabulous Mogul* (London: Derek Verschoyle, 1955).
87. Hunt added that Ali was "my chief informant on this matter." "Notes on Politics in Hyderabad," 1 November 1922, Mss Eur F/2/2210, OIOC.
88. Nizam to Sita Rambhupal, 21 February 1923, R/1/1/1469, OIOC.
89. "Notes on Politics in Hyderabad," 1 November 1922, F/2/2210, OIOC.
90. Nizam to Sita Rambhupal, 16 September 1922, R/1/1/1469, OIOC. "Jatpole" also appears as "Jetpol" in some records. I have used Jatprole as a compromise spelling between Telugu and Urdu translations.
91. Sita Rambhupal to Nizam, 22 September 1922, R/1/1/1469, OIOC.
92. "Notes on Politics in Hyderabad," 1 November 1922, Mss Eur F/2/2210, OIOC.

Chapter 4: The Court of Wards in Hyderabad

1. For example, a "major portion" of the annual expense incurred by the Court of Wards for civil litigation in 1931 was caused by the Wanaparthi succession case as Sarala Devi employed counsel from British India. See *Report of the Administration of the Court of Wards Department of H.E.H. the Nizam's Government for the Year 1340 Fasli* (Hyderabad-Deccan: Government Central Press, 1932), p. 20.
2. Before the formal establishment of the Court, estates operated at the mercy of the Nizam. For instance, when the last Gurgunta raja died in 1890, leaving behind two widows and a daughter, the estate was forcibly removed from these rightful heirs by the *talukdar* accompanied by sepoys. The ranis had to resort to legal action to regain their estate. *Hyderabad in 1890 and 1891*, p. 74.
3. This summary of the history of England's Court of Wards is taken from the excellent work by H.E. Bell. Also, Blackstone gives a summary of English landholdings but no real mention of the Court of Wards. William Blackstone, *The Commentaries on the Laws of England of Sir William Blackstone*, 4th ed., vol. 2 (London: John Murray, 1876), pp. 50–65, and especially pp. 57–58.
4. H.E. Bell, *An Introduction to the History and Records of the Court of Wards & Liveries* (Cambridge: Cambridge University Press, 1953), p. 119.
5. Ibid., p. 121. It is interesting to compare these educational goals with those of Hyderabad's Court of Wards that sought to impart the "best English" education to its wards.
6. Two centuries later in Hyderabad, the record shows that several wards were "insane," but we are left wondering on what basis this was determined.
7. This was a practice common amongst the Mughals as well as countless other noble families. For example, Shah Jahan in 1625 sent his two young sons

Dara Shukoh and Aurangzeb to Jahangir as part of a lenient settlement to end the latter's circuitous flight into the Deccan. John Richards, *The Mughal Empire* (Cambridge: Cambridge University Press, 1995), p. 115.

8. Walter Kelly Firminger, ed., Affairs *of the East India Company (Being the Fifth Report from the Select Committee of the House of Commons 28th July, 1812)*, vol. 2 (1812; repr., Delhi: Neeraj Publishing House, 1917), p. 75.
9. John Herbert Harington, *An Elementary Analysis of the Laws and Regulations Enacted by the Governor General in Council*, 3 vols. (Calcutta: Company Press, 1817), pp. 103–23. Also: C.D. Maclean, *Manual of the Administration of the Madras Presidency*, vol. 1 (Madras: Government Press, 1885), pp. 173–75.
10. Barton to GOI, 7 December 1925, R/1/1/1469, OIOC.
11. McLane, *Land and Local Kingship in Eighteenth-Century Bengal*, p. 226 and 315.
12. Chatterjee, *A Princely Imposter?* p. 61.
13. Price, *Kingship and Political Practice in Colonial India*, p. 164.
14. Ibid., p. 165.
15. Yang, "An Institutional Shelter: The Court of Wards in Late Nineteenth-Century Bihar," p. 247.
16. Stephen Henningham, "The Raj Darbhanga and the Court of Wards, 1860–1879: Managerial Reorganization and Elite Education," *The Indian Economic and Social History Review* 19, no. 3 and 4 (1982): p. 347.
17. Theodore Tasker and Richard Chenevix-Trench served as director general and Revenue member, respectively, for much of the Court's existence. Much of the success of the Court (in staving off the Nizam's *nazr* demands, and returning estates to their owners) can be credited to these men.
18. This is the last year that records seem to be available.
19. The remains of the Court now employ two people who are responsible for helping settle the endless litigation between heirs to the estates.
20. *Report of the Administration of the Court of Wards Department of H.E.H. the Nizam's Government for the Year 1336 Fasli* (Hyderabad-Deccan: Government Central Press, 1928), p. 1. Prior to this, the Court's findings were submitted in an Administration Report.
21. "Opinion of Richard Trench," 28 July 1930, Revenue Department, APSA.
22. The earliest attempt and failure to maintain a physical home for the wards comes from 1894, the Court's first year in Hyderabad, when a "Wards Institute" was opened, only to fail for lack of funds three years later. *Report on the Administration of His Highness the Nizam's Dominions for the Four Years 1304–1307 Fasli*, vol. 1 (Madras: Lawrence Asylum Press, 1899), p. 88.
23. *Report on the Administration of His Highness the Nizam's Dominions for the Year 1324 Fasli* (Hyderabad: A.V. Pillai and Sons, Gladstone Press, 1916), p. 11.
24. *H.E.H. the Nizam's Government: Report on the Working of the Departments under the Director General of Revenue* (Hyderabad: Central Jail Press, 1915–1916), p. 6.

25. *Report on the Administration of H.E.H. the Nizam's Government for the Year 1347 Fasli* (Hyderabad-Deccan: Government Central Press, 1940), p. 13.
26. *Report of the Administration of the Court of Wards Department of H.E.H. the Nizam's Government* (Hyderabad-Deccan: Government Central Press, 1940), p. 1.
27. *Report of the Administration of the Court of Wards Department of H.E.H. the Nizam's Government for the Year 1340 Fasli*, p. 8.
28. *Report of the Administration of the Court of Wards Department of H.E.H. the Nizam's Government for the Year 1337 Fasli* (Hyderabad-Deccan: Government Central Press, 1929), p. 24.
29. *Report of the Administration of the Court of Wards Department of H.E.H. the Nizam's Government for the Year 1339 Fasli* (Hyderabad-Deccan: Government Central Press, 1931), p. 1.
30. "The Hyderabad Court of Wards Act," In *Hyderabad Code*, vol. 2 (Hyderabad: Avon Printing, 1956), p. 419.
31. Ibid., p. 420.
32. Ibid., p. 428.
33. Ibid., p. 423.
34. Ibid., p. 432.
35. Unlike in the English Court of Wards, the Hyderabad Act does not lay down any guidelines to determine mental competence such as counting, knowing one's parents, and so on.
36. Under Osman Ali Khan, estates within the Court were a prime source of income in the form of *nazr*, and he seemed reluctant to release estates when it could be avoided. We see this with Gadwal (and twelve other estates), examined in the chapter 5.
37. "The Hyderabad Court of Wards Act," p. 467.
38. For some description of this exchange within the Raj and the titles that were frequently conferred, see Roper Lethbridge, *The Golden Book of India* (London: Sampson Low, Marston & Company, 1900), pp. i–xv.
39. Under the sixth Nizam in 1890–1891, upon recognition of his heirship, the raja of Anagundi was suddenly forced to pay a *peshkush* of Rs. 18,000. This was in contradiction to reports by both the *subhedar* of the area, and of A.J. Dunlop who reported that the raja could in no way pay the amount. *Hyderabad in 1890 and 1891*, p. 139.
40. Kishen Pershad to First Assistant Resident, 17 February 1904, Foreign Department, NAI.
41. Barr to Secretary to the Government of India, Foreign Department, 29 March 1904, Foreign Department, NAI.
42. *Report of the Administration of the Court of Wards Department of H.E.H. the Nizam's Government for the Year 1336 Fasli*, p. 14.
43. "Transcript of the interview with Shri J. Rameshwar Rao for Oral History Division, Nehru Memorial Museum and Library," 8 August 1991, NML, pp. 30–31.

44. *Report of the Administration of the Court of Wards Department of H.E.H. the Nizam's Government for the Year 1340 Fasli*, p. 5.
45. *Report of the Administration of the Court of Wards Department of H.E.H. the Nizam's Government for the Year 1336 Fasli*, p. 8. *Report of the Administration of the Court of Wards Department of H.E.H. the Nizam's Government*, p. 11.
46. Barton to GOI, 7 December 1925, R/1/1/1469, OIOC. Later, the young raja objected when the Court began the process of assessing the samasthan. He argued that he would have the samasthan assessed when he attained majority. The government ignored his request and carried out an assessment. Later assessments were left to the raja.
47. As early as 1925, the Court of Wards was one of the "problems" foremost in the Resident's mind. William Barton, Resident at Hyderabad from 1925 to 1930, listed, "Abuses of the Court of Wards administration and confiscation of private estates, chiefly through two Revenue officials (Fasih Jung and Rahim Yar Jung), who pandered to the greed of the Nizam." Hyderabad Affairs, Resident to Glancy, 2 November 1933, summary of Barton's letter of 11 December 1925, R/1/1/2425, OIOC.
48. 5 May 1927, R/1/1/1675, OIOC.
49. Crump to Thompson, 19 May 1927, R/1/1/1639, OIOC.
50. *Report of the Administration of the Court of Wards Department of H.E.H. the Nizam's Government for the Year 1338 Fasli* (Hyderabad-Deccan: Government Central Press, 1930), p. 3.
51. *Report of the Administration of the Court of Wards Department of H.E.H. the Nizam's Government for the Year 1337 Fasli*, pp. 21–22. Rajapet was in the Court of Wards as of 1926, and recommended for release.
52. For an account of her life, see: Cornelia Sorabji, *India Calling: The Memories of Cornelia Sorabji, India's First Woman Barrister*, ed. Chandani Lokugé (New Delhi: Oxford University Press, 2001). And, for Sorabji's time in London, see: Antoinette Burton, *At the Heart of Empire* (Berkeley: University of California Press, 1998), pp. 110–51.
53. *Report of the Administration of the Court of Wards Department of H.E.H. The Nizam's Government for the Year 1338 Fasli*, p. 5.
54. Ibid.
55. Ibid.
56. Ibid., p. 6.
57. *Report of the Administration of the Court of Wards Department of H.E.H. the Nizam's Government for the Year 1343 Fasli* (Hyderabad-Deccan: Government Central Press, 1935), p. 2.
58. 16 April 1930, Mss Eur, D/7982, OIOC.
59. This and the following data come from: "Wanaparthy 13 Khurdad '50F." 17 April 1941. M. Farooq, CW. Hyderabad.
60. *Report of the Administration of the Court of Wards Department of H.E.H. the Nizam's Government for the Year 1340 Fasli*, p. 12.

61. *Report of the Administration of the Court of Wards Department of H.E.H. the Nizam's Government for the Year 1341 Fasli* (Hyderabad-Deccan: Government Central Press, 1933), p. 16.
62. *Report of the Administration of the Court of Wards Department of H.E.H. the Nizam's Government*, p. 17. In today's Indian army, the battalion with its origins in Wanaparthi still recalls that historic connection. Jatania, Prachi. *A Bombay-Born Battalion Turns 150.* <cities.expressindia.com>, 2003. Accessed 28 March 2004.
63. Sarala Devi to *Nazim*, 1 February 1931, and *Nazim* to Sarala Devi, 9 March 1931, WFP.
64. Sarala Devi to *Nazim*, 16 March 1931, WFP.
65. Dr. Rao to Sarala Devi, 12 March 1931, WFP.
66. Sarala Devi to *Nazim*, 16 April 1931, WFP.
67. Tasker to Sarala Devi, 31 July 1931, WFP.
68. Sarala Devi to Tasker, 2 August 1931, WFP.
69. Barton to GOI, 15 October 1925, R/1/1/1462, OIOC.
70. 16 January 1972, Mss Eur D7985, OIOC.
71. It was not only the samasthans that paid *nazr* while under the Court; the *paigahs* also were subject to exaction. In 1929, at the investigation and recommendation of the Paigah Committee, it was found that the Kurshid Jah Paigah owed nearly Rs. 84,000 in *nazr* and *peshkush* that it had not paid while under the Court. The amount was paid to the Nizam when the estate was released from the Court. See: Mirza Yar Jung, *Paigah Committee Report of 1347 H–1929* (Hyderabad: 1929), p. 31.
72. Barton to GOI, 7 March 1927, R/1/1/1675, OIOC.
73. A nineteenth-century example of such a legal implosion comes from the estate of Venkatadri Naidu of Guntur district. His estate, worth some 5.5 million pounds sterling was frittered away in the courts. See Frykenberg, *Guntur District, 1788–1848*, p. 44.
74. Venkata Swetachalapati Ranga Rao, *Advice to the Indian Aristocracy* (Madras: Addison and Co., 1905), p. 195.

Chapter 5: The Death of Kings, the Birth of a Nation

1. John McLeod, *Sovereignty, Power, Control: Politics in the States of Western India*, 1916–1947 (Leiden: Brill, 1999), p. 189.
2. Gupta has produced a series of studies on several small and some larger states. Among many, H.L. Gupta, "Banswara Successions, 1838 and 1844," *Journal of Indian History* 42, no. 3 (1964): 763–70.
3. Michael H. Fisher, *Indirect Rule in India* (Delhi: Oxford University Press, 1991), pp. 65 and 144.
4. Robbins Burling, *The Passage of Power: Studies in Political Succession* (New York: Academic Press, 1974), p. 257. Burling looks at succession in South

Asia by examining the Maratha empire, pp. 53–84. In a different work, Reinhard Bendix has looked at the transformation of societies from monarchies to democracies, and the process of modernization. See Reinhard Bendix, *Kings or People* (Berkeley: University of California Press, 1978).

5. Burling, *The Passage of Power: Studies in Political Succession*, p. 261.
6. Shastri, *Wanaparthi Samasthan Charitra*. A copy of the unpublished manuscript is at the APSA Secretariat Branch, Revenue Department, Hyderabad.
7. Shastry adds that he came to Wanaparthi for an event where he received Rs. 25 *sambhaawana* (money given to Brahmans for their blessing at an event), but at Gadwal he received Rs. 50. Many of the samasthans were known for supporting artistic and literary endeavors. For Wanaparthi, see: Reddy, *Wanaparthi Samasthan Telugu Sahityaseva*. For the other samasthans: Donappa, *Andhra Samasthamulu Sahitya Poshammu*.
8. The daughters were Nanchar Amma who married Gopal Reddy, *Deshmukh* (officer exercising limited police or revenue authority over a district) of Chinchod, and Janamma, who married Ram Linga Reddy, Raja Sirnapalli samasthan.
9. "Will and Testament," 20 October 1922, WFP.
10. "Statement Zameema 'BEY' as per Circular No 34 of 1331 Fasli," 19 October 1922, WFP.
11. This is another example of the linkages between the samasthans in Hyderabad State and the Madras Presidency.
12. Maharaja to Ram Dev Rao and Ram Krishna Rao, 23 November 1922, WFP.
13. Sarala Devi was the daughter of the raja of the Managala samasthan in the Madras Presidency, and her father at times assisted her in the succession dispute.
14. "Judgement of the Nazim Sahib of Atiyat," 8 January 1930, Revenue Department, APSA.
15. "Opinion of Richard Trench," 28 July 1930, Revenue Department, APSA.
16. John Herbert Harington, *An Elementary Analysis of the Laws and Regulations Enacted by the Governor General in Council*, vol. 1 (Calcutta: Company Press, 1818).
17. The exception to this might be the Gopalpet samasthan that seems to have been related to Wanaparthi, and might have begun as part of Wanaparthi's land given to a family member to begin their own estate. At another time, Wanaparthi lost part of its territory to the Mughals, but the core area around Sugur and Wanaparthi town remained part of the samasthan.
18. "Nawab Aquil Jung Bahadur" Revenue Department, APSA.
19. "Opinion of Richard Trench," 28 July 1930, Revenue Department, APSA.
20. "Nawab Mirza Yar Jung Bahadur," 22 December 1930, Revenue Department, APSA.
21. "Nawab Mirza Yar Jung Bahadur," 22 December 1930, Revenue Department, APSA.
22. For Muslim litigants, Hyderabad followed the Hanafi school of Islamic law. For instance, in the succession dispute in the *paigah* families, the law was

followed and amended only when it went against the orders of the Nizam. Reilly, *Report of the Paigah Commission*, p. 104.

23. Revenue Gashti No. 38 of 1299F in "Nawab Mirza Yar Jung Bahadur," 22 December 1930, Revenue Department, APSA.
24. R.B. Sethi, *The Hindu Succession Act*, 4th ed. (Allahabad: Law Book Co., 1970), p. 103.
25. Ibid., p. 31.
26. Ibid., p. 32.
27. "Judgement of the Nazim Sahib of Atiyat," 8 January 1930, Revenue Department, APSA.
28. "Nawab Mirza Yar Jung Bahadur," 22 December 1930, Revenue Department, APSA.
29. "Judgement of the Nazim Sahib of Atiyat," 8 January 1930, Revenue Department, APSA.
30. Untitled, 19 October 1924, WFP.
31. According to Shastry, the first fifty-four pages of the manuscript were printed, in Telugu, at the press in Wanaparthi.
32. "Statement of Venkat Shastry Continued," 1 September 1930, WFP.
33. Ibid.
34. "Statement of Venkat Shastry Continued," 1 September 1930, WFP. The underline is in the original.
35. "Nawab Aquil Jung Bahadur," WFP.
36. "Opinion of Richard Trench," 28 July 1930, Revenue Department, APSA.
37. "Order on the petition of Rameshwar Rao for review of the second appellate judgment of the Atyat Committee in the Inam and Succession enquiry of the Wanpurti Samasthan," 21 July 1932, Revenue Department, APSA.
38. Trench, unlike his colleague Tasker, seems to have led a more public and sometimes controversial life in Hyderabad. His position on this case was no exception. In the summer of 1931, the newspapers circulated a story that Trench, before beginning his official position as committee member, had already expressed his opinion in favor of Ram Dev Rao. As the committee's work got underway, Trench made a personal statement before both sides of the case, stating that he had, in casual conversation with one of the committee members, expressed his private and uninformed opinion on the case. He went on to state that this premature opinion in no way would hamper his professional duties he was about to undertake. Both sides of the case saw no harm in Trench's statement and proceeded. "The Wanaparthi Case." *The Hindu*, 27 July 1931. And "A Correction." *The Hindu*, 3 July 1931.
39. *Firman*, 1 June 1933, WFP.
40. Sita Rambhupal's wife, Venkatalakshamma, and Rambhupal's wife, Lakshmi Devamma, both administered the samasthan simultaneously. The leadership of these women (and the role of women in general) in the samasthan would become an important argument in Maharani Adi Lakshmi's legal case, the wife and widow of Sita Rambhupal II.
41. "The Hyderabad Court of Wards Act," pp. 416–17.

42. Ibid., p. 419.
43. *Firman*, 15 May 1924, R/1/1/1469, OIOC.
44. Nizam to Sita Rambhupal, 20 June 1922, R/1/1/1469, OIOC.
45. Sethi, *The Hindu Succession Act*, p. 94. Succession between male heirs at one time was based on religious merit as derived from performing funeral rights. This practice was gradually dismissed as a means of determining heirship, and codified laws were set in place instead. Also in the laws of Manu it is stated, "There is no distinction between a son's son and a daughter's son in worldly matters, for a daughter's son also saves him in the world beyond, just like a son's son." *The Laws of Manu*, trans. (London: Penguin, 1991), p. 214.
46. Ayyangar was born at Kumbakonam and educated in Madras. He served in the Residency courts from 1900, and was a leading advocate in south India. Krishna Swamy Mudiraj describes him thus: "He hails from a family of distinction which had for generations been at the helm of affairs in the Gadwal Samasthan. He is one of those rare intellects from the south and, during his unceasing successful career at the bar, endeared himself to his clients, his colleagues in the Bar and to the bench." Mudiraj, *Pictorial Hyderabad*, p. 464 D.
47. Barton to GOI, 7 December 1925, R/1/1/1469, OIOC.
48. Barton to GOI, 7 December 1925, R/1/1/1469, OIOC. This "dread of high-handed interference" is something we see at Jatprole.
49. To see how the British wanted to "avoid disorder," see: McLeod, *Sovereignty, Power, Control*, p. 192.
50. For a discussion of loyalty and the peace gained from such loyalty, see: Gupta, "Banswara Successions, 1838 and 1844," p. 764.
51. Petitions were sent to the Nizam lobbying for the release of the samasthan, and the press also joined with the maharani in opposition to the Nizam's decision.
52. *Firman*, 31 December 1924 and Russell to GOI, 16 January 1925, R/1/1/1462, OIOC.
53. Precedent is similar to "custom" as argued in the Wanaparthi succession.
54. "Confidential Note by Diwan Bahadur Aravamudu Ayyangar" R/1/1/1469, OIOC.
55. Eaton, *A Social History of the Deccan, 1300–1761*, pp. 177–202.
56. Barton to Thompson, 3 September 1925, R/1/1/1462, OIOC. Barton speculates that C.R Reddy possibly organized the memorial. Reddy (1880–1951) was a member of the Madras Legislative Council and a prominent educationalist in Andhra.
57. "Enclosure No. 1. Memorandum," R/1/1/1469, OIOC.
58. Russell to GOI, 16 January 1925, R/1/1/1462, OIOC.
59. Russell to GOI, 3 February 1925, R/1/1/1462, OIOC.
60. "Congress," in *Report on English Papers Examined by the Criminal Investigation Department, Madras*, No. 17 (Madras: Government of Madras, 1925), TNSA.
61. Gadwal, like the other samasthans, maintained a small armed force of about 300 men, but they seem to have not been deployed beyond guarding the palace.

62. Barton to GOI, 15 October 1925, R/1/1/1462, OIOC.
63. Barton to GOI, 7 December 1925, R/1/1/1469, OIOC.
64. "Congress," in *Report on English Papers Examined by the Criminal Investigation Department, Madras*, No. 14, TNSA.
65. Ibid., No. 16, TNSA.
66. "Swadeshabhimani," in *Report on English Papers Examined by the Criminal Investigation Department, Madras*, No. 17, TNSA.
67. "Andhra Patrika," in *Report on English Papers Examined by the Criminal Investigation Department, Madras*, No. 17, TNSA.
68. "Tamil Nadu," in *Report on English Papers Examined by the Criminal Investigation Department, Madras*, No. 18, TNSA.
69. In his article, Copland has argued that Hyderabad was relatively free from communal tension until about this time. Ian Copland, " 'Communalism' in Princely India: The Case of Hyderabad, 1930–1940," *Modern Asian Studies* 22, no. 4 (1988): 783–814.
70. "The Hyderabad Court of Wards Act," p. 420.
71. Barton to GOI, 7 December 1925, R/1/1/1469, OIOC.
72. "Note by the Counsel of the present Rani of Gadwal" R/1/1/1469, OIOC.
73. Fitze to GOI, 2 March 1926, R/1/1/1469, OIOC.
74. Someshwar Rao would play an important role in defending the rights of the samasthans some two decades later. This we see in the conclusion.
75. "Copy of a confidential note by Diwan Bahadur Aravamudu Ayyangar, Counsel for the Rani of Gadwal, on the Gadwal Case," R/1/1/1469, OIOC.
76. 24 January 1933, Mss Eur D/7982, OIOC. Tasker visited Gadwal 24 January 1933, and it was in his notes from that visit that we learn about his prior visit, and relations between the rani and the different *talukdars*. No evidence of any discord between the rani and the *talukdars* is evident, communal or otherwise. It was not uncommon for Hindu rajas or ranis to have Muslim *dewans*, as was the case in Jatprole and Wanaparthi during the same time.
77. Lothian to Watson, 2 March 1928, R/1/1/1740, OIOC.
78. *Report of the Administration of the Court of Wards Department of H.E.H. the Nizam's Government for the Year 1337 Fasli*, p. 5.
79. Ibid., p. 5.
80. At the time of the release of Gadwal from the Court of Wards, the general secretary of the Bombay Reddy League sent a telegram to the Nizam thanking him for installing the rani, referred to as the "religious head, [of the] Reddi community." General Secretary to Nizam, 22 March 1928, Political Department, APSA.
81. The birth was duly noted by the Resident who continued to keep watch over events within Gadwal. Barton to GOI, 31 May 1928, R/1/1/1740, OIOC.
82. 24 January 1933, Mss Eur D/7982, OIOC.
83. *Deccan Chronicle*, 8 December 1940. p. 8.
84. *FNR*, 2 December 1940, R/1/1/3486, OIOC.

85. His life is detailed in a biography published one year later. Ramasubbaravu, *Sri Surabhi Venkatalaksmaraya Nijam Navajyant Bahaddarvari Jivitamu.*
86. Jagannath Rao II was himself adopted from Gurujala in the Guntur district of the Madras Presidency.
87. Sastrulu, *Sri Surabhivari Vamsa Charitramu*, p. 117.
88. Sastri, *A Family History of Venkatagiri Rajas*, p. 101.
89. Venkata Swetachalapati Ranga Rao, *A Revised and Enlarged Account of the Bobbili Zemindari*, 2nd ed. (Madras: Addison and Co., 1907), p. 136.
90. See the synopsis of Dilthey's ideas in: Ranajit Guha, "Introduction," in *A Subaltern Studies Reader 1986–1995*, ed. Ranajit Guha (New Delhi: Oxford University Press, 2000), p. 1–33.
91. Row, *Biographical Sketches of the Rajahs of Venkatagiri*, pp. 83–85.
92. Rao, *A Revised and Enlarged Account of the Bobbili Zemindari*, p. 140.
93. For more on hunting in Bobbili and Jatprole under Lakshma Rao, see: M. Radhakrishna Sarma, "Animal-Hunting—A Study in Perceptions," in *Social Evils in Andhra Desa 17th and 18th Centuries, A.D.*, ed. R. Soma Reddy, M. Radhakrishna Sarma, and A. Satyanarayana (Hyderabad: Osmania University, 1999), p. 106.
94. Sastrulu, *Sri Surabhivari Vamsa Charitramu*, pp. 120–23.
95. Row, *A Revised and Enlarged Account of the Bobbili Zamandari*, p. 126.
96. Rao, *Advice to the Indian Aristocracy*, p. 24.
97. Lakshma Rao to Pithapur, 5 February 1921, CW.
98. Lakshma Rao to Pithapur, 29 November 1926, CW.
99. 9 April 1925, Religious Affairs Files, APSA.
100. 9 April 1925, Religious Affairs Files, APSA.
101. Copland, *State, Community and Neighbourhood in Princely North India, C. 1900–1950*, p. 23.
102. Ibid., p. 36.
103. Where no male heirs were born over a period of generations at a samasthan, oral histories exist that "explain" the phenomenon. For Jatprole, the story goes, one raja had a penchant for beautiful young girls. One day, a new Brahman girl was in the village, and went unknowingly to the village well, within sight of the raja's palace. She was abducted and raped, but before being put to death, she cursed the raja that neither he nor his family will have male heirs for many generations.
104. This document in the Court of Wards files was badly damaged in the right margin where one inch of the paper and text was torn. I have inserted in brackets what appears to be missing.
105. Jatprole papers, 20 June 1915, CW.
106. Venkat Lakshma Rao was 50 years old at the time.
107. Jatprole papers, 20 June 1915, CW.
108. Ibid.
109. For another example of pride as an issue in a succession case, see Gupta, "Dungapur Succession, 1846," pp. 87, 90.

110. This statement by Tasker has been passed on through the family, who shared it with the author. After an exhaustive search for the actual document, none was found. However, all evidence points to its existence: Jatprole's administration *was* excellent, and the rani was made Regent. She went on to become an outstanding administrator of the samasthan, frequently touring its *taluks* and enjoying a high degree of respect.
111. Keyes to GOI, 8 September 1931, R/1/1/2100, OIOC.
112. "Secret Handing over Note," Mss Eur F13131B, OIOC.

Conclusion

1. Osman Ali Khan, 13 February 1937 in *H.E.H The Nizam's Government, Report of the Royal Commission on Jagir Administration and Reforms* (Hyderabad: H.E.H The Nizam's Government, 1947), p. 6.
2. V.P. Menon, *Integration of the Indian States* (Hyderabad: Orient Longman, 1956), pp. 317–18.
3. H.E.H., *Report of the Royal Commission on Jagir Administration and Reforms*, 117–18.
4. Ibid.
5. Government, *Report of the Royal Commission on Jagir Administration and Reforms*, pp. 117–18.
6. This event has been adequately covered by several scholars, most recently by Benichou, in *From Autocracy to Integration*. For a different perspective, see Fareed Mirza, *Police Action in the Erstwhile Hyderabad State* (Hyderabad: [Privately published by the author], 1976).
7. V.P. Menon was involved in the financial compensation awarded to the samasthans and *jagirdars* whom he claims were "justly treated." Menon, *Integration of the Indian States*, pp. 385–86.
8. Samasthan Representatives to J.N. Chaudhury, 19 February 1949, WFP. The samasthans represented include: Gadwal, Wanaparthi, Jatprole, Amarchinta, Paloncha, Domakonda, Gopalpet, Anagundi, Dubbak, Papanapet, Gurgunta, and Sirnapalli.
9. Samasthan Representatives to J.N. Chaudhury, 26 February 1949, WFP.
10. Ibid.
11. Samasthan Representatives to Secretary Ministry of States, 31 May 1949, WFP.
12. Ibid.
13. The fate of the other samasthans is less clear. A lengthy list of nobles and their handover dates was published on 14 September, but beyond titles of "raja" and "rani," it is unclear who signed over their territories, and which samasthans they might have represented. Government of Andhra Pradesh, *Jagir Administration*, Vol.1 (Hyderabad: Government Central Press, 1968), pp. 73–85.
14. Rameshwar Rao to General Chaudhuri, 10 September 1949, WFP.

15. General Chaudhuri to Rameshwar Rao, 12 September 1949, WFP.
16. Lytton to Salisbury, 11 May 1876. Cohn, "Representing Authority in Victorian India," p. 149.
17. General Chaudhuri to Rameshwar Rao, 12 September 1949, WFP.
18. Speech by Rameshwar Rao, 15 September 1949, WFP.
19. Ibid.
20. *Welcome Address*. 15 September 1949. Sree Panchacharya Press, Mahbubnagar. WFP.
21. *Deccan Chronicle*. 16 September 1949.
22. Government of Andhra Pradesh, *Jagir Administration*, pp. 19–20.
23. This and other supporting documentations were typed and bound but not published. Rameshwar Rao to Chief Minister Hyderabad State. 20 March 1950 in *Translations of Some Sanads and Documents by Translation Department of Hyderabad*, WFP.
24. "The Hyderabad Jagirs (Commutation) Regulation, 1359F," in *Jagir Administration*, vol. 2 (Hyderabad: Government Central Press, 1963), p. 23.
25. K.M. Munshi, *The End of an Era* (Bombay: Bharatiya Vidya Bhavan, 1957), p. 16. Munshi himself seems to have been unclear about the subtle differences between Hyderabad's landholding nobility. He refers to the raja of Wanaparthi as head of the largest "Hindu *jagirdar*"—Wanaparthi was neither the largest of the samasthans nor a *jagirdar* (p. 94).
26. Mukherjee, *A Bengal Zamindar*, p. xxiii.
27. "Hindu 'principalities' surviving in Hyderabad State" Mss Eur D798/62, OIOC.

Bibliography

Unpublished Sources

Private Papers

Oriental and India Office, British Library, London (OIOC)
Bowring Collection, Eur Mss G38
Davidson Collection, Eur Mss D728
Elliot Collection, Eur Mss F48
Hunt Collection, Eur Mss F222
Keyes Collection, Eur Mss F131
Mackenzie General Collection
Munro Collection, Eur Mss F151
Tasker Collection, Eur Mss D798
Wyld Collection, Eur Mss B320
Yule Collection, Eur Mss E357

Nehru Memorial Library, New Delhi (NML)
Rameshwar Rao interview transcripts, Oral History Division
Wanaparthi Family Papers, Hyderabad (WFP)

Official Records

Oriental and India Office, British Library, London (OIOC)
Crown Representative Records (R/1)
Board Collection (F/4)
Residency Records (R/2)
Records of the Political and Secret Department of the India Office (L/P&S)

Tamil Nadu State Archive, Chennai (TNSA)
Political Department Files
Criminal Investigation Files

Andhra Pradesh State Archive, Hyderabad (APSA)
Ceremonials Files

Political and Private Secretary Files
Political Department Files
Political Secretary Files
Private Secretary Files
Religious Affairs Files
Revenue Files

Court of Wards, Hyderabad (CW)
Gadwal Files
Jatprole Files
Wanaparthi Files

National Archive of India, New Delhi (NAI)
Foreign and Political Department Files

Unpublished Manuscripts and Theses

Chander, Sunil. "From a Pre-Colonial Order to a Princely State: Hyderabad in Transition, C. 1748–1865." Ph.D. thesis, Cambridge University, 1987.

Ramulu, M. "Gadwal Samasthanam: A Study." MA thesis, Telugu University, 1989.

Roosa, John. "The Quandary of the Qaum: Indian Nationalism in a Muslim State: Hyderabad 1850–1948." Ph.D. thesis, University of Wisconsin, 1998.

Shah, Alison Mackenzie. "Constructing a Capital on the Edge of Empire: Urban Patronage and Politics in the Nizams' Hyderabad, 1750–1950." Ph.D. thesis, University of Pennsylvania, 2005.

Somanna, Chinna. "The Economic History of the Samsthanas in Mahaboobnagar District (1900–1948)." MA thesis, Osmania University, 1994.

Wood, Peter. "Vassal State in the Shadow of Empire: Palmer's Hyderabad, 1799–1867." Ph.D. thesis, University of Wisconsin, 1981.

Published Works in Telugu and Urdu

Donappa, Acharya Tumati. *Andhra Samasthamulu Sahitya Poshammu.* Hyderabad: Pravardana Publications, 1969.

Krishna, Rachayata. *Wanaparthi Samasthana Charitra.* Kurnool: Hyderabad Printers, 1948.

Ramasubbaravu, Vajapeya Yajula. *Sri Surabhi Venkatalaksmaraya Nijam Navajyant Bahaddarvari Jivitamu.* Hyderabad: Kovvuru, 1929.

Reddy, A. Mohan. *Wanaparthi Samasthan Telugu Sahityaseva.* Hyderabad: Orient Longman, 1998.

Saksenah, Raman Raj. *Qadim Dakani Saltanaten Aur Samastan.* Hyderabad: Husami Book Depot, 1996.

Sastrulu, V. Sadasiva. *Sri Surabhivari Vamsa Charitramu.* Madras: Saradamba Vilasa Press, 1913.

Shastri, Namatari Venkat. *Wanaparthi Samasthan Charitra*. Hyderabad: Orient Longman, 1992.
Sri Raja Prathama Rameshwara Rayalu. Hyderabad: Orient Longman, 1990.
Varma, K. Satayanarayan, and C. Papayashastri. *Andhra Bhoja Shri Suryaraya Maharaja Prashti*. Pithapuram, 1966.
Wanaparthi Samasthana Paripalana Vidhanamu. Wanaparthi: Wanaparthi State, 1948.

Official Publications

The Chronology of Modern Hyderabad 1720–1890. Hyderabad: Central Records Office Hyderabad Government, 1954.
The Coronation Durbar Delhi 1903. Official Directory (with Maps). Delhi: Foreign Office Press, 1903.
The Imperial Gazetteer of India. Vol. V. Oxford: Clarendon Press, 1908.
The Imperial Gazetteer of India. Vol. XXIV. Oxford: Clarendon Press, 1908.
The Imperial Gazetteer of India. Vol. XIX. Oxford: Clarendon Press, 1908.
Jagir Administration. Vol. I and II. Hyderabad: Government Central Press, 1968.
Note Regarding the Visit of Their Excellencies Lord & Lady Willingdon to Hyderabad in November 1933. Hyderabad-Deccan: Government Central Press, 1937.
Report of the Administration of the Court of Wards Department of H.E.H. the Nizam's Government for the Year 1336 Fasli. Hyderabad-Deccan: Government Central Press, 1928.
Report of the Administration of the Court of Wards Department of H.E.H. The Nizam's Government for the Year 1338 Fasli. Hyderabad-Deccan: Government Central Press, 1930.
Report of the Administration of the Court of Wards Department of H.E.H. The Nizam's Government for the Year 1340 Fasli. Hyderabad-Deccan: Government Central Press, 1932.
Report of the Administration of the Court of Wards Department of H.E.H. The Nizam's Government for the Year 1341 Fasli. Hyderabad-Deccan: Government Central Press, 1933.
Report of the Administration of the Court of Wards Department of H.E.H. the Nizam's Government. Hyderabad-Deccan: Government Central Press, 1940.
Report of the Royal Commission on Jagir Administration and Reforms. Hyderabad: H.E.H. The Nizam's Government, 1947.

Newspapers and Magazines

Deccan Chronicle
Englishman
New York Times
Time

Published Sources

Abd-er-Razzak. "Narrative of the Journey of Abd-Er-Razzak." In *India in the Fifteenth Century Being a Collection of Narratives of Voyages to India*, edited by R.H. Major, 1–49. Delhi: Deep Publications, 1974.

Ackerley, J.R. *Hindoo Holiday*, edited by Eliot Weinberger. New York: New York Review Books, 2000.

Aitchison, C.U. *A Collection of Treaties, Engagements and Sanads*. Vol. IX. Calcutta: Superintendent Government Printing, 1909.

Ali, Cheragh. *Hyderabad (Deccan) under Sir Salar Jung*. Vol. 1. Bombay: Education Society's Press, 1885.

Anderson, Benedict. *Imagined Communities*. London: Verso, 1991.

Barnett, Richard. *North India between Empires: Awadh, the Mughals, and the British, 1720–1801*. Berkeley: University of California Press, 1980.

Barton, William. *The Princes of India*. London: Nisbet & Co. Ltd., 1934.

Bawa, Vasant Kumar. *Hyderabad under Salar Jung I*. New Delhi: S.Chand & Company Ltd., 1996.

———. *The Last Nizam*. New Delhi: Viking, 1992.

———. *The Nizam between the Mughals and British: Hyderabad under Salar Jung I*. New Delhi: S.Chand and Co., 1986.

Bayly, Susan. *Saints, Goddesses and Kings Muslims and Christians in South Indian Society 1700–1900*. Cambridge: Cambridge University Press, 1989.

Bell, H.E. *An Introduction to the History and Records of the Court of Wards & Liveries*. Cambridge: Cambridge University Press, 1953.

Bendix, Reinhard. *Kings or People*. Berkeley: University of California Press, 1978.

Benichou, Lucien D. *From Autocracy to Integration*. Hyderabad: Orient Longman, 2000.

Blackstone, William. *The Commentaries on the Laws of England of Sir William Blackstone*. 4th ed. Vol. 2. London: John Murray, 1876.

Briggs, Henry George. *The Nizam*. 2 vols. 1985 ed. Delhi: Manas Publications, 1861.

Bruce, Colin, John Deyell, Nicholas Rhodes, and William Spengler. *The Standard Guide to South Asian Coins and Paper Money*. Iola, Wisconsin: Krause Publications, 1981.

Buckler, F.W. "The Oriental Despot." In *Legitimacy and Symbols: The South Asian Writings of F.W. Buckler*, edited by M.N. Pearson, 176–87. Ann Arbor: The University of Michigan, 1985.

Burling, Robbins. *The Passage of Power: Studies in Political Succession*. New York: Academic Press, 1974.

Burton, Antoinette. *At the Heart of Empire*. Berkeley: University of California Press, 1998.

Burton, Reginal. *A History of the Hyderabad Contingent*. Calcutta: Central Printing Office, 1905.

Campbell, A. Claude. *Glimpses of the Nizam's Dominions*. Philidelphia: Historical Publishing Co., 1898.

Cannadine, David. "The Context, Performance and Meaning of Ritual: The British Monarchy and the 'Invention of Tradition,' C. 1820–1977." In *The Invention of Tradition*, edited by Eric Hobsbawm and Terence Ranger, 101–64. Cambridge: Cambridge University Press, 1983.

———. *Ornamentalism: How the British Saw Their Empire*. London: Penguin Group, 2001.

Chaudhuri, Nani Gopal. *British Relations with Hyderabad*. Calcutta: University of Calcutta, 1964.

Chauhan, R.R.S. *Africans in India: From Slavery to Royalty*. New Delhi: Asian Publication Services, 1995.

Chatterjee, Partha. *A Princely Imposter?* Princeton: Princeton University Press, 2002.

Chetty, N.G. *A Manual of the Kurnool District in the Presidency of Madras*. Madras: R. Hill, 1886.

Cohen, Benjamin B. "Gifts or Greed? Nazr in the Reign of Hyderabad's Osman Ali Khan." In *Paradigms in Indian History*, edited by V. Sadanandam. 105–16. Hyderabad: Itihasa Prabhasa Publishers, 2004.

Cohn, Bernard. "Representing Authority in Victorian India." In *The Invention of Tradition*, edited by Eric Hobsbawm and Terence Ranger, 165–209. Cambridge: Canto, 1983.

———. *Colonialism and Its Forms of Knowledge*. Princeton: Princeton University Press, 1996.

———. "Political Systems in Eighteenth Century India: The Banaras Region," *Journal of the American Oriental Society* 82, no. 3 (1962): 312–19.

Copland, Ian. " 'Communalism' in Princely India: The Case of Hyderabad, 1930–1940." *Modern Asian Studies* 22, no. 4 (1988): 783–814.

———. *State, Community and Neighbourhood in Princely North India, C. 1900–1950*. New York: Palgrave Macmillan, 2005.

Dalrymple, William. *White Mughals: Love and Betrayal in Eighteenth-Century India*. London: HarperCollins Publishers, 2002.

Das, Rahul Peter. "Little Kingdoms and Big Theories of History." *Journal of the American Oriental Society* 117, no. 1 (January–March 1997): 127–34.

Defremery, C., B.R. Sanguinetti, and H.A.R. Gibb, eds. *The Travels of Ibn Batutta, A.D. 1325–1354*. Vol. III. Cambridge: Cambridge University Press, 1971.

"A Description of the Diamond-Mines, as It was Presented by the Right Honourable, the Earl Marshal of England, to the R. Society." *Philosophical Transactions* XII (1677): 907–16.

Dirks, Nicholas. "Colonial Histories and Native Informants: Biography of an Archive." In *Orientalism and the Postcolonial Predicament*, edited by Carol A. Breckenridge Peter van der Veer, 279–313. Philadelphia: University of Pennsylvania Press, 1993.

Dirks, Nicholas. *The Hollow Crown*. Cambridge: Cambridge University Press, 1987.

Diver, Maud. *Royal India*. New York: D. Appleton-Century Company, 1942.

Eaton, Richard. *A Social History of the Deccan, 1300–1761: Eight Indian Lives*. Cambridge: Cambridge University Press, 2005.

Edney, Matthew H. *Mapping an Empire*. New Delhi: Oxford University Press, 1999.

Elphinstone, Mountstuart. *The History of India*. 3rd, 1966 ed. Allahabad: Kitab Mahal, 1849.

Ferishta, Mahomed Kasim. *History of the Rise of the Mahomedan Power in India till the Year A.D. 1612*. Translated by John Briggs. 4 vols. Calcutta: R. Cambray & Co., 1910.

Firminger, Walter Kelly, ed. *Affairs of the East India Company (Being the Fifth Report from the Select Committee of the House of Commons 28th July, 1812)*. 3 vols. 1st ed. 1917. Repr. 1983, Delhi: Neeraj Publishing House.

Fisher, Michael H. *A Clash of Cultures: Awadh, the British, and the Mughals*. New Delhi: Manohar, 1987.

———. *Indirect Rule in India*. Delhi: Oxford University Press, 1991.

Fortescue, John. *Narrative of the Visit to India of Their Majesties King George V. and Queen Mary and of the Coronation Durbar Held at Delhi 12th December 1911*. London: Macmillan and Co., 1912.

Fraser, Hastings. *Memoir and Correspondence of General James Stuart Fraser*. London: Whiting & Co., 1885.

———. *Our Faithful Ally the Nizam*. London: Smith, Elder and Co., 1865.

Frykenberg, Robert E. "The Coronation Durbar of 1911: Some Implications." In *Delhi through the Ages*, edited by Robert E. Frykenberg, 369–90. Delhi: Oxford University Press, 1986.

———. *Guntur District, 1788–1848. A History of Local Influence and Central Authority in South India*. Oxford: Clarendon Press, 1965.

———. "Introduction." In *Land Control and Social Structure in Indian History*, edited by Robert E. Frykenberg, xii–xxi. Madison: University of Wisconsin Press, 1969.

———. "On Roads and Riots in Tinnevelly: Radical Change and Ideology in Madras Presidency During the 19th Century." *South Asia* 14, no. 2 (1981): 34–52.

Furer-Haimendorf, Christoph von. *The Aboriginal Tribes of Hyderabad*. 2 vols., vol. 2. The Reddis of the Bison Hills. London: Macmillan & Co., Ltd, 1945.

Ganapathi, Racharla. *Subordinate Rulers in Medieval Deccan*. Delhi: Bharatiya Kala Prakashan, 2000.

Geertz, Clifford. *Negara: The Theatre State in Nineteenth-Century Bali*. Princeton, NJ: Princeton University Press, 1980.

Gommans, Jos. "The Silent Frontier of South Asia C. 1100–1800." *Journal of World History* 9, no. 1 (1998): 1–24.

Gordon, Stewart. "Introduction: Ibn Battuta and a Region of Robing." In *Robes of Honour Khil'at in Pre-Colonial and Colonial India*, edited by Stewart Gordon, 1–30. New Delhi: Oxford University Press, 2003.

———. "Scarf and Sword: Thugs, Marauders, and State-Formation in 18th Century Malwa." *The Indian Economic and Social History Review* 6, no. 4 (1969): 403–30.

Gribble, J.D.B. *A History of the Deccan*. Vol. 1. 1896; New Delhi: Rupa & Co., 2002.

Guha, Ranajit. "Introduction." In *A Subaltern Studies Reader 1986–1995*, edited by Ranajit Guha, 1–33. New Delhi: Oxford University Press, 2000.

Gupta, H.L. "Banswara Successions, 1838 and 1844." *Journal of Indian History* 42, no. 3 (1964): 763–70.

Harington, John Herbert. *An Elementary Analysis of the Laws and Regulations Enacted by the Governor General in Council*. Vol. 1. Calcutta: Company Press, 1818.

———. *An Elementary Analysis of the Laws and Regulations Enacted by the Governor General in Council*. Vol. 3. Calcutta: Company Press, 1817.

Hasan, S. Nurul. "Zamindars under the Mughals." In *Land Control and Social Structure in Indian History*, edited by Robert E. Frykenberg, 17–32. Madison: University of Wisconsin Press, 1969.

Hassan, Syed Siraj ul. *Castes and Tribes of the Nizam's Dominions*. 2 vols. New Delhi: Vintage, 1990.

Henningham, Stephen. "The Raj Darbhanga and the Court of Wards, 1860–1879: Managerial Reorganization and Elite Education." *The Indian Economic and Social History Review* 19, nos. 3 and 4 (1982): 347–63.

The History of Surabhi Family and the Rajah Saheb of Jatprole. Madras: The Indian Encyclopedias Compiling & Publishing Coy.

Husain, Mazhar. *Hyderabad District Gazetteers: Mahbubnagar*. Hyderabad-Deccan: Government Central Press, 1940.

———. *Hyderabad District Gazetteers: Raichur*. Hyderabad-Deccan: Government Central Press, 1941.

———. *List of Uruses, Melas, Jatras, Etc. in H.E.H. the Nizam's Dominions 1349f (1940 A.D.)*. Hyderabad: Government Central Press, 1940.

Hyderabad in 1890 and 1891. Bangalore: Caxton Press, 1892.

Imadi, Saidul Haq. *Nawab Imad-Ul-Mulk*. Hyderabad: The State Archives Government of Andhra Pradesh, 1978.

Joshi, P.M. "The Raichur Doab in Deccan History—Re-Interpretation of a Struggle." *Journal of Indian History* 36, no. 3 (1958): 379–96.

Jung, Mirza Yar. *Paigah Committee Report of 1347 H-1929*. Hyderabad, 1929.

Karaka, D.F. *Fabulous Mogul*. London: Derek Verschoyle, 1955.

Kaye, John. *The Life and Correspondence of Major-General Sir John Malcolm*. Vol. 1. London: Smith, Elder, and Co., 1856.

Khalidi, Omar. *The British Residents at the Court of the Nizams of Hyderabad*. Wichita, Kansas: Haydarabad Historical Society, 1981.

———. *The Romance of the Golconda Diamonds*. Middletown, New Jersey: Grantha Corporation, 1999.

———, ed. *Hyderabad: After the Fall*. Wichita: Hyderabad Historical Society, 1988.

Khalidi, Omar, ed. *Memoirs of Cyril Jones*. New Delhi: Manohar, 1991.
Khan, Mirza Mehdy. *Census of India, 1891. Volume XXIII. His Highness the Nizam's Dominions*. London: Eyre and Spottiswoode, 1894.
———. *Imperial Gazetteer of India Provincial Series Hyderabad State*. Calcutta: Superintendent of Government Printing, 1909; Rept., Atlantic Publishers, New Delhi, 1991.
Khan, Zahid Ali, ed. *Images of Hyderabad*. Hyderabad: Siasat, 1994.
Kooiman, Dick. *Communalism and Indian Princely States*. New Delhi: Manohar, 2002.
Lawson, Phillip. *The East India Company: A History*. London: Longman, 1993.
Leonard, Karen. "The Deccani Synthesis in Old Hyderabad: An Historiographic Essay." *Journal of the Pakistan Historical Society* 21, no. 4 (1973): 205–18.
———. "The Hyderabad Political System and Its Participants." *Journal of Asian Studies* 30, no. 3 (1971): 569–82.
———. *Social History of an Indian Caste*. Hyderabad: Orient Longman, 1994.
Lethbridge, Roper. *The Golden Book of India*. London: Sampson Low, Marston & Company, 1900.
Luther, Narendra. *Hyderabad a Biography*. New Delhi: Oxford University Press, 2006.
Lynton, Harriet Ronken. *My Dear Nawab Saheb*. Hyderabad: Disha Books, 1991.
Lynton, Harriet Ronken, and Mohini Rajan. *Days of the Beloved*. Berkeley: University of California, 1974.
MacKenzie, John M. *The Empire of Nature*. Manchester: Manchester University Press, 1988.
Maclean, C.D. *Manual of the Administration of the Madras Presidency*. Vol. 1. Madras: Government Press, 1885.
Major, R.H., ed. *India in the Fifteenth Century*. New York: Burt Franklin. [First published in 1857, Reprinted in 1964.]
Manucci, Niccolao. *Storia Do Mogar or Mogul India*. Translated by William Irvine. Rept., Calcutta: Indian Editions, 1966.
Mayer, Adrian C. "The King's Two Thrones." *Man (N.S.)* 20, no. 2. (1985): 205–21.
McLane, John. *Land and Local Kingship in Eighteenth-Century Bengal*. Cambridge: Cambridge University Press, 1993.
McLeod, John. *Sovereignty, Power, Control: Politics in the States of Western India, 1916–1947*. Leiden: Brill, 1999.
Menon, V.P. *Integration of the Indian States*. Hyderabad: Orient Longman, 1956.
Metcalf, Thomas. *Land, Landlords, and the British Raj*. Berkeley: University of California Press, 1979.
Michell, George, and Mark Zebrowski. *Architecture and Art of the Deccan Sultanates*. Cambridge: Cambridge University Press, 1999.
Mirza, Fareed. *Police Action in the Erstwhile Hyderabad State*. Hyderabad: [Privately published by the author], 1976.

Moon, Penderel. *The British Conquest and Dominion of India*. Vol. 2. New Delhi: India Research Press, 1999.

Mudiraj, K. Krishnaswamy. *Pictorial Hyderabad*. Vol. 2. Hyderabad: Chandrakanth Press, 1934.

Mukherjee, Nilmani. *A Bengal Zamindar*. Calcutta: Firma K.L. Mukhopadhyay, 1975.

Munshi, K.M. *The End of an Era*. Bombay: Bharatiya Vidya Bhavan, 1957.

Munshi, Qadir Khan. *Tarikh-E-Asaf Jahi*, translated by Zaib Hyder, edited by N.R.V. Prasad. Hyderabad: Andhra Pradesh Government Oriental Manuscript Library and Research Institute, 1994.

Ota, Nobuhiro. "Beda Nayakas and Their Historical Narratives in Karnataka during the Post-Vijayanagara Period." In *Kingship in Indian History*, edited by Noboru Karashima, 163–94. New Delhi: Manohar, 1999.

Prasad, Rajendra. *The Asif Jahs of Hyderabad*. New Delhi: Vikas Publishing House, 1984.

Price, Pamela. *Kingship and Political Practice in Colonial India*. New York: Cambridge University Press, 1996.

———. "Warrior Caste 'Raja' and Gentlemen 'Zamindar:' One Person's Experience in the Late Nineteenth Century." *Modern Asian Studies* 17, no. 4 (1983): 563–90.

Raj, Sheela. *Medievalism to Modernism*. London: Sangam Books, 1987.

Rajayyan, K. *South Indian Rebellion: The First War of Independence 1800–1801*. Mysore: Wesley Press, 1971.

Ramulu, M. "Gadwala Samsthanam—A Historical Perspective." *Itihas* vol. 16, no 1. (January–June 1990): 117–24.

Ramusack, Barbara. *The Indian Princes and Their States*. Cambridge: Cambridge University Press, 2004.

Rao, Velcheru Narayana, David Shulman, and Sanjay Subrahmanyam. *Textures of Time Writing History in South India 1600–1800*. New Delhi: Permanent Black, 2001.

Rao, Venkata Swetachalapati Ranga. *Advice to the Indian Aristocracy*. Madras: Addison and Co., 1905.

———. *A Revised and Enlarged Account of the Bobbili Zemindari*. 2nd ed. Madras: Addison and Co., 1907.

Ray, Bharati. *Hyderabad and British Paramountcy 1858–1883*. Delhi: Oxford University Press, 1988.

Regani, Sarojini. *Nizam-British Relations: 1724–1857*. Hyderabad: Booklovers Private Limited, 1963.

Reilly, H.D.C. *Report of the Paigah Commission*. Hyderabad, 1345 H.

Richards, John. *Mughal Administration in Golconda*. Oxford: Clarendon Press, 1975.

———. *The Mughal Empire*. Cambridge: Cambridge University Press, 1995.

Richards, J.F., and V. Narayana Rao. "Banditry in Mughal India: Historical and Folk Perceptions." In *The Mughal State 1526–1750*, edited by Muzaffar Alam and Sanjay Subrahmanyam, 491–519. New Delhi: Oxford University Press, 1998.

Row, T. Rama. *Biographical Sketches of the Rajahs of Venkatagiri*. Madras: Asiatic Press, 1875.

Row, Venkata Swetachalapati Ranga. *A Revised and Enlarged Account of the Bobbili Zamandari*. Madras: Addison and Co., 1900.

Sarma, M. Radhakrishna. "Animal-Hunting—A Study in Perceptions." In *Social Evils in Andhra Desa 17th and 18th Centuries, A.D.*, edited by R. Soma Reddy, M. Radhakrishna Sarma, and A. Satyanarayana, 102–10. Hyderabad: Osmania University, 1999.

Sarma, M. Somasekhara. *History of the Reddi Kingdoms*. Waltair: Andhra University, 1948.

Sastri, Alladi Jagannatha. *A Family History of Venkatagiri Rajas*. Madras: Addison Press, 1922.

Sastry, P.V.P. *The Kakatiyas of Warangal*. Hyderabad: Government of Andhra Pradesh, 1978.

Saunders, C.B. "Administration Report of Hyderabad for 1869–1870, by C.B. Saunders, Esq., C.B., Resident at Hyderabad." In *Hyderabad Affairs*, edited by Syed Mahdi Ali, 266–86. Bombay: Times of India Steam Press, 1869–1870.

Schmitthenner, Peter L. *Telugu Resurgence C.P. Brown and Cultural Consolidation in Nineteenth-Century South India*. New Delhi: Manohar, 2001.

Sethi, R.B. *The Hindu Succession Act*. 4th ed. Allahabad: Law Book Co., 1970.

Sewell, Robert. *A Forgotten Empire*. 2nd ed. New Delhi: National Book Trust, 1970.

Sherwani, H.K. *History of the Qutb Shahi Dynasty*. New Delhi: Manoharlal Publishers, 1974.

Shulman, David. "On South Indian Bandit Kings." *The Indian Economic and Social History Review* 17, no. 3 (1980): 283–306.

Siddiqui, Abdul Majeed. *History of Golconda*. Hyderabad: The Literary Publications, 1956.

Singh, K.S., ed. *People of India: Andhra Pradesh*. Vol. 13, Part 3. New Delhi: Affiliated East-West Press, 2003.

Sitapati , P. "Introduction." In *Enugula Veeraswamy's Journal*, edited by P. Sitapati and V. Purushottam. pp. 1–23. Hyderabad: Andhra Pradesh Government Oriental Manuscripts Library & Research Institute, 1973.

Sorabji, Cornelia. *India Calling: The Memories of Cornelia Sorabji, India's First Woman Barrister*, edited by Chandani Lokugé. New Delhi: Oxford University Press, 2001.

Spear, Percival. *Twilight of the Mughuls*. Karachi: Oxford University Press, 1973.

Stein, Burton. *Peasant State and Society in Medieval South India*. Delhi: Oxford University Press, 1980.

———. *Vijayanagara*. Cambridge: Cambridge University Press, 1993.

Sundarayya, P. *Telangana People's Struggle and Its Lessons*. Calcutta: Desraj Chadha, 1972.

Talbot, Cynthia. *Precolonial India in Practice: Society, Religion, and Identity in Medieval Andhra*. Oxford: Oxford University Press, 2001.

Taylor, Philip Meadows. *Confessions of a Thug*. 1st ed. 1839. Oxford: Oxford University Press, 1986.

———, ed. *The Story of My Life*. Repr. 1986 ed. New Delhi: Asian Educational Services, 1882.

Temple, Richard. *Journals Kept in Hyderabad, Kashmir, Sikkim, and Nepal*. Vol. 1. London: W.H. Allen & Co., 1887.

Thornton, Thomas Henry. *General Sir Richard Meade and the Feudatory States of Central and South India*. London: Longmans, Green, and Co., 1898.

Thurston, Edgar. *Castes and Tribes of Southern India*. Vol. 7. Madras: Government Press, 1909.

Tripathi, Ram Prasad. "The Turko-Mongol Theory of Kingship." In *The Mughal State 1526–1750*, edited by Muzaffar Alam and Sanjay Subrahmanyam, 115–25. New Delhi: Oxford University Press, 1998.

Varshney, Ashutosh. *Ethnic Conflict and Civic Life*. New Haven: Yale University Press, 2002.

Veeraswamy, Enugula. *Enugula Veeraswamy's Journal (Kasiyatra Charitra)*, translated by P. Sitapati. Hyderabad: Andhra Pradesh Government Oriental Manuscripts Library & Research Institute, 1973.

Waghorne, Joanne Punzo. *The Raja's Magic Clothes: Revisioning Kingship and Divinity in England's India*: University Park: Pennsylvania State University Press, 1994.

Wagoner, Phillip. " 'Sultan among Hindu Kings': Dress, Titles and the Islamicization of Hindu Culture at Vijayanagara." *The Journal of Asian Studies* 55, no. 4 (1996): 851–80.

———. *Tidings of the King*. Honolulu: University of Hawaii Press, 1993.

———. "Precolonial Intellectuals and the Production of Colonial Knowledge." *Comparative Studies in Society and History* 45, no. 4 (2003): 783–814.

Watson, Adam. *The War of the Goldsmith's Daughter*. London: Chatto & Windus, 1964.

Wiebe, Paul D. *Christians in Andhra Pradesh*. Madras: The Christian Literature Society, 1988.

Wink, André. *Al-Hind*. Vol. II. New Delhi: Oxford, 1999.

———. "From the Mediterranean to the Indian Ocean: Medieval History in Geographic Perspective." *Comparative Studies in Society and History* 44, no. 3 (2002): 416–45.

———. *Land and Sovereignty in India*. London: Cambridge University Press, 1986.

Yang, Anand. "An Institutional Shelter: The Court of Wards in Late Nineteenth-Century Bihar." *Modern Asian Studies* 13, no. 2 (1979): 247–64.

Yazdani, Zubaida. *Hyderabad During the Residency of Henry Russell, 1811–1820*. Oxford: University Press, 1976.

Index